THE FUTURE
OF THE WORLD
ECONOMY

A United Nations Study
by Wassily Leontief *et al.*

NEW YORK
OXFORD UNIVERSITY PRESS
1977

Preface

This report is intended to present the preliminary results of a study, made under the auspices of the United Nations, on the impact of prospective economic issues and policies on the International Development Strategy for the Second United Nations Development Decade. The detailed model of the world economy described in this report is far from a finished piece of work. Additional time and resources are urgently needed to verify and correct the initial estimates of its parameters and to refine its structure. Some of the conclusions presented in the report are drawn from numerical solutions of the model. These conclusions may have to be revised as corrections and improvements are introduced. Elaborations and extensions were recommended by the *ad hoc* Expert Group that reviewed the system. These should broaden the scope and value of its applications.

In the computations for the central scenarios, regional growth rates of Gross Domestic Product were fixed by assumption. These growth rates were chosen for exploratory purposes. They do not represent official United Nations goals and should certainly not be interpreted as predictions of future trends.

Primary financial support for the study was provided by the Government of the Netherlands through a grant to the United Nations in 1973, following discussions with the then Under-Secretary-General for Economic and Social Affairs, Mr. Philippe de Seynes. Additional financial support, which permitted a number of consultants to prepare special analyses, was provided by the United Nations and the Ford Foundation. Fundamental research on input-output analysis was sponsored by a grant from the United States National Science Foundation to Brandeis and Harvard Universities. These grants afforded partial support for work on the world model.

The team of principal investigators responsible for building the world input-output model and for the computation of the projections included in this report was under the direction of Wassily Leontief and included Anne P. Carter and Peter Petri (of Brandeis University), with Joseph J. Stern (of Harvard University) serving as a co-ordinator for the project. Richard Drost (of Brandeis University) wrote the programmes with which the various computations were performed. All of the computations were performed at Brandeis University on the PDP-10 at the Feldberg Computer Center. Ira Sohn (of New York University) assisted Professor Leontief in the final stages of preparation of the report.

Many offices and organizations of the United Nations family generously provided statistical information and relevant reports. The authors are especially grateful to the Economic Commission for Europe of the United Nations, which prepared a special study of interindustry relations in Europe; the Food and Agriculture Organization of the United Nations, for generously making available a large amount of data on the agricultural sector in various regions of the world; the International Labour Office and the Population Division of the United Nations Secretariat for providing demographic data. In addition, the World Bank gave us access to its vast amount of data pertaining to the developing economies.

In the original conception of the study, it was hoped that research organizations in various countries, especially the developing countries, would be asked to undertake specific studies and data collections. Actually, this proved to be difficult, partly because the time available to complete the study was too short to permit effective liaison to be established between the research staff at Brandeis and Harvard Universities and overseas research institutes. Nevertheless, the assistance of the Development Centre of the Organisation for Economic Co-operation and Development (OECD) which distributed the project outline and interim reports to the members of its world-wide network of research institutions is gratefully acknowledged. As is suggested in the report, further analysis of the environmental problems can and indeed must call upon the statistical and analytical talents of research institutions throughout the world.

The authors are pleased to note that the General Assembly in two important resolutions, 3345 (XXIX) on research on the interrelationships between population, resources, environment and development, and 3508 (XXX) on long-term economic trends and projections, has already called for United Nations work in this area. In this context the Department of Economic and Social Affairs of the United Nations Secretariat is initiating a major activity, under the title "Project 2000", which is designed, in collaboration with the regional commissions and other organizations of the United Nations system, to examine alternative patterns of development through the remainder of the twentieth century and their policy implications.

During the course of the nearly three years of work, numerous administrative and substantive matters arose requiring guidance and interpretation. At United Nations Headquarters, Jacob L. Mosak, Director of the Centre for Development Planning, Projections and Policies and Deputy to the Under-Secretary-General for Economic and Social Affairs, helped guide the project; Dallas H. Steinthorson, Principal Officer, and subsequently Stanislav M. Menshikov, Assistant Director of the Centre, helped to maintain liaison with the United Nations. Mr. Menshikov and Munidasa Kodikara, Senior Officer of the Centre, assisted on a number of substantive matters and parts of the report. Mr. Hiroshi Niida, Senior Officer, also assisted in the initial stage of the project. Their help is gratefully acknowledged. United Nations experts commented on the work in progress and shared their views and knowledge during a number of meetings.

Without the support, knowledge and assistance of the many persons who contributed directly and indirectly to the research effort, the work would have been more difficult and the result less satisfying. None is, of course, responsible for any shortcomings of the study or for any interpretations of the statistical resources which they so generously supplied. Responsibility for the factual analysis rests solely with the authors. The report is put forward in the hope that it will stimulate further thought and work on the quantitative analyses of long-term global development policy.

Explanatory notes

The following symbols have been used in the tables throughout the report:

Three dots (...) indicate that data are not available or are not separately reported
A dash (—) indicates that the amount is nil or negligible
A blank in a table indicates that the item is not applicable
A minus sign (−) indicates a deficit or decrease, except as indicated
A full stop (.) is used to indicate decimals
A slash (/) indicates a crop year or financial year, e.g., 1970/71

Use of a hyphen (-) between dates representing years, e.g., 1971-1973, signifies the full period involved, including the beginning and end years.

Reference to "tons" indicates metric tons, and to "dollars" ($) United States dollars, unless otherwise stated.

Annual rates of growth or change, unless otherwise stated, refer to annual compound rates.

Details and percentages in tables do not necessarily add to totals, because of rounding.

*
* *

The designations employed and the presentation of material in this publication do not imply the expression of any opinion whatsoever on the part of the Secretariat of the United Nations concerning the legal status of any country, territory, city or area or of its authorities, or concerning the delimitation of its frontiers or boundaries.

CONTENTS

INTRODUCTION AND SUMMARY

The basis for the present report is a study on the environmental aspects of the future world economy. This study includes—as a principal feature—a set of alternative projections of the demographic, economic and environmental states of the world in bench-mark years 1980, 1990 and 2000.

The detailed methodology and substantive findings of the study are released in parts one and two of the present report. This introduction is meant to give a short history of the project and to summarize the findings and conclusions of the study having the most immediate interest for the current deliberations on the future of the International Development Strategy and ways of implementing the new international economic order.

The setting of the project

The International Development Strategy adopted in 1970 expressed concern with the environment and stated that national and international efforts should be intensified "to arrest the deterioration of the human environment and to take measures towards its improvement, and to promote activities that will help maintain the ecological balance on which human survival depends".[1]

Since 1970, environmental concerns have received increasing attention. At the international level, these have been most notably manifest in the 1972 United Nations Conference on the Human Environment,[2] in the founding, in the same year, of the United Nations Environment Programme (UNEP) and in its subsequent activities, in an intensification of environmental programmes of United Nations organizations, in the establishment in 1974 of the International Habitat and Human Settlements Foundation (General Assembly resolution 3327 (XXIX)), and in the decision to hold a United Nations conference on human settlements in 1976 (General Assembly resolutions 3001 (XXVII) and 3128 (XXVIII)). At the national level, many Governments have adopted more numerous and more effective environmental policies. The interest of people and Governments has intensified rapidly and in many directions.

Within the United Nations governing bodies, member States have decided that environmental policies should imply for the International Development Strategy no weakening of the thrust to make the world, in its economic and social aspects, a more just and rational home for mankind. On the contrary, a number of resolutions of the General Assembly and the Economic and Social Council, especially Assembly resolution 3002 (XXVII) of 15 December 1972, emphasized that environmental policies should enhance the attainment of the goals and objectives of the Strategy and should ensure that the development priorities of the developing countries set out in the Strategy were in no way adversely affected or distorted.

At present, the whole question of the environment and the Strategy clearly falls within the broad range of considerations which led to the Declaration on the Establishment of a New International Economic Order and the corresponding Programme of Action and to General Assembly resolution 3362 (S-VII) on development and international economic co-operation. In particular, the General Assembly decided that modifications to the Strategy must take account of that Declaration and Programme of Action.

In accordance with these principles, the United Nations initiated in 1973 a study on the impact of prospective economic issues and policies on the International Development Strategy, on which the present report is based. The objective of the study was to investigate the interrelationships between future economic growth and prospective economic issues, including questions on the availability of natural resources, the degree of pollution associated with the production of goods and services, and the economic impact of abatement policies. One question specifically asked by the study was whether the existing and other development targets were consistent with the availability and geographic distribution of resources. To the extent that some resources are limited should the desired growth be modified? Does increasing concern with pollution and protection of the environment as a whole seriously affect economic development and call for a re-examination of various national and international development targets? These and other questions were to be investigated within the framework of this study.

Although the 1970s have been designated as the Second United Nations Development Decade, certain policies, especially those relating to environmental factors, are more realistically viewed from a longer-term perspective. While the potential impact of environmental constraints may not impinge to any substantial extent on development over the medium-term, the cost of postponing actions that take account of such potential factors may be great.

The impact exerted by environmental conditions and policies on the growth and structure of the world economy generally becomes apparent only gradually and in the long run. Environmental conditions and policies, however, are highly pertinent to the International Development Strategy for the Second United Nations Development Decade, despite the Strategy's single-decade format. This is because, despite this format, the Strategy is coming to be viewed more and more as a contribution to a cumulative, long-run process, as evidenced, for example, by its recent linking in General Assembly decisions with the concept of a new international economic order.

This approach is significantly new, because despite the

---

[1] *International Development Strategy: Action Programme of the General Assembly for the Second United Nations Development Decade* (United Nations publication, Sales No. E.71.II.A.2), para. 72.

[2] *Report of the United Nations Conference on the Human Environment* (United Nations publication, Sales No. E.73.II.A.14).

other ways in which it was a historic step forward, the present Strategy was originally concerned with the perspective of a single decade without explicitly taking into account longer-range problems such as those that have recently come to the fore in the context of the conferences on environment, on population and on food, and most importantly, in the context of the decisions on a new international economic order. In this respect, the climate of opinion prevailing today differs significantly from that of 1970, and may, therefore, call for a reassessment of the underlying thrust of the Strategy. Accordingly, while the goals and objectives of the International Development Strategy have been reaffirmed and have been complemented by related decisions, there has arisen at the same time a feeling that the long-term implications of present international policies deserve closer scrutiny. Such scrutiny could throw useful light on some future consequences of present policies, and conversely, could help disclose some needs for action in the 1970s imposed by mankind's future requirements.

The global model

To provide a quantitative basis for the study, a global economic model of the world economy has been constructed. The purpose of the model is to display various possible interrelationships, as the world economy evolves over future decades, between environmental and other economic policies. With respect to time horizons, the world economy of 1970 is depicted and compared with hypothetical pictures of the world economy in 1980, 1990 and 2000.

Despite its global scope, the model displays an unusual degree of detail. The world economy is divided into 15 regions—namely, four developed market regions (North America, Western Europe (high-income), Japan and Oceania); two developed centrally planned regions (the Union of Soviet Socialist Republics and Eastern Europe); six developing market regions (Latin America (medium-income), Latin America (low-income), the Middle East and African oil countries, Asia (low-income), Africa (arid) and Africa (tropical)); one region including the countries of Asia with centrally planned economies; and two medium-income regions (Western Europe (medium-income) and Southern Africa).

Each region is described in terms of 45 sectors of economic activity. In agriculture, four specific subsectors are analysed—namely, livestock products, grains, high-protein crops and roots. With respect to mineral resources, special accent is placed on copper, bauxite, nickel, zinc, lead, iron ore, petroleum, natural gas and coal. Manufacturing activities are divided into 22 sectors, such as food processing, primary metals, textiles, fertilizer, various types of machinery and equipment. There is separate treatment of utilities and construction, trade and services, transportation and communication. The model describes emissions of eight types of major pollutants and five types of pollution-abatement activities.

Though each of the 15 regions is treated separately, the model also brings them together through a complex linkage mechanism, including exports and imports of some 40 classes of goods and services, capital flows, aid transfers, and foreign interest payments. The model also permits a detailed analysis of prospective changes in technology, cost of production and relative prices.

The model was constructed in the first instance for the study of development in relation to environmental questions. The principal environmental policies considered are those concerning pollution, constraints on the extraction of mineral resources and the production of food. However, as can be clearly seen from the above description, the model is basically a general-purpose economic model and is thus applicable to the analysis of the evolution of the world economy from other points of view.

Because of these features of the global model, the scope of the study was broadened to include, in addition to environmental aspects, some other problems of economic development. Based on results of model computations, the study investigates in a very broad framework such problems as food and agriculture, mineral resources, pollution and pollution abatement, structural changes in the economies, balance of payments and changes in international economic relations. It is hoped that the model will have a continuing life in which fresh data are used as they become available and in which the model is eventually applied to other development questions.

The degree of detail in the model is advantageous since it permits the use of data specific to individual industries in particular regions, and consequently results in conclusions of relatively specific policy significance. This will provide a basis for continuing contributions to the quantitative analysis of the evolving world economy, such as that requested in General Assembly resolution 3345 (XXIX), entitled "Research on the interrelationships between population, resources, environment and development", and especially in General Assembly resolution 3508 (XXX), which calls for long-range projections of economic development, first at the regional and then at the global level.

The International Development Strategy and alternative scenarios of development

As a bench-mark against which to measure the future impacts of environmental and other economic policies, hypothetical pictures (scenarios) of the world economy are needed. Most of the alternative scenarios analysed in this study embody various assumptions about rates of growth of population and of gross product *per capita*.

One possible scenario was to use growth targets set by the International Development Strategy for the Second United Nations Development Decade. These targets, for the developing regions as a whole, are set at 6 per cent per annum for gross product and 3.5 per cent for gross product *per capita*, assuming an average 2.5 per cent annual growth of population.[3]

The targets were reaffirmed in 1975 at the seventh special session of the General Assembly in the resolution adopted on development and international economic co-operation.[4]

The International Development Strategy does not set targets for growth in developed countries. However, if previous long-term trends in these countries were extrap-

---

[3] *International Development Strategy: Action Programme of the General Assembly for the Second United Nations Development Decade* (United Nations publication, Sales No. E.71.II.A.2), paras, 13-15.
[4] General Assembly resolution 3362 (S-VII) of 19 September 1975, preamble.

olated, they would mean an annual growth of about 4.5 per cent in gross product and 3.5 per cent in gross product *per capita*.

If the minimum targets of growth for the developing countries, as set by the International Development Strategy, were implemented continuously throughout the remaining decades of this century, and if the growth rates prevailing in the developed countries during the past two decades were to be retained in the future, then the gap in *per capita* gross product between these two groups of countries, which was 12 to 1 on the average in 1970, would not start diminishing even by the year 2000. It is true that gross product in the developing countries would continue to expand somewhat faster than in the developed countries, and thus the share of the developing countries in total world product would increase. However, because of the much higher growth rates of population, the expansion of gross product *per capita* would be no faster in the developing countries than in the world as a whole.

This outcome is clearly contrary to the spirit of the International Development Strategy and the Declaration on the Establishment of a New International Economic Order, which call for the correction of inequalities and the redressment of existing injustice, making it possible to narrow the gap between the developed and developing countries and to ensure steadily accelerating economic and social development and justice for present and future generations.[5] It is for this reason that the International Development Strategy laid stress on the necessity to accelerate growth starting with the second half of the current decade in order to make at least a modest beginning towards narrowing the income gap between developed and developing countries.

For these considerations the study turned to different scenarios, in which growth rates of gross product *per capita* were set in such a way as to reduce, roughly by half, the income gap between the developing and the developed countries by the year 2000, with a view towards closing the income gap completely by the middle of the next century. It was felt that these scenarios were more consistent with the spirit of the International Development Strategy and the aims of the Declaration on the Establishment of a New International Economic Order.

Table 1 summarizes the basic differences between the two approaches and can be used to illustrate some of the basic features of the more consistent approach, which leads to a reduction of the average income gap from 12 to 1 in 1970 to about 7 to 1 in the year 2000.

To reach this goal, a substantially higher rate of growth of *per capita* gross product would be necessary in the developing countries. The study assumed that these higher rates could not be achieved immediately but that the acceleration would have to be a gradual step-by-step increase, starting with the current actual rates of growth in most of the developing regions. An exception was made for the Middle East and African oil countries, where a gradual decline from the currently very high growth rates (13-14 per cent) was considered a more realistic assumption. Under scenario C, illustrated in table 1, growth rates of population were based on the United Nations "low" projections. However, other

[5] General Assembly resolution 3201 (S-VI) of 1 May 1974, preamble.

TABLE 1. HYPOTHETICAL SCENARIOS OF WORLD ECONOMIC DEVELOPMENT

	Scenario	Developed countries	Developing countries
Growth rates (percentage):			
Gross product . .	I[a]	4.5	6.0
	C[b]	3.6	6.9
Population . . .	I	1.0	2.5
	C	0.6	2.0
Gross product *per capita* .	I	3.5	3.5
	C	3.0	4.9
Income gap in the year 2000[c]	I	12 to 1	
	C	7 to 1	

[a] I indicates scenario based on extrapolation to the year 2000 of International Development Strategy targets for gross product increase in developing countries and extrapolated long-term historical rates in developed countries.

[b] C indicates scenario based on substantial reduction of gap in gross product *per capita* between developing and developed countries.

[c] Average *per capita* gross domestic product of the developed regions, as related to the average *per capita* gross domestic product of the developing regions.

scenarios, using the "medium" United Nations projections, were also found to be consistent with the basic goal of reducing the income gap.

With respect to developed countries a different rule was followed for projecting the growth rate of gross product. It was assumed that, as individual developed regions achieve higher levels of gross product per head of population, their growth rate of product *per capita* would decline. Thus, the growth rate of 4 per cent *per capita* would apply to regions in the $3-4,000 income *per capita* range (in 1970 constant prices), a 3 per cent growth rate in the $4-5,000 range, 2.5 per cent in the $5-6,000 range and so forth. This has the effect of bringing down the average growth rate of gross product in the developed countries to 3.6-4 per cent in the final three decades of this century from the long-term trend of 4.5 per cent. It was felt that an assumption of gradually declining growth rates in the developed countries would be more realistic than would a simple extrapolation of their past performance.

Under such conditions of accelerated growth in most developing regions, in 1970-2000 average *per capita* gross product would increase 4 times in the Middle East and African oil countries, 3.6 times in the developing market economies of Asia and about 2.5 times in the non-oil countries of Africa.

Even under these relatively optimistic assumptions, by the year 2000 average gross product *per capita* would only reach about $400 (in 1970 prices) in non-oil Asia and Africa, while other developing regions would be able to enter the $1-2,000 range. This is owing to the relatively low current levels of *per capita* income in non-oil Asia and Africa, and to the current divergence in growth rates of different developing regions. Only in the early part of the next century could one realistically envisage more equality in average *per capita* incomes among the various developing regions.

To achieve the relatively low income target of $500 *per capita* by the year 2000, non-oil regions of Africa and Asia would have to increase their gross product annual growth rates to more than 6.5-7.5 per cent as compared to the 5.5-6.5 range assumed in the study. While such higher growth rates are not impossible, especially favourable conditions relating to trade and payments, transfer of technology and technical assistance would have to be created for the development of these areas. Under all circumstances it is clear that the income situation in these areas will continue to be acute in this century, and that more attention and concerted international effort favouring development of these regions is necessary.

Conditions of growth (I): food and agriculture

The first question that the study addresses itself to is whether the hypothetical scenario of world development just described is feasible, given the well-known constraints on growth, such as the availability of mineral reserves, the potential for food production and the levels of industrial and consumer pollution of the natural environment.

It is important to stress that the study proceeds from assumptions of population growth, as projected by the United Nations. According to these projections, which are based on a detailed analysis of fertility, mortality, age structure, urbanization and other basic factors underlying and determining population dynamics, growth of population is not an exponential process, or an exponential explosion, in which a constant growth rate is maintained. Rather these projections show that population growth rates first tend to increase, then to decline, after certain levels of income and degrees of urbanization are reached.

It follows from these projections that population growth rates in the developed regions will be falling already in the remaining quarter of this century, and that a stable state of population will be reached after 2025. The coming quarter century will, however, evidence a continuation of the very high rate of population expansion experienced in the developing regions between 1950 and 1975. However, population growth rates will start decreasing here in the first quarter of the next century, and a stable state probably will be reached after 2075. This outcome would be achieved not through mass starvation, but through demographic change occurring at relatively high levels of economic development.[6]

Whatever changes in population growth rates might occur in the future, it remains certain that there will be an extremely steep increase in total world population in 1975-2000 (by about 60 per cent), and particularly in the developing regions (about twofold). Thus, the pressure of increasing population upon the food producing potential of the world will remain enormous.

As stated in the International Development Strategy for the Second United Nations Development Decade, a 4 per cent rate of annual growth of agricultural production is consistent with a gross product growth rate of 6 per cent.[7] Assuming higher over-all growth rates of the economies of the developing regions (an average of 7 per cent), and with full provision for changes in the structure of personal consumption (including the reduction of the share of food in total consumption, accompanying the increase in income levels), the average annual increase of agricultural production in the coming decades would have to be about 5 per cent.

This assumes that the current levels of dependence by developing regions on imports from developed regions would not increase. If this dependence were increased, the burden of higher food imports on the balance of payments of non-oil Africa and Asia would rise substantially. However, it should be borne in mind that the difference between a 4 and 5 per cent growth rate in agricultural output would be, by 2000, larger in absolute terms than the total agricultural output in 1970. This clearly shows the difficulty of using imports of food as a major source of any substantial and continuous increase. The major thrust of food supply in the developing regions will have to come from an increase in their own agricultural output.

A 5 per cent annual growth of agricultural output is equivalent to a 4.3-fold increase in 30 years. This is quite a formidable task. However, a 4 per cent annual growth would compound to a 3.2-fold increase in the same period, and even a mere 2.5 per cent increase, consistent with maintaining at least today's very low food consumption levels, would necessitate a 2.1-fold increase of output by the end of the century. In addition, agricultural production in the developed regions as a whole would have to increase by at least 60 per cent in 30 years to assure an average rise in their agricultural consumption *per capita* of only 1 per cent per annum.

Will this task of expanding agricultural output be feasible? As shown in the study, all the developing regions have fairly large reserves of arable land which can be brought into cultivation, given adequate investment and institutional arrangements. It is physically possible to increase the land area under cultivation in the developing market regions as a whole by some 229 million hectares by the year 2000, or by 30 per cent as compared to the actual arable land total of 1970. Presumably, many substantial measures of public policy in the areas of land reclamation and irrigation, public and private investment, credit facilities, supply of necessary machinery and equipment, resettlement of agricultural labour and others would have to be taken in order to turn this physical possibility into a reality.

Even after mobilizing available excess arable land resources, land productivity (including crop yields and cattle productivity) would have to be increased at least threefold in the developing regions if the more optimistic target of a 5 per cent annual growth in agricultural output is to be achieved. If the more modest target of 4 per cent is retained, land productivity would still have to increase about 2-2.5 times. With a marginal growth of 2.5 per cent, and assuming full utilization of additional land, the necessary increase in land productivity is estimated at 60 per cent.

It should be added that, according to the study, even in the developed regions, where possibilities of expanding arable land are sometimes very limited, land productivity would have to increase by 60 to 100 per cent to satisfy their growing demand for agricultural products. Thus, the task of a new "green revolution" is not one that exists exclusively in the developing areas. But it is there that it is most acute and least supported, as of now, by adequate policies and resources.

The major task of drastically increasing land productivity within a 30-year time horizon is not without precedent in the recent history of world agriculture. In the United States of America agricultural output per unit of total land area under cultivation has increased on the average by 80 per cent in 1971-1975, as compared to 1941-

---

[6] See *Concise Report on the World Population Situation in 1970-1975 and Its Long-Range Implications* (United Nations publication, Sales No. E.74.XIII.4), pp. 58 and 59.

[7] Although this target date was not achieved during the first half of the Decade, the World Food Conference held in Rome in 1974 reaffirmed the target for the second half of the Decade.

1945. Crop yields of wheat have increased by 90 per cent, and of corn 2.8 times within the same time period. In the Soviet Union agricultural output per unit of cultivated land has increased on the average by 79 per cent in 1971-1974, as compared to 1946-1950. Crop yields of grains are on the average twice as high as in the earlier period, while yields of cotton have increased 2.6-2.8 times.

Starting from a relatively high level, Japan has been able to increase its average rice yield in the last 30 years by about 30 per cent. Possibilities of much faster growth due to intensive irrigation were demonstrated recently in some developing South-east Asian countries where absolute yield levels were quite low before these programmes were started. Thus, in both the Philippines and Thailand average rice crop yields were increased by about 50 per cent between 1960 and 1970, which is equivalent to increasing 3.4 times in a 30-year period. In most developing countries crop yields are still far below those of Japan, and in all of them they are even farther from the 8 tons per hectare potential that is considered possible given the present state of technology, an irrigation rate of close to 100 per cent and adequate organization.

According to some estimates, the total investment necessary to bring the average crop yield in Asia to half the maximum (4 tons per hectare) would be over $60 billion, including investment into irrigation, fertilizer plants, farm machinery, transport equipment and the like.[8] It may be useful to note that similar schemes implemented in the Soviet Union have brought about a 45 per cent increase in average rice yields in the past 10 years, and that those yields have increased 2.3 times as compared to the late 1950s.

In wheat the progress in the 1960s was spectacular, both in the developed and in some developing countries. In Mexico, where the "green revolution" was initiated, crop yields of wheat increased 2.2 times between 1960 and 1970. In the same period, on a much larger scale, but in the substantially more complicated environment of India and Pakistan, the average wheat yield was increased by 50 per cent, which is equivalent to a 3-fold increase over a span of 30 years. In the Syrian Arab Republic in only five years (from 1970 to 1975) total agricultural production increased by 50 per cent, and the amount of irrigated land doubled.

With all the possible caveats about the unpredictability of weather conditions and the problems involved in implementing technological revolutions in agriculture, it is clear from these examples that, at least with respect to the major food staples, the doubling and trebling of land productivity is a realistic technical and organizational possibility. It is well known that crop yields and cattle productivity are, as a rule, relatively low in the developing countries. Thus, an increase of land productivity in these regions to current levels reached in the developed and some of the developing countries would be a significant contribution to meeting the targets discussed earlier.

This task clearly involves substantial investment into land improvement, irrigation, fertilizer production and distribution, research and development—especially the development of those kinds of plants and animals which yield best results in the peculiar natural environment of the regions and countries in question—education for farmers and the like. Given the large excess labour potential in these regions a lot can be achieved by intensifying labour inputs into soil improvement and plant cultivation. Adequate provision would need to be made for foreign aid in the promotion of higher agricultural production and for the international transfer of progressive technology where applicable.

The success of the new technological revolution in agriculture of the developing regions depends to a large extent on land reform and other social and institutional changes, which are necessary to overcome non-technological barriers to increased land use and productivity. It also depends on creating, by special measures of agricultural policy, a favourable economic environment for agricultural development, including incentives directed towards eliminating inefficiencies in the use of land, labour and technology. If these conditions are met, then the formidable task of feeding the rapidly increasing population of the planet and of improving diets in all regions of the world will be fulfilled.

Conditions of growth (II): adequacy of mineral resources

According to the study, there will be a tremendous growth in the world consumption of minerals between 1970 and 2000. The demand for copper is expected to increase 4.8 times, for bauxite and zinc 4.2 times, nickel 4.3 times, lead 5.3 times, iron ore 4.7 times, petroleum 5.2 times, natural gas 4.5 times and coal 5.0 times.

These estimates were adjusted, wherever possible, to take into account the influence of future technologies on resource development and consumption. Account was taken of potential savings of primary resources through increased recycling. The maximum potential for recycling of many materials under continuing growth, estimated to be about 55 per cent, was assumed to be achieved in all regions by the end of the century. In spite of the new, more rational and economic ways of using mineral resources, the world is expected to consume during the last 30 years of the twentieth century from 3 to 4 times the volume of minerals that has been consumed throughout the whole previous history of civilization. Are the finite reserves of minerals in the earth's crust adequate to sustain this demand?

The study points to the uncertainties of estimating both future stocks of mineral resources and future demands for minerals. Resources already known to exist will be supplemented to an unknown extent by new discoveries in the future, as they were in the past. The degree to which technological change will affect mining and extraction costs is unknown. Substitution among minerals may result from changes in relative prices and from technological change in industries using these minerals. Because of the highly speculative character of estimates of regional and world resource endowments, a very cautious and conservative approach was used in making the basic calculations for this study—namely, the available current estimates of reserves of minerals known to exist at present were used as a basic benchmark without any provision for new discoveries or major new potential sources, such as undersea nodules.

When measured against this extremely conservative bench-mark it was found that only two of the metallic minerals considered in this study, lead and zinc, are expected to "run out" by the turn of the century,

[8] *Far Eastern Economic Review*, 23 January 1975.

provided that the assumptions of future demand are correct and that proven reserves of mineral resources do not increase from their current estimates. However, other investigators have expressed concern about adequacies of other minerals such as asbestos, fluorine, gold, mercury, phosphorus, silver, tin and tungsten.

In a less conservative scenario the estimated endowments of metallic resources found to be relatively scarce either in the world as a whole or in some of the regions were augmented by "hypothetical" and "speculative" reserves cited in geological investigations. In this variant, world reserves of copper were increased about 2.5 times, reserves of nickel 2 times, reserves of lead 1.5 times and reserves of zinc 1.2 times. Iron ore and bauxite were found to be in abundant supply.

Of the energy resources, coal is relatively plentiful even under conservative endowment estimates, while natural gas endowments furnish only a small proportion of energy for the developing countries. In the case of petroleum, available estimates of world reserves were found to be roughly 1.3 times the estimates of cumulative world demand through 2000. However, estimates of oil reserves are increasing rapidly, and it is very difficult to reconcile the various conflicting estimates of possible future changes in their regional distribution.

Thus, known world resources of metallic minerals and fossil fuels are generally sufficient to supply world requirements through the remaining decades of this century, and probably into the early part of the next century as well. However, the adequacy of the world endowment does not necessarily ensure against regional shortages and high prices, nor does it guarantee smooth economic transitions to dependence on shale oil, gasified coal and other "new" energy sources.

As far as regional distribution is concerned, it was found that in the absence of major new discoveries, Western and Eastern Europe, "medium-income" Latin America, arid Africa, and non-oil Asia will remain net importers of most basic minerals in the foreseeable future. Because of balance-of-payments difficulties these regions may have to consider mineral reserve exploration among their top priorities for economic growth. This is especially true of non-oil Asia and Africa, and parts of Latin America.

The study took into account the fact that even in some cases in which mineral resources were relatively abundant in physical terms they will be more costly to extract in the future. As the more accessible reserves of particular minerals become exhausted, the next layer involving higher extraction costs begins to be exploited. To some extent this can be modified by increasing the efficiency of mineral extraction and by new discoveries of highly productive reserves.

Thus, the general response to the question posed earlier is that mineral resource endowment is generally adequate to support world economic development at relatively high rates but that these resources will most probably become more expensive to extract as the century moves towards its conclusion.

Conditions of growth (III): economic cost of pollution abatement

Any scenario of accelerated economic development has to deal with the problem of rapidly increasing pollution, which accompanies the growth of industry, transportation, urban agglomerations and even technical progress in agriculture. It is felt in some quarters that in the long run, and most certainly before the turn of the century, this would lead to insurmountable physical constraints on any further economic growth. The two most pertinent questions in this respect are (1) whether the growth of pollution is at all avoidable and (2) whether the costs of pollution abatement are too high and present a significant constraint on resources for consumption and investment.

The answer to the first question is by now pretty obvious: for many types of industrial and urban pollution, technologies are currently in existence which make it possible to significantly reduce the actual emission of pollutants to at least manageable levels.

The present study estimates, on a world-wide basis, and for each region separately, the future emission of some of the major pollutants: particulate air pollution, biological oxygen demand, nitrogen water pollution, phosphates, suspended solids, dissolved solids, urban solid wastes and pesticides. Abatement activities represented in the study consist of the commonly recognized treatment for particulate air pollution, the primary, secondary and tertiary treatment of water pollution, and the land filling or incineration of urban solid wastes.

Not all the pollutants that are treated by currently used abatement processes are completely abated. For example, processes for the elimination of airborne waste leave unabated around 1 per cent of the pollution in the treated pollutants, and in the case of water pollution 20 per cent of suspended solids. Although the concern for the impact of pollution on the environment has led to rapid technological progress in the abatement processes, for many pollutants, such as sulphur, nitrogen oxides, carbon monoxide and hydrocarbons in the case of airborne waste, pesticides and manure-waste dumping, agricultural pollutants and radioactive waste, no abatement processes are as yet commercially available. Owing to the lack of necessary statistics, the study did not attempt to cover the very important problem of pollution of the open seas. In spite of these limitations, the scope of this study lays the basis for a generalized economic analysis of the problem.

As in the case of minerals, a very cautious and conservative approach was followed. The 1970 standards of pollution abatement in the United States of America were used as a general yardstick, and four hypothetical scenarios were applied for current and future periods, according to the following rule: in any region with a *per capita* gross product of more than $2,000 (1970 constant dollars) the 1970 standards of the United States would have to be fully applied. In other words, these regions would first have to abate pollutants in the same proportions that they were abated in the United States in 1970, and then they would have to increase their abatement activities in such a way as to keep net emissions of pollutants at the level established when the full 1970 United States standards were first applied. The regions falling into this category for the whole period under study are North America, Western Europe (high-income), Japan and Oceania. For these regions it is assumed that pollution will not get worse, in absolute terms, than it was in 1970, if United States standards are universally applied. Any absolute reduction in net pollution emissions would be contingent on better abatement technologies and higher abatement costs.

For regions in the $700 to $2,000 *per capita* income bracket, which in 1970 included all other developed and

6

medium-income regions, it was assumed that the proportion of pollutants abated would have to be equal to half of the United States proportions in 1970. According to the study, two of these regions—namely, the Soviet Union and Eastern Europe—would reach the United States abatement standards by 1980; in the other regions concerned, progress in pollution abatement would be significantly slower.

For regions with a gross product of less than $700, no abatement was envisaged. This was based on the assumption that pollution does not, as a rule, present serious problems at the stage of development in question, except for certain industrial areas and urban centres, and that, on the other hand, such countries would be the hardest pressed as far as resources for investment and consumption are concerned.

In 1970 all of the developing regions in the study fell into this purely hypothetical "no-abatement" category. It was found that some of them, like parts of Latin America and the Middle East and African oil countries, would have to introduce pollution-abatement activities as early as 1980. However, it was thought that in non-oil Asia and Africa the "no-abatement" scenario would remain well into the next century. The net emission of pollutants in these regions would, of course, increase more or less in proportion with their gross products and even faster, posing relevant problems for policy makers.

The study goes on to measure the costs of maintaining these relatively conservative abatement standards. For regions in which the maximum standards of abatement were applied, total costs (including investment and current costs) of abatement procedures included in the study, amounted to 0.7-0.9 per cent of gross product. Since the study, thus far, covers only about one half of actual abatement, according to current United States standards, the total costs of all abatement activities would be in the area of 1.4-1.9 per cent of gross product. This is consistent with available estimates of national expenditures for pollution abatement and control in the United States of America—about 1.6 per cent of gross national product in 1972.[9] Where more liberal abatement standards were applied, the total costs of all abatement activities would amount to 0.5-0.9 per cent of gross product. Thus, a developing country contemplating pollution-abatement activities would have to consider diverting one half to one per cent of its gross product from consumption or investment in production facilities.

The share of capital stock used for abatement purposes is estimated by the study to be in the area of 2.5 to 4 per cent for full coverage of the abatement activities considered. The actual estimated private investment for pollution abatement in the United States of America was about 5 per cent of total private expenditure for new plant and equipment in 1973-1975.[10] Public expenditures for pollution abatement and control would have to be added to this estimate to make it more comparable with the findings of the present study.

For developing regions planning a limited implementation of pollution-abatement techniques, a realistic estimate of the share of investment diverted from other purposes would not, on the average, be larger than 2 to 4 per cent.

[9] *Survey of Current Business*, February 1976, p. 8.
[10] *Survey of Current Business*, July 1975, p. 15.

Thus, the findings of the study are that although pollution is a grave problem for humanity, it is a technologically manageable problem, and that the economic cost of keeping pollution within manageable limits is not unbearable. This does not mean that in the future the world can avert all environmental disruption at moderate cost, or that even modest levels of abatement expenditures may not be considerable, particularly for countries that are just entering the intermediate stages of industrialization. What it means is that the pollution and pollution-abatement problem does not pose an insurmountable barrier for accelerated development along the lines considered in the study.

Conditions of growth (IV): investment and industrialization

The study points to other significant problems of resource allocation which accompany the path of accelerated development. Stepped-up rates lead to a substantial increase of the share of investment in gross product and in the share of producer goods in total output. As shown in the study, the ratio of gross fixed investment to total final internal use (sum of investment, private and public consumption) would need to increase from 20 per cent on the average in 1970 to 41 per cent in 2000 in the Middle East and African oil countries, from 17-20 to 31-33 per cent in Latin America, and from 15 to 23-25 per cent in non-oil Asia and Africa.

The proportion of gross product devoted to investment depends on the rate of growth and pattern of gross product and the coefficients relating the stock of capital in the form of plant, equipment and inventories to the level of production by economic sector. It appears from the calculations in this model that growth rates of 4-6 per cent can be accomplished with an average investment ratio of 20 per cent or less. Growth rates of 7-8 per cent point to investment ratios of about 30 per cent, while sustained growth rates of 9-10 per cent or more cannot be accomplished unless the investment ratio goes up to 35-40 per cent. These ratios are far in excess of the minimum 20 per cent target recommended by the International Development Strategy for the Second United Nations Development Decade.

Current rates of total savings in the developing countries can be augmented at least to a limited extent by reallocating to saving and investment channels some of public consumption in countries in which the rate of public consumption currently allocated to non-civilian purposes is too high. However, because of high demand for public expenditure for various civilian purposes (i.e., education, health services, social security etc.), a large part of the reallocation for investment will have to come out of private consumption. The share of personal consumption expenditure in total final internal use will probably have to be brought down from 68-71 per cent in most developing regions in 1970 to about 60 per cent in non-oil Asia and Africa, to 55-57 per cent in Latin America, and close to 50 per cent in the oil countries of the Middle East and Africa.

The relative decline in the share of personal consumption would lead to an initial slowdown in the increase of *per capita* consumption. However, this disadvantage would, within the period under investigation, lead to much higher levels of both personal consumption and *per capita* consumption through faster growth of total production than would be possible with lower ratios of investment.

The study shows that currently prevailing private and public savings would be clearly inadequate to finance the necessary levels of investment. Substantial relevant measures of taxation and credit and monetary and fiscal stimulation of savings will have to be taken, and institutional changes made, facilitating an accumulation of resources for investment and directing them into those sectors which are essential for the process of accelerated development. Active policy in the investment sphere is desirable, including the setting of investment priorities and the increase, where necessary, in the role of public investment and of the public sector in production and in the infrastructure of the economy.

Special measures would have to be taken to facilitate a more equal distribution of income in the developing countries, so that the benefits of faster growth of average *per capita* income are shared fully, and on a priority basis, by the poorest groups in these countries. Government action may be needed to see to it that high private earnings derived from accelerated development are directed more and more into equitable and productive uses.

As shown in the study, agriculture and extraction will be expanding at slower rates than total gross product once over-all growth is higher than 4 per cent per annum. At the same time, total output of manufacturing industries is expected to expand at higher rates than gross product—namely, 6-7 per cent in non-oil Africa, 7.5-8 per cent in non-oil Asia, 8.5-9 per cent in Latin America, and 14 per cent in the oil producing countries of Asia and Africa.

One distinctive feature of industrialization in the developing regions is the generally lower growth rates of light industry, when compared to those of heavy industry, including machinery equipment and industrial materials (i.e., steel, rubber, chemicals, etc.). This general rule, as shown in the study, is a logical consequence of the growth of the investment ratio and of the decline in the share of personal consumption in total final use.

The tendency of heavy industry to grow more rapidly is well pronounced in all developing regions, according to the study. Growth rates of this sector would reach 7-8.5 per cent in non-oil Africa, 8-8.5 per cent in non-oil Asia, 9-10 per cent in Latin America and 16-17 per cent in the oil countries of Asia and Africa. An accent on heavy industry is essential for industrialization and economic development on the broad regional, though not necessarily on the small country, basis. This opens vast horizons for co-operation and specialization between developing countries, especially in the priority sectors of machinery, equipment and basic industrial materials. The study also shows that because of its substantial current share in total industrial production, light industry in many cases will still remain a larger part of manufacturing than either equipment and machinery or industrial materials in the period before 2000.

The changes in the industrial structure of the various regions reflect their differences in mineral resource endowment, as well as the relative difficulty of developing machinery and equipment as compared to industrial materials production. However, a much larger share of domestic machinery and equipment production would be necessary if the developing regions were to drastically reduce their current dependence on this category of imports.

Changes in world trade and potential payments gap

Accelerated Dev [handwritten annotation]

The study goes on to discuss the implications of accelerated development for international economic relations. Under the most favourable scenario analysed in the study, the share of developing market regions in world gross product would increase from 11 per cent in 1970 to 22 per cent in 2000; their share in world output of manufacturing industries, from 6 to 17.5 per cent.[11] If the countries of Asia with centrally planned economies were added to the developing market regions, the changes in the shares would be from 15 to 28 per cent in gross product and from 9 to about 24 per cent in manufacturing output.

According to the study, the countries with centrally planned economies as a whole would increase their share of world gross product from 23 to 27 per cent and of world manufacturing output from 22 to 29 per cent, while the shares of those with developed market economies (including medium-income regions) would fall from 66 to 51 per cent of gross product and from 70 to 49 per cent of manufacturing output. Though the over-all redistribution of product shares in the coming decades would be substantial, the changes in shares would not involve any absolute reduction either in product or in *per capita* income of any of the developed regions. The redistribution of shares would be a natural outcome of different growth rates in various regions in the world in the course of their mutual co-operation in global economic development.

If the targets set by the International Development Strategy for the 1980s and historical trends were used as a basis for extrapolation into the future, the total share of developing countries (both those with market and centrally planned economies) in the world gross product would reach 22 rather than 28 per cent, and in manufacturing output 17 rather than 24 per cent. For the developing market regions as a whole the shares would be in this case 16 per cent of gross product, and 11-12 per cent of manufacturing output. Even these increases would be significant when compared to the relatively small changes in shares which occurred during the previous 30 years.

Continued world economic growth will lead to a brisk expansion of international trade. According to the study, the total physical volume of world trade, measured in 1970 prices, would increase in 1970-2000 at an annual rate of 6.0 per cent. This is substantially higher than the average over-all growth rate of world gross product, 4.8 per cent. It is projected that in the year 2000, 14.5 per cent of world gross product would cross national borders as compared to 10.6 per cent in 1970.

There would be a particularly rapid expansion of trade in manufactured goods (about 7 per cent per annum), while growth in agricultural trade (at 2.9 per cent) and in mineral resources (at 5 per cent) is projected to be less than the average for all trade. Estimated in 1970 prices, the share of manufactured products in total world trade turnover would increase from 62 per cent in 1970 to 79 per cent in 2000, the share of agricultural goods and minerals would decrease from 38 to 21 per cent.

---

[11] This may be compared with a target of 25 per cent for the year 2000, set at the United Nations Industrial Development Organization Conference on Industrial Development, held at Lima in 1975.

An accelerated rate of development would easily increase the share of developing countries in world imports. Assuming normal decreases in import dependence, the share of developing market regions in total imports of goods in the more optimistic scenario is expected to increase from 16 per cent in 1970 to about 31 per cent in 2000. However, their total share in world exports of goods is not projected to rise as fast, leaving a large potential trade deficit in some regions. All in all, by 2000 the potential balance-of-trade deficit of the developing market regions would amount to some $67 billion, at price levels taking expected changes in relative prices into account. This over-all deficit, however, consists in part of much larger trade deficits for several resource-poor developing regions.

If current trends persist, only a rather modest increase in net aid flows to the developing countries could be counted on. The net capital inflow to the developing regions would increase substantially, but when debt service payments are accounted for, the net financial gain of the developing regions from capital imports would turn out to be very small.

The study then goes on to discuss two drastically different possibilities. One alternative consideration was to estimate world economic development under the assumption that the individual developing regions (with the exception of the Middle East and other major resource exporters) maintained fully balanced payment positions with the outside world (i.e., their balance-of-payments totals would be equal to zero), and that no drastic changes in the economic relations between developed and developing countries would occur. This alternative is examined in scenario A in Chapter VII. Another assumption inherent in this scenario is that full employment is maintained in the developed countries.

Under this scenario, as shown in the study, the average growth rate of gross product in the developed countries would be 3.9 per cent, and only 5.4 per cent in the developing countries, significantly lower than the target set by the International Development Strategy. Due to the difference in population growth rates, the income gap between the two groups of countries would, by the year 2000, remain roughly where it was in 1970.

Conditions of growth (V): towards a new world economic order

Another alternative is to try to close the balance-of-payments deficit of the developing countries by promoting significant changes in the character of economic relations between the developed and the developing countries. The study attempts to estimate the magnitudes involved in various changes that would help close the potential balance-of-payments gap of the developing countries. These changes include the following:

(a) A faster change in relative prices of primary commodities vis à vis manufactured goods;

(b) A decrease in the dependence of the developing countries on imports of manufactured goods;

(c) An increase in the share of the developing countries in world exports of manufactured goods;

(d) Larger aid flows;

(e) Changes in flows of capital investment.

The study shows that on a purely technological basis and taking into account the relative scarcity of some minerals, the prices of natural resources would tend to increase, relative to the prices of manufactured goods,

in the closing decades of the twentieth century. Under the assumption of conservative mineral endowments the average relative prices of minerals would increase some 2.7 times between 1970 and 2000 and the average price of agricultural goods by 14 per cent, while the average price for manufactured goods would decline by 6.8 per cent. Prices of mineral resources in 2000 would be 2.9 times higher in relation to manufactured goods than they were in 1970, and agricultural commodities would be 1.2 times as expensive.

These price changes would take a long time to happen. Most of them would occur in the 1980s or the 1990s. When these slow price changes are accounted for, it turns out that the over-all balance of payments of the developing market regions would emerge with a surplus by 1990 but would have a deficit in 2000. However, the payments position of the individual developing regions would be very different. While the oil-producing countries of the Middle East, Africa and Latin America would have an over-all trade surplus of $15 billion in 1980 and more than $100 billion in both 1990 and 2000, all the other developing market regions would have an over-all deficit of $18 billion in 1980, $80 billion in 1990 and over $150 billion in 2000.

A combination of factors in the first half of the 1970s has in fact brought about drastic changes in absolute and relative prices very much in advance of what would be expected according to the study. These movements have not been uniform. While the price of petroleum in 1975 was 4.7 times higher than in 1970 in relation to the average prices of final consumption in the United States of America, the price of copper fell by 35 per cent, and the price of wheat (in a bad crop year) increased some 90 per cent, which is much more than the study considers likely by 2000 (31 per cent). Because prices fluctuate widely in the short run it was unrealistic to use current commodity prices for computations. However, other fairly realistic assumptions were made to evaluate the impact of faster price changes on the balance of trade and payments.

It was thus assumed that the relative prices, as computed for 2000, already would be paid in international trade in 1980 and 1990. This assumption brings about significant changes in the balance of trade of the developing countries. Most of the difference is due to the 3.5-fold increase in the price of petroleum. The net addition to the balance of trade of the developing regions, as a whole, is $57 billion in 1980 and $36 billion in 1990. The balance of trade of the developing regions as a whole becomes positive in 1980, and increasingly so in 1990, but a deficit is in order for 2000.

Actually, the price changes assumed in these variants do not favour all developing regions. The Middle East, African and Latin American oil regions, and also the metallic mineral exporting region, tropical Africa, are the beneficiaries, achieving in some cases substantial export surpluses in their trade balances. However, non-oil developing regions, and also those that are not large exporters of metallic minerals—namely, most of Latin America and Asia—do not directly benefit from these changes and have to pay the higher prices for minerals, of which they are largely net importers. While this additional burden is already quite large in 1980, it would become very substantial by 1990 and especially by 2000.

One way of alleviating this additional burden would be to introduce a scheme, under which the oil-importing developing regions would be financially compensated for the higher oil prices they have to pay. The study estimates that under such schemes, if generally implemented, some $11 billion in 1980, $22 billion in 1990 and $58 billion in 2000 would be redistributed in favour of oil-importing developing regions, mostly in Asia and Latin America.

The study also estimates the foreign-income increases to the developing countries stemming from the implementation of international commodity schemes, under which the prices of some agricultural goods, of which the developing countries are substantial net exporters, and of mineral resources other than oil, are raised starting in 1980. The over-all effect would be an increase in the export earnings of the developing regions of about $20 billion in both 1980 and 2000, and about $30 billion in 1990. These increases would be rather smoothly distributed between various developing regions, excluding the Middle East and arid Africa. Most of the additional earnings would be due to higher prices of copper, iron ore and products of tropical agriculture.

With all of these price changes put into effect, the projected payments situation of most developing regions would be brought into balance in 1980. However, because of the acceleration of their development in the 1980s and 1990s in all of these regions, except the Middle East and tropical Africa, fairly large payments deficits would re-emerge by 1990, and especially by 2000.

Special computations were made to estimate the effects of changes in import dependence and larger export shares of those developing regions which are not at present richly endowed with mineral resources. In one of the scenarios (scenario M) ratios of import dependence were reduced in Latin America (medium-income), Asia (low-income) and Africa (arid) for a variety of manufactured goods—namely, textiles and apparel, furniture, paper, wood, chemicals, cement, glass and all categories of machinery and equipment. It was assumed that it would be possible to reduce their projected rates of import dependence by 10 per cent in 1980, by 18 per cent in 1990 and by 26 per cent in 2000.

At the same time it was asked what the result would be if the shares of these regions in total world exports of products of light industry increased by 10 per cent in 1980, by 22 per cent in 1990 and by 35 per cent in 2000. It was also assumed that Latin America (medium-income) would be able to substantially increase its share of exports of agricultural commodities. The total savings in the balance of trade of the three developing regions in question was estimated at $8 billion in 1980, $34 billion in 1990 and $73 billion in 2000.

Additional advantages would accrue to the developing countries if developed regions increased their dependence on imports through policies directed towards general liberalization of their tariff and non-tariff barriers, and especially through preferential policies in favour of the developing countries. The strongest effect, however, would be produced by a combination of both liberalized trade policies in the developed countries and the increased competitive power of the products of the developing countries. The combined effect of both changes in relative prices and foreign trade policies would be to practically close the balance-of-payments gap of the developing regions which do not currently have large exportable surpluses of oil and metallic minerals.

The study also estimates the possible magnitudes involved in larger foreign-aid flows. It was assumed that gross aid flows from the developed countries in relation to their gross product would increase step by step from their current levels. This increase would not be uniform but would reflect the different starting levels and *per capita* incomes of the various developed regions. Thus, the gross aid ratio would increase from 0.85 per cent in 1970 to 1 per cent in 1980 and 2 per cent in 2000 in North America. It would remain at its current 1.5 per cent in both 1980 and 1990 and increase to 2 per cent in Western Europe (high-income). In Japan it would be increased from 0.45 per cent in 1970 to 0.75 per cent in 1980 and 1.5 per cent in 2000. In the regions with centrally planned economies it would constitute 0.5 per cent in 1980, 0.7 per cent in 1990 and 2 per cent in 2000.

These measures would have the effect of increasing net aid flows to the developing countries by $3 billion in 1980, $15 billion in 1990 and $47 billion in 2000. More than half of the increase would be canalized into non-oil Asia, with the remainder evenly distributed between Latin America and non-oil Africa. The over-all effect of the increases in aid would be lower than the effect of better trade policies.

Finally, the study undertook to estimate some hypothetical changes in the movement of capital. A better mix of capital flows to the developing countries (including a larger share of loan and portfolio equity investment versus direct investment) might help to create a more favourable atmosphere for such flows, both in the developed and developing countries, and would thus serve as a factor promoting the transfer of modern technology to the developing regions. It was assumed that under these conditions gross capital outflows from the developed market regions would increase by some 20 per cent in both 1990 and 2000, while the average rate of return on such investment to the developed regions would be reduced by 2 per cent so as to lessen the burden of debt service and foreign income outflows from these countries.

It was found that the total net effect of these changes in favour of the developing regions would be about $7 billion in 1990 and $18 billion in 2000. These increments are relatively small financially when compared to other changes discussed previously but would involve substantial transfers of technology and funds for investments. The total effect of the various measures discussed is roughly to achieve the balance-of-payments equilibrium in the developing countries even under conditions of accelerated growth. It should be stressed that these measures are dependent on significant changes in the current economic relations between the developed and the developing countries, which are called for by the resolutions of the General Assembly at the sixth and seventh special sessions.

Summary

The findings of this study can be briefly summarized as follows:

(*a*) Target rates of growth of gross product in the developing regions, set by the International Development Strategy for the Second United Nations Development Decade, are not sufficient to start closing the income gap between the developing and the developed countries. Higher growth rates in developing countries in the 1980s and 1990s, coupled with slightly lower rates in the developed countries (as compared to their long-term trends), would reduce, at least by half, the average income gap by 2000;

(*b*) The principal limits to sustained economic growth and accelerated development are political, social and institutional in character rather than physical. No insurmountable physical barriers exist within the twentieth century to the accelerated development of the developing regions;

(*c*) The most pressing problem of feeding the rapidly increasing population of the developing regions can be solved by bringing under cultivation large areas of currently unexploited arable land and by doubling and trebling land productivity. Both tasks are technically feasible but are contingent on drastic measures of public policy favourable to such development and on social and institutional changes in the developing countries;

(*d*) The problem of the supply of mineral resources for accelerated development is not a problem of absolute scarcity in the present century but, at worst, a problem of exploiting less productive and more costly deposits of minerals and of intensive exploration of new deposits, especially in the regions which are not currently known to be richly endowed with vast mineral resources, so as to reduce the unevenness in the distribution of such reserves between the various regions of the world;

(*e*) With current commercially available abatement technology, pollution is not an unmanageable problem. It is technically possible to keep net emissions of pollution in the developed regions at their current levels. Full application of relatively strict abatement standards would be less of a general problem in most of the developing regions in this century and would be largely limited to abatement activities in certain industrial areas and to urban solid-waste disposal. However, even if relatively strict abatement standards were gradually applied in the developing regions, the over-all economic cost of pollution abatement is not estimated to exceed 1.5-2 per cent of gross product—that is, it does not present an insurmountable barrier for economic development of these regions;

(*f*) Accelerated development in developing regions is possible only under the condition that from 30 to 35 per cent, and in some cases up to 40 per cent, of their gross product is used for capital investment. A steady increase in the investment ratio to these levels may necessitate drastic measures of economic policy in the field of taxation and credit, increasing the role of public investment and the public sector in production and the infrastructure. Measures leading to a more equitable income distribution are needed to increase the effectiveness of such policies. Significant social and institutional changes would have to accompany these policies. Investment resources coming from abroad would be important but are secondary as compared to the internal sources;

(*g*) Accelerated development points to the necessity of a faster growth, on the average, of heavy industry, as compared to the over-all rates of expansion for the manufacturing industry. This is certainly true on the broad regional if not on a small country basis, increasing the possibilities of industrial co-operation between the developing countries. In many regions, however, light industry would remain a leading manufacturing sector for a long time, providing, among other things, a basis for a significant increase in the exports of manufactured products from the developing countries;

(*h*) Accelerated development would lead to a continuous significant increase in the share of the developing regions in world gross product and industrial production, as compared to the relative stagnation of these shares in recent decades. Because of the high income elasticity of the demand for imports this would certainly entail a significant increase in the share of these regions in world imports to support internal development. However, the increase in their share of world exports is expected to be slower, owing to severe supply constraints in the developing regions and the relatively slower pace at which the competitive strength of their manufacturing industries would be built up. For those reasons accelerated development poses the danger of large potential trade and payments deficits in most of the developing regions;

(*i*) There are two ways out of the balance-of-payments dilemma. One is to reduce the rates of development in accordance with the balance-of-payments constraint. Another way is to close the potential payments gap by introducing changes into the economic relations between developing and developed countries, as perceived by the Declaration on the Establishment of the New International Economic Order—namely, by stabilizing commodity markets, stimulating exports of manufactures from the developing countries, increasing financial transfers and so on;

(*j*) A relatively stable increase in the prices of minerals and agricultural goods exported by the developing countries, as compared to prices of manufactured goods, is one way of increasing the export earnings of these countries and closing their potential payments deficit. Higher mineral and agricultural prices are also called for, owing to technological requirements and the relative scarcity of natural resources, which makes them relatively more costly as time goes by. However, because of the uneven way in which mineral resources are currently distributed between various developing regions, these price changes would be of advantage to some regions, while placing an additional economic and financial burden on the others. Special schemes, providing for financial compensation to the net importing developing regions would be a possible way to reduce these imbalances;

(*k*) For developing regions which are not large net exporters of minerals or agricultural goods, the main way to reduce the potential trade imbalance is to significantly decrease their import dependence on manufactured products in the course of industrialization, while at the same time increasing their share of world exports of some manufactured products, particularly those emanating from light industry. Building up the competitive strength of such products in the world market is an important prerequisite, combined with the reduction of tariffs and other barriers imposed on the exports of the developing regions to the developed regions. An increase in the flow of aid to the developing regions; measures to create a more favourable climate for and a better mix of capital investment flows to these regions; a reduction in the financial burden arising from foreign investment in these regions are important but are secondary measures as compared to the necessary changes in the commodity markets and trade in manufactured products;

(*l*) To ensure accelerated development two general conditions are necessary: first, far-reaching internal changes of a social, political and institutional character in the developing countries, and second, significant changes in the world economic order. Accelerated development leading to a substantial reduction of the income gap between the developing and the developed countries can only be achieved through a combination of both these conditions. Clearly, each of them taken separately is insufficient, but when developed hand in hand, they will be able to produce the desired outcome.

11

Part One

APPRAISING THE FUTURE

The subject of the present report is the future or rather several alternative futures of the world economy. It describes the different paths along which the different parts of the world economy could advance either rapidly or slowly or, indeed, along which they could be forced to retreat, as the case may be, through 1980 and 1990 towards 2000.

The future can rarely be predicted with precision; and the future of such a complex phenomenon as the world economy is particularly difficult to anticipate or even to visualize. When nothing is known about such a phenomenon nothing can be proven to be impossible. But as the actual state of the system and its structural properties becomes known and the forces and relations that govern its development and change become better understood, many of the originally envisaged futures are eliminated from the range of realistic possibilities. At the same time the distant outlines of the possible emerge more clearly and in more detail as increased knowledge and understanding are brought to bear on the subject.

However, even if the inner workings of the world economic system were fully understood and the external factors which will affect its development possibilities over the next quarter of a century were fully known, a gradual elimination of the options that first appeared to be open but upon further examination turned out to be closed cannot reduce the originally envisaged wide range of possibilities to a single inevitable path. One reason for this is that some of the factors upon which the course of future developments can be shown to depend will be controlled by purposeful national or international action guided by more or less rational political choice.

The allocation of the current output of goods and services among consumption, productive investment and government uses, the erection of new or the elimination of old barriers to international trade, more intensified measures against environmental disruption, the initiation of public health measures designed to affect long-run demographic trends—these are only a few examples of the policy actions that can be expected to have quite obvious direct as well as less obvious indirect effects on development prospects in all parts of the world. As Professor Jan Tinbergen so eloquently emphasized many years ago, no thoughtful rational choice between alternative courses of action, in the socio-economic or in any other sphere, is possible without systematic, detailed and, one should add, objective understanding of the complex sets of those direct and indirect repercussions that each of them is bound to bring about.

That is one reason why this report does not present a single projection of the future course of development for the world economy but rather a set of alternative, tentative projections. The other reason is simply ignorance. Even if specific policy measures directed towards influencing future population trends, the rates of growth of the less developed and the more developed countries, the future rate of exploitation of basic mineral resources and of investment in the production of food-stuffs were firmly set, the consequences of any of these policies could be anticipated only to a limited extent. This is not so much because of a lack of appropriate analytical tools as because of insufficient factual knowledge: for instance, the estimates made by experts of as yet untapped reserves of mineral and even agricultural resources differ from each other not by 50 but in some instances by as much as several hundred per cent. Great uncertainty is attached to estimates of future population trends and still greater to the nature and direction of future technological change.

Some of the missing data can and should be secured through additional factual research; other data, such as estimates of the quantitative specifications of technologies that might be used 10, 20 or 30 years from now—although they too can be improved—are bound to be of a contingent kind.

13

Chapter I

THE INPUT-OUTPUT STRUCTURE OF PRODUCTION AND CONSUMPTION

The input-output method used in the present study provides the means of describing the complex and highly differentiated structure of the world economy in great detail. Each of the 15 regions into which all the developed and less developed countries are grouped for the purposes of this analysis is visualized as a set of 48 producing and consuming sectors connected with each other and with the economies of other regions by steady flows of services and goods.[12] Extractive industries absorb, in addition to inputs received from other sectors, renewable or non-renewable primary—that is, natural—resources. Households absorb consumer goods and supply labour; the public sector is represented by government activities of several different kinds. Pollutants are treated as by-products of regular production or consumption processes, and their elimination (abatement) as a special type of "productive" activity. Besides the flows of current inputs, each sector employs also "stocks" of buildings, machinery, inventories of raw and semi-fabricated materials (usually referred to, respectively, as fixed and working capital) and—in the case of the household sector—residential housing, sewage systems and the like.

The "cooking recipe" (technological mix) used in a particular industry at any given place and time determines the amounts of all the inputs, including labour, required to produce a given amount of its output. In the case of households, it is the "consumption recipe", which depends on the income level and the combination of biological needs, social conditions and cultural standards, that determines the contents of a typical household shopping basket.

A set of regional input and consumption coefficients describes the combination of goods and services required by each one of the productive sectors of a particular economy per unit of its output and, in the case of private or public households, per unit of their aggregate expenditures and income.

For the purposes of numerical computation, the schematic image of the world economy described above is reduced primarily but not exclusively to a system of linear input-output equations. This analytical tool has been designed with a view towards being able to absorb, with as little distortion as possible, large variegated sets of quantitative data. Array upon array of technical "mixes" describing the present or the projected future input requirements of all the different branches of mining, agriculture, manufacturing and various service industries, as well as the contents of typical shopping baskets of private and public households in each of the 15 different groups of countries had to be fitted into the structural framework of an analytical description of the world economy and committed to the electronic memory of a large computer. So were alternative estimates of the total stocks of different mineral and other natural resources. The technical coefficients permitting estimation of the amounts of various pollutants generated in many of the production and consumption processes were ascertained too, as were the input requirements of processes designed to suppress or at least reduce the flows of these undesirable by-products of regular economic activities. Separate estimates had to be made of the key urban environmental amenities (e.g., water supply and liquid and solid waste collection) and housing. They too were included in the analytical design and entered into the computer.

---

[12] See Annex I for a discussion of the geographical classification scheme.

Chapter II

INTERNATIONAL TRADE, PRICES AND FINANCIAL TRANSACTIONS

The economies of individual regions are linked with each other through flows of internationally, or rather, interregionally traded goods. While the inputs and outputs of services and goods classified as "domestic" must be balanced within each region, the consumption of internationally traded goods has to be balanced only for the world as a whole. Export surpluses and import surpluses of each commodity or commodity group must add up to zero on the international scale. The world-wide input-output system must contain a set of equations stating this in algebraic terms.

In principle the composition of each region's exports and imports should be examinable and consequently also predictable in terms of comparative production costs and the structure of demand. However, the lack of sufficiently detailed factual information precludes, at this stage of analysis, the possibility of explaining interregional commodity flows in such fundamental terms.

The quantity of a particular type of commodity, such as steel, exported from a given region, such as North America, is treated as a fixed share of aggregate world exports (which, of course, are equal to aggregate world imports) of that commodity. The quantity of steel imported into the North American region is, on the other hand, regarded as representing a given share of the total amount of steel consumed in that region. Thus, the domestic outputs and the global input—or rather its separate regional components—are the variables that enter into the determination of the internal input-output balances of the trading regions. With sets of appropriate "trade coefficients" incorporated in our system of equations, any projected change in regional inputs and outputs of internationally traded goods will thus be accompanied by appropriate shifts in each region's pattern of exports and imports. Moreover, the quantities of internationally traded goods flowing into and out of every region are related to—and determined simultaneously with—their flows between the different sectors of each region.

In terms of this approach, all the exports of a particular commodity can be viewed as if they were delivered to a single international trading pool and all the imports as if they were drawn from that pool. The world-wide trading balance (to be distinguished from the monetary payments balance, considered below) requires that the sum total of all regional exports of each commodity delivered to its pool equals the sum total of all regional imports drawn from that pool. The fact that this formulation does not involve any analysis of bilateral (i.e., region to region) trade flows, should be viewed, at this stage, as its strength rather than its weakness. Detailed analysis and explanation of the network of interregional shipments—involving the consideration of such factors as differential transportation costs—can and should be separated from the analysis of long-run patterns of what might be called the interregional division of labour. The introduction of prices and income variables leads, as explained below, to the important question of the total value of the exported and imported goods and the problem of capital flows and of other types of international transfers.

The same sets of technical coefficients that govern the physical relationships between the inputs and the outputs within the structural framework of a particular economy also determine the relation between prices of various goods and services, on the one hand, and the "value added"—that is, the wages, rents, profits earned and taxes paid by the industries that produce them—on the other. Given the price received by an industry for a unit of its output and the prices paid by it for the inputs purchased from other industries, one obviously can determine how much of its receipts will remain (after all these purchases have been made) to be paid out as value added or, if worse comes to worse, how much subsidy (negative value added) that industry will have to receive in order to keep going.

Given the value added to be paid out by each industry (per unit of its output), one can reverse the question and ask what prices would have to be charged for the products of different industries so as to enable each of them to balance its revenue with its total outlay—the latter defined so as to include payments for purchased supplies, as well as the value added. This latter approach is used to compute, by solving the appropriate set of price/value-added equations, the corresponding prices of their products from the given—or rather the projected—values added paid out by producing sectors of advanced industrialized areas (exemplified by the North American region). Such computations naturally must also take into account the expected changes in the technical input coefficients. Prospective changes in the prices of various raw materials derived in this way will necessarily reflect the rise in the capital and other input requirements of primary extractive industries expected to be brought about by the depletion of the more accessible resources and the consequent shift to inferior reserves of natural resources.

Having determined the prices of internationally traded goods on the basis of conditions expected to prevail in the highly developed regions, we can then turn around and insert these prices in the equations describing the price/value-added relations reflecting the technology and resource endowments assumed to exist at that time in other, less developed regions. With prices considered as given, the solution of these equations yields the values added—that is, the net income comprising wages, profits and rents that can be expected to be earned by the various industries in the less developed countries.

Extractive industries exploiting rich natural deposits in some of the less developed areas can be expected to yield in the future, as they already do now, much higher values added (rents and profits) than their counterparts operating under much less favourable natural conditions in the developed industrialized countries. The opposite will probably be true in the case of some of the manufactured goods. Squeezed between world prices reflecting the advanced technology and labour skills of the developed regions and high domestic costs, industries producing such goods for export in the less developed countries can be expected to yield only very low or even negative values added. In the latter case, they could exist only if supported by direct or indirect subsidies.[13]

This, incidentally, is a situation that could not have been envisaged if the principle of cost minimization had been formally applied on a world-wide scale. The simultaneous operation of high-cost and low-cost facilities under conditions in which the latter could actually satisfy the entire demand obviously violates that principle. It is equally obvious, however, for many different reasons, that such situations not only prevail now but will continue to exist also in the future.

The trade balance of a country or region in the model depends on the quantities of goods imported and exported and on the prices at which they have been purchased or sold. Unlike outputs which are treated as

physical quantities only, export and import totals, as well as trade balances, are computed in current prices. In addition to the items entered in the balance of trade, the balance of payments includes such financial transactions as capital transfers (securities and loans), international interest and other income payments and official aid. These variables are incorporated in the system of input-output equations, which also contain all the structural data used in deriving the alternative projections of possible future states of the world economy presented in this report.

For the purpose of developmental projections, the balance of trade of a particular region can be treated either as one of the given variables and its gross national income as one of the unknown variables, or vice versa. After having set, for example, numerical gross product targets for less developed areas, one can determine what import surplus under given structural conditions the attainment of these targets would entail. Or, to reverse the process, having fixed the allowable import surplus of a region, one can compute the attainable level of gross national product. In other formulations of the problem, both the payments deficit or surplus and the level of consumption of the less developed countries are treated as variables dependent, for instance, on the given prices of the raw materials that these countries sell and the manufactured goods that they buy on international markets.

---

[13] It has been impossible to carry out a full analysis of the price and rent implications of the world system within the time limitations of the present report. Such an analysis is, however, planned.

Chapter III

FLEXIBILITY AND INTERDEPENDENCE WITHIN THE EXISTING STRUCTURAL CONSTRAINTS

The model as a whole contains more variables than equations. The structural relations described in it can thus be satisfied by many (strictly speaking, infinitely many) different combinations of the unknown magnitudes that enter into it. By fixing the magnitudes of some of the variables from the outside one by one, we can reduce the total number of unknowns so as to make that number equal to the number of equations and thus arrive at a unique solution. By varying the magnitudes of one or several of the externally fixed variables, it is thus possible to obtain a series of alternative projections showing in each case how the dependent variables would have to shift so as to preserve the internal balance of the system within its given structural framework.

Because of the general interdependence among all parts of the system, the level of each type of economic activity in each corner of the world, so long as it has not been fixed by assumption, is bound to respond in one way or another to every primary change introduced in any other part of the system. Many of the remote indirect repercussions turn out to be so small that they could be neglected, while others on the contrary are much larger than one would intuitively expect them to be.

For purposes of scientific explanation or projection one would be inclined to observe, or to fix by assumption, the magnitudes of what might be called causal factors and use the analytical system to ascertain their necessary effect. For purposes of practical action, however, the relation between causes and effects can also be approached from the other end. In explaining, for example, the means of narrowing the gap between the levels of *per capita* consumption in the less developed and the more advanced regions, the inquiry might move not from causes to effects but from desired effects to the causes capable of bringing them about. Instead of fixing, among other factors, the magnitude of variables that represent the level of capital transfer from developed to the less developed areas or, say, the stringency of anti-pollution standards imposed on industries operating in the latter groups of countries, and then computing the corresponding income levels, we can start out by postulating the target income levels for all regions and then proceed — by solving the appropriate system of equations — to find out what combinations of larger capital transfer would permit the attainment of these predetermined goals.

In examining the state of the world economy as projected by the model, we do not necessarily need to know which of the variables were fixed in advance — that is, before the computation started — and which were treated as unknowns to be derived. The total picture would remain the same if the roles were reversed — that is, if some of the numbers obtained through the original solution were considered as given, while some of those originally fixed were treated as unknowns.

A description of a particular hypothetical state of the world economy can be interpreted as providing answers to all kinds of questions. In fixing developmental goals such as have been defined in the context of the Second United Nations Development Decade, variables that describe the future state of the economic system are usually designated as target variables. These typically are the levels of *per capita* gross domestic product (GDP), private and public *per capita* consumption and their respective rates of growth. The number of variables that in one context or another can be viewed as representing causal factors, such as domestic savings, external balance, labour force participation, prices of raw materials and so on is quite large. Hence, after inserting in the system the prescribed or desired magnitudes of target variables, one will often find that the number of the remaining unknowns exceeds the number of equations. This means that many different combinations of causal instrumental factors could bring about, within the given set of technical and structural limitations, the attainment of the same prescribed goals.

At this point one might ask, why not maximize? Why not find out what combination of causal or policy-controlled variables would, for example, maximize the level of consumption or the welfare index defined in some specific terms? The response to this question is fundamentally the same that was given above to the question about the optimal international division of labour. Any attempt at general over-all maximization would inevitably drive a system beyond the valid limits of the simplified analytical formulation erected on a still relatively weak and fragmentary data base and certainly beyond the range of what can be expected actually to happen.

It is more a question of analytical convenience than of fundamental difference when one speaks, on the one hand, of given magnitudes or unknown variables (for example, regional income levels, international trade flows, capital transfers) and, on the other hand, of numerical coefficients describing the structural characteristics of the system (for example, technical input coefficients of various industries, estimated reserves of raw materials and the like). What is treated today as a given structural characteristic of the economic system, tomorrow might be explained in terms of some more fundamental factors and relations, the existence of which empirical inquiry has as yet not been able to ascertain or to measure with sufficient precision.

The system is described in terms of sets of linear equations and the computer programme developed to solve them enables not only the authors of the present report but also its prospective users to ask and to answer — with minimal computational effort — such questions as, how an unknown (for instance, the investment level of a particular less developed area) would react not only to shifts in the values of some externally fixed variables (such as the level of foreign aid received) but also to a structural change (such as a reduction in the magnitude of a technical coefficient describing the amount of electrical power used per unit of output by the chemical industry).

The input-output model of the world economy on which this report is based is capable of answering a great variety of questions. Since that system is complex and large, the formulation of specific questions and the interpretation of answers that come out of the computer in the form of figures is a task that has to be approached with great care and circumspection. Alternative conjectures concerning future population trends, prospective technological advances or not yet ascertained reserves of mineral resources can be combined with each other in many different ways. Similarly, each one of the possible combinations of national and international policies are bound to have different effects on the direction of economic and social developments in all parts of the world. Taken together, alternative sets of basic factual and policy assumptions can yield a great number of different developmental paths for the world economy as a whole and for each of its interdependent regions.

The general analytical approach, the computer programme and the data bank developed for the purpose of this report can be used to explore any number of internally consistent paths of the world economy from its present state into the future. The analysis that follows is based on a detailed consideration of eight alternative projections. Each delineates a different long-run course of investment and consumption, exports and imports, pollution and abatement activities, as well as many other economic variables in each of the developed and less developed regions from 1970 through 1980 and 1990 to 2000. Some of these projections are based on more and some on less optimistic assumptions about the amounts of the existing, not yet exploited reserves of natural resources; some reflect higher and others lower estimates of the future rates of population growth; some illustrate the implications of stringent, others of lax abatement policies. Alternative outlooks for the future allocation of international import markets between the developed and less developed areas is given special consideration.

Seven of the eight projections are anchored in given sets of developmental targets described in terms of specific levels of *per capita* GDP to be attained by various less developed and developed regions in 1980, 1990 and 2000. In other words, the projections belonging to these groups represent alternative paths—all steep, some hardly traversable—towards the attainment of the same set of developmental goals.

The eighth projection, which turns out to be rather pessimistic, does not involve setting up mandatory income targets. It is derived on the assumption that the division of current income between saving and consumption, both in the developing and the developed areas, would be governed in the future by the same patterns of behaviour that have been observed up to now and that the flow of capital and of official aid from the developed countries will continue to be governed by the same economic considerations that seem to have determined it in the past. A juxtaposition of the income levels that the developing and the developed regions can be expected to attain under these assumptions, with the income targets set by the United Nations, and a comparison of the rates of investment, the patterns of international trade and, in particular, the configurations of international indebtedness and balances of payments that correspond to the different developmental paths provides a concrete tangible basis for appraising the fundamental contrast between the old international economic order and the proposed new one.

Chapter IV

FORMULATION OF A MULTIREGIONAL WORLD INPUT-OUTPUT SYSTEM

A concise mathematical formulation of the multiregional input-output system employed in this report is contained in Annex IV. The schematic overview of its structure, presented below, should suffice for a general understanding and a correct interpretation of the principal conclusions.

The 2,625 equations contained in the model consist of 15 interconnected regional sets, one for each of the 15 regional blocks. Each regional set consists of 175 equations that describe—in terms of 269 variables—the interrelations between the production and consumption of various goods and services and, in particular, of specific natural resources within a particular region; 229 of these variables are region specific, while 40 represent the export-import pools of internationally traded goods and the balance or imbalance, as the case may be, of that region's international financial transactions.

Regional breakdown

The 15 regions and the abbreviated designations which are used for each in many of the tables of the present report, as well as the total population of each region and average *per capita* GDP figures for the year 1970 are listed in table 2; a complete list of the countries included

in each region is presented in Annex I. Basically, the geographic groupings reflect a reasonable degree of homogeneity in the economic variables that characterize those nations combined in a single regional unit. A primary criterion employed in this classification scheme was the level of economic development as measured by *per capita* income levels and the share of manufacturing activity in total GDP. Further aggregation was based on the identification of certain variables that are of particular importance to the present study. Thus, the major oil-exporting countries were grouped together and, for African nations, a distinction was made between those receiving less than 10 inches of rainfall annually and those receiving more. As might be expected, the criteria outlined were not applied without exceptions. In general, the regional groupings respect continental boundaries so as to facilitate the comparison of the projected results with the economic data produced by various international agencies. An exception to this rule was made for the oil-producing countries of the Middle East and Africa, which were grouped into one region. In a few other instances, geopolitical considerations overrode the economic basis for aggregation.

Table 3 (at end of volume) presents in schematic form a block of equations pertaining to a single region. The

TABLE 2. CLASSIFICATION OF REGIONS[a]

Name of region	Abbreviated designation	Identifying number	Population 1970 (millions)	Per capita GNP 1970 (1970 dollars)
Developed . . . . : *DC*				
North America	NAH	1	229.1	4625
Western Europe (high-income)	WEH	4	282.0	2574
Soviet Union	SUH	6	242.8	1791
Eastern Europe	EEM	7	105.1	1564
Western Europe (medium-income)[b] . .	WEM	5	108.1	698
Japan	JAP	9	104.3	1916
Oceania	OCH	15	15.4	2799
Africa (medium-income)[b]	SAF	14	21.5	786
Developing group I (Developing with major mineral resource endowment) . . . . . : *LDC-I*				
Latin America (low-income) . . .	LAL	3	90.0	443
Mid-East Africa (oil producers) . . .	MDE	11	126.5	286
Africa (tropical)	TAF	13	141.4	168
Developing group II (Other developing) . . . . . : *LDC-II*				
Latin America (medium-income) . .	LAM	2	191.4	594
Asia (low medium-income) . . .	ASL	10	1023.2	120
Africa (arid)	AAF	12	131.2	205
Asia (centrally planned)	ASC	8	808.4	167

[a] Complete list of countries included in each region is presented in Annex I. Classification influenced by the level of development the regions are likely to reach by 2000.
[b] Classified in developing group II in the print-out of scenario A, which appears in Annex VI.

letter or symbol placed in each cell of the table represents the coefficients of variables (named at the heads of the relevant columns) that enter into the linear equations (or a linear approximation of a non-linear equation) described by each row. Thus, for example, the symbol, @, at the intersection of row 50 and column 81 stands for the set of technical coefficients that represents inputs of traded goods (XT) per unit of output of non-traded goods (XNT). Note, however, that this very large table is itself still in summary form: the variable XT actually represents the class of 19 traded goods; the variable XNT represents the class of 6 non-traded goods; and the symbol @ represents the coefficients of a 19×6 portion of the regional input-output table. A key to the symbols for the various coefficients in the table and a key to the symbols representing the variables accompanies table 3.

The equations, or groups of similar equations, represented by a particular row in table 3 can be conveniently identified by the name of the "leading" variable that this equation explains or defines in terms of some other variables. Abbreviations of these identifying variables are entered in the left-hand column of the key to rows in table 3. All other variables are listed in abbreviated form in the key to columns in table 3. All variables are listed in full in Annex III.

Some of the variables are measured in appropriate physical units, the others in value (dollar) units. For the base year 1970, all valuations are in 1970 United States prices; for the years 1980, 1990 and 2000—depending on the context—values are expressed either in current-year relative dollar prices or in constant 1970 dollars. Dollar figures describing the values of outputs, inputs, exports, imports or stocks of particular goods in base year—that is, 1970—prices can be interpreted as measurements of their physical amounts.[14]

An equation or a group of similar equations can be reconstituted from each row by multiplying each coefficient entered along the row (not forgetting to take into account the sign) with the variable identified by the symbol located above it in the top row of the table, and then setting the sum or the terms so formed to equal zero.[15]

For example, the equation corresponding to the first row of coefficients reads:

---

[14] The unit used in such measurement is defined as the amount of that commodity that could be purchased for \$1 at its 1970 price.

[15] Certain variables are identified as "slacks". Their meaning and their use requires explanation. Formally, a "slack" is an extra additive variable introduced into an equation. There are several different reasons for using this device. If a slack is treated as one of the unknowns (the magnitude of which can be determined simultaneously with the magnitude of all the other variables), the final result will be the same as would have been obtained if the equation in question were simply eliminated from the system; except that the magnitude of the slacks as it came out in the numerical solution will indicate by how much the relationship into which it was inserted would have to change in order to be compatible with the rest of the system.

A general computer programme for manipulating a large system that contains equations which are kept in force for some solutions and have to be suppressed for some others can thus be greatly simplified by the use of slacks. If the value of slack entered into an equation (and with it into the computer programme) is set to be zero, that equation is kept in force. To switch it out one simply has to treat the slack as one of the unknown variables.

Treated as an exogenously determined variable, a slack can also be conveniently employed to introduce a change in the shape of the equation (and consequently of the relationship described by it) in which it enters—for instance, an upward or a downward shift in a curve.

$$-M_1 * GDP + CONS + INVS + GOV + EXPRT$$
$$- IMPRT + P_1 * URBAN + P_2 * ABATE$$
$$+ INVCH = 0$$

where $M_1 = 1 + M_2$

M_2 = per cent of GNP spent on pollution abatement in 1970

P_1 = *per capita* cost of urban service

P_2 = abatement costs per unit of pollution abated

This equation can be transformed into an explicit definition of gross domestic product, as used in the model:

$$GDP = \frac{1}{1+M_2} (CONS + INVS + GOV + EXPRT$$
$$- IMPRT + P_1 * URBAN + P_2$$
$$* ABATE + INVCH)$$

Each equation, or group of equations, represented in table 3 can be transformed to explain the variables, or groups of variables, that give their names to the rows of the table.

A complete list of all the variables appearing in the multiregional system and the abbreviations used in all tabulations is presented in Annex III. The equations contained in the system are tabulated in their explicit algebraic form in Annex IV.

Macroeconomic balances

Equations 1 through 9 describe balances for the macroeconomic variables. They show how the principal elements of the regional accounts—regional GDP, gross investment, employment and the like—are related to the levels of other activities in the system and to each other. The multiplication of GDP with M_1 in the first term of equation 1 compensates (as can be verified by appropriate substitutions) for the cost of abatement, $P_2*ABATE$, that is already included in the conventional measure of the gross domestic product for the base year 1970. Since regional accounts for future years are also expressed in 1970 prices only an increase in the proportion of pollution abated (M_2) will be registered as an increase in GDP. To take account of the abatement expenditures in GDP, any increment in the rate of abatement over that actually realized in 1970 (i.e., M_2) is multiplied by the 1970 "prices" (i.e., the unit cost) of abatement and summed into the Gross Domestic Product. Inventory change is treated as analogous to investment, but in compliance with standard conventions it is recorded as a distinct element of GDP.

Personal consumption of specific goods is treated as a function of income *per capita*. The coefficients in columns 2 and 9 are terms in the linear approximations of the consumption functions for the region. The coefficients, C, of column 2 measure the amounts of specific agricultural products (AGS), metal and energy resources (RSS) and industrial products (XT and XNT) consumed per dollar of additional total expenditure. The coefficients in column 9 represent the population term in the linearized consumption functions. They show, for any given level of consumption expenditure, how the amounts of the various specific products will increase or decrease with an increase in population (with the total consumption expenditure held constant). Housing is treated as household investment. The capital coefficients, K, in columns 2 and 9 represent the consumption expenditure and income terms that determine the stock of housing required at any given spending and population level. Expenditures on collection of household liquid and solid wastes and water supply are specified as "urban amenities". Their level in any given region depends on the size of the urban, rather than the over-all population.

The second equation determines DSAVE—that is, the positive or negative excess of desired private saving over the actual volume of investment. It is essentially a slack variable (see foot-note 14). While government saving is set equal to government investment, the desired—that is, potential—supply of private savings is determined as a given per cent of GDP plus net inflows of foreign capital and foreign aid. For a single region, unless explicitly set equal to zero, a positive or negative DSAVE can exist. By the internal logic of the system, it has to be matched by a shortfall or an excess of the actual, as compared to the normal (corresponding to the normal saving ratio) level of consumption, a positive or negative (as the case may be) element in aid and capital flows, or some combination of the two.[16]

Each year's investment is the sum of four components: equipment, plant, land development and irrigation investment. Rows 75, 76 and 87 through 91 of table 3 show further details of the treatment of investment in this system. In any given year, the stocks of plant and equipment capital required to support current production are determined by capital coefficients (K). Investment required over a 10-year period (say, between 1970-1980) must cover depreciation as well as the difference between current requirements and the stock of capital at the beginning of the decade. Equation 91 keeps track of the requirements of arable land, but the levels of investment in land development and irrigation are set exogenously in the present system.[17] Columns 97 through 101 show the industrial composition of the four different types of domestic investment—that is, the proportional allocation of a dollar's worth of equipment investment among the sectors producing machinery, electrical machinery and the like, and the industrial composition of inventory change.

Row 8 contains labour coefficients, representing employment per unit of output in the various industrial, household and government sectors. Only in the developed countries are labour coefficients specified for agriculture. Thus, total regional employment includes the entire employed labour force in the developed regions but excludes the agricultural labour force in the lower-income regions.

Input-output balances

Rows 11 through 69 of table 3 describe the input-output balances of the system. Rows 50-68 show the total requirements of 19 internationally traded manu-factures per unit of output of the corresponding domestic producing sectors. The purchasers of these inputs include household consumers, government and investment, as well as other industrial sectors. Separate rows identify specific products measured in physical units—that is, specific agricultural products (AGS) and specific resource products (RSS). Residual agriculture (AGR—that is, all agricultural production except animal and milk products, cereals, high-protein crops and root crops), residual resources (RSR—that is, all minerals other than the six metals and three energy resources specifically enumerated) and food and resource processing margins (AGM and RSM, see the key to columns accompanying table 3 at end of volume) are also shown separately, but they are measured in 1970 value units.

Pollution and abatement equations

Equations 13 through 31 are the pollution balances of the system. Rows 11 through 15 are the equations for setting the levels of abatement activities. Rows 16 through 23 contain the emissions coefficients, which measure the quantities (metric tons of biological oxygen demand, suspended solids, particulate matter and the like) emitted per unit of output of each economic activity. Emissions coefficients are specified for urban households as well as for all agricultural and industrial processes. Net total emissions (EMA) measure the volume of each pollutant that is emitted minus the amount treated by the abatement sectors (ABATE). However, abatement activities in turn generate pollution and hence can eliminate only a fraction of the pollution that they treat. Thus, particulate abatement eliminates more than 99 per cent of the emissions treated, while primary water treatment eliminates only 80 per cent of the suspended solids and none of the nitrogen pollution in the water it treats. The coefficients in rows 24 through 31 measure residual pollution after treatment by the abatement processes. This pollution (EMNA) is not abatable in the sense that it is the proportion of treated emissions remaining after treatment. The variable EMTOT is the sum, for each pollutant, of untreated emissions and residual emissions after the abatement processes have been applied. Thus, EMTOT measures the total volume of emissions that remains to render whatever damage or discomfort can be attributed to pollution.

While world-wide environmental consciousness is growing rapidly, proven abatement technologies are acknowledged to be available for only a very limited list of pollutants. For the rest (since no abatement is technically feasible at present), the level of gross emissions by producers and households is necessarily equal to the level of net emissions. The levels of emissions of these pollutants can be estimated by the multiplication of the emissions coefficients for non-abatables by the levels of industrial and household pollution determined through solution of the model. Developmental projections presented in this report contain such estimates for one non-abatable pollutant (pesticides) only.

Investment balances

Required stocks of plant and equipment (SPLT, SEQP) are computed by multiplying sectoral production levels by their respective capital coefficients (rows 84 and 99). For 1970, investment in plant and equipment

---

[16] The balance of payments is a slack variable as described previously.

[17] It is not possible at this stage to develop satisfactory projections for agricultural yields in various parts of the world. For the time being, land-input coefficients (the inverses of yield ratios) were held at 1970 levels; the model therefore computes how much land would be required in the absence of yield improvements. Alternatively, the projection can also be viewed as showing the combination of yield improvements and/or increases in cultivated area needed to realize the projected levels of agricultural output.

(equations 75 and 76) is determined by multiplying the required stocks by the sum of the growth rate and the estimated rates of replacement of the stocks in question. In later years, replacement investment is still considered a fixed percentage of the capital stock in place, while investment for expansion is computed as the difference between required capital (SPLT, SEQP) and that in place 10 years earlier (HPLT, HEQP), referred to in some tables as historical stocks.

Since the differences between the output levels of two different years, and consequently the corresponding capital stock, are in many cases treated as unknowns to be determined through the solution of the system of (non-linear) equations, the computations described above may involve the use of iteration—that is, of a method of step-wise successive approximations.

Equations 78 through 86 cumulate the consumption of mineral resources over successive decades. Information on cumulative resource extraction provides a basis for projecting the future costs of extraction: as the more accessible reserves of a particular mineral in a given region become exhausted, the next layer involving higher extraction costs begins to be exploited.

International transaction equations

The remaining equations in the table determine the imports and exports of the various types of goods and services discussed above. This system does not identify the region of origin of any region's imports, nor the destination of any region's exports (see p. 15 above). Instead, every exporter sells to a "pool" of traded goods, from which importing regions draw their imports. Equations 92 through 131 deal with imports. In general, imports are specified as a given ratio of imports to domestic output. The import/output ratios, A, are derived from a set of import coefficients,[18] each one of which represents the proportion of total domestic consumption of a particular commodity that is satisfied by imports in a particular region. Imports of services, primarily foreign travel, are tied directly to GDP, and imports of transportation to total imports. Thus, every region draws an amount from the world pool of specific products in accordance with its domestic consumption and its import coefficients.

Each region is assigned a given share of the total export pool for each commodity. Equations 132 through 172 state that a region's exports of each kind of output is a given proportion, B, of the total world pool. World pools are represented by the pool variables, PAGS, PAGR, PRSS and so on.

In comparing a table that describes the composition of the exports of a region with one that lists the imports of that region, we find that in most instances the region appears to be an importer and exporter of the same goods. This reflects the process of classification by which different kinds of goods are grouped together. More-over, when the exports and the imports of the countries combined in a single region are aggregated, the flow of goods traded between any two countries often are not netted out but rather are listed both as exports and imports of that region. Hence, coefficients and export shares generally depict gross rather than net trade. An exception is made for specific metal and energy resources, which are treated on a net basis. Their margins, however, are carried on a gross basis. Thus, a region can be both an importer and an exporter of metal refining services, but it can only appear as either a net importer or a net exporter of metal content. Resource refining margins traded by any region are assumed to be equal to their 1970 volumes plus a specified proportion of imports or exports of specific resource products in excess of the base year. Agricultural margin trade is computed by multiplying the trade in each of the specific agricultural products by a region-specific processing margin per-centage. Interregional financial transfers are separated into capital flows, which change a region's international indebtedness and thus also generate interest payments and aid payments, which are treated as pure grants.

The balance of payments, BAL, is the sum total of deficits or surpluses, as the case may be, of the following three external accounts—the difference between the value of exports and imports of the region, EXPRT-IMPRT; the difference between the capital inflows and the capital outflows of the regions, ECAP-MCAP; the difference between the foreign aid obtained and supplied by the region, EAID-MAID—and the net foreign income payments (mainly interest payments) received or made by the region. In other words, the balance of payments, BAL, by definition, is the net compensating flow of foreign short-term credit. It represents a gap (positive or negative) between the long-term financial intakes and outlays of a given region.

The cumulative level of indebtedness which constitutes the base for the determination of annual interest pay-ments is computed so as to include not only cumulative ordinary capital flows but also cumulative annual positive or negative balances of payments, as defined above.

Implementation

The task of assembling data for the world system involved two major endeavours: the estimation of structural coefficients for each region in the base year, 1970, and the projection of changes in these base-year coefficients for the years 1980, 1990 and 2000. Both of these efforts posed serious problems and it would be presumptuous to claim any degree of statistical authority even for the base-year data.[19] Estimates of future co-efficients are, for obvious reasons, even more uncertain. Nevertheless, it is our belief that the estimates, while rough, are generally plausible, and that they provide a solid base for future improvements. Many international, regional and national institutions, including statistical,

---

[18] By import coefficients we mean imports/total regional use. For computational convenience, the model actually uses import ratios (imports/regional output), even though the concept of the import coefficient is more satisfactory for analytical purposes. The two concepts are related by a simple algebraic formula as long as regional outputs are non-zero.

[19] In many respects the 1970 solution was made to be consistent with actual 1970 data; in other respects it was found more meaning-ful to construct and use "normal 1970" data, that is, data that exclude peculiarities due to 1970 alone. For example, most balance-of-payments statistics are based on 1969-1971 averages due to the great variability of some of these measures. Also, investment and inventory change are based on 1961-1970 growth rates rather than on actual 1970 observations. This facilitates comparisons between 1970 and the later projections.

research and other types of institutions, contributed specialized information to this effort. Their co-operation was important, yet much remains to be done. The full potential of this initial study will be realized only if it stimulates various institutions to undertake efforts to improve the data at all levels of the system.

The analytical structure requires systematic estimation of a comprehensive set of input-output accounts, including current and capital account transactions, exports and imports and the balance of payments for each of the 15 regions of the world. In addition to the conventional production accounts in value units, balances in physical units were constructed for four types of agricultural products (livestock, cereals, high-protein crops, root crops), fish, six metals (iron, copper, aluminium, nickel, zinc, lead), three fossil fuels (coal, petroleum, natural gas), eight pollutants (particulate air pollution, suspended solids, biological oxygen demand, phosphorus, nitrogen, dissolved solids, solid wastes, pesticides) and fertilizer.

Detailed data on trade flows were obtained from United Nations sources. These were aligned and aggregated in accordance with the regional and product specifications of the world system to provide estimates of import coefficients and export shares for all traded commodities, including the specific agricultural products. The trade coefficients for the metal and energy resources were not readily attainable from the United Nations statistics; they were reconstructed from other sources, as were the aid and capital flows for the base year. The United Nations statistics furnished base-year values for most of the macro variables of the system: GDP, population, urban population government expenditures and labour force. The Food and Agriculture Organization of the United Nations (FAO) furnished data on the production and consumption of specific agricultural products and on some of the major agricultural inputs.

Regional input-output tables and the input structures for agriculture, mining and pollution abatement were not so readily available. While input-output tables are published for more than 70 countries, there are no comprehensive regional accounts. Individual country tables are constructed with differing classifications and accounting conventions and expressed in terms of their own price units. Years of painstaking analysis and data refinement would be necessary before we could combine individual country tables to construct meaningful regional tables. Furthermore, for several of the developing regions there were only one or two country tables available, and for China and some of the African regions there was none. The same sort of problems made it impossible to observe directly the composition of consumption and investment expenditures in each region. In the absence of adequate region-specific data it was necessary to estimate many, but by no means all, of the structural coefficients of the system as functions of *per capita* gross national product on the basis of cross-country regressions. The basic strategy consisted of reconciling and adjusting the prices of a small group of input-output tables and consumption vectors and determining how individual coefficients or groups of coefficients vary with income levels in the sample of comparable tables.

Table 4 summarizes the methods used to estimate the base-year data and to project the model's coefficients into the future. Each of the blocks in the diagram represents a set of coefficients in the world model. The "texture" of each block—whether it is dotted, cross-

hatched etc.—denotes the kind of methodology used to estimate the base-year coefficients. The numbers (1, 2, 3 or 4) refer to the methods used to project the coefficients for the base year into the future.

The great majority of the parameters were estimated on the basis of cross-national regressions of specific coefficients or weighted sums of coefficients on national *per capita* income (taken to represent an index of the over-all level of the economic and technical development of the country in question). While information from the input-output tables and other economic statistics of 15 or more countries were consulted in cross-sectional analysis, the actual regressions were often computed on the basis of only eight countries—namely, those for which the Kravis study provided some basis for an international price standardization.[20] Coefficients that were estimated from cross-national regressions were entered into the system as reference tables for each of 11 "bench-mark" levels of *per capita* income.

This procedure was used for estimating those coefficients indicated on the diagram by unmarked (plain) cells, including those for energy and capital inputs into agriculture, investment, consumption structures, an urban amenities vector and the industry input-output tables. Thus, for example, the input-output coefficients for a given region are assumed to depend only on its income level rather than on other region-specific characteristics. Such an assumption does not, of course, take into account potentially great differences in the sectoral input proportions among regions with similar income levels but with different consumption habits or technologies.

Input-output tables do not normally include the detail on mining and resource processing margins requisite for the present system. Therefore, the coefficients for mining and resource consumption had to be estimated from special studies. To estimate each region's input structure for mining we began with the input coefficients for mining from the detailed, 485-sector input-output table for the United States of America and modified each column to take into account interregional differences in the average costs of extracting each specific resource. In the case of most of the metals, interregional differences in mining costs were not known directly. In these cases we assumed that cost differences were proportional to interregional differences in the average grades of the particular ore mined. The regional labour costs for mining were estimated by the same methods as the other labour coefficients in the system.

The specific resource-consumption per unit of output of each industrial sector was first estimated from unpublished, detailed time series information from the United States of America, obtained from the United States Bureau of Mines. The detailed energy-consumption coefficients for the United States were available from special studies made by the Center for Advanced Computation at the University of Illinois. Since the intensity of consumption of the specific resources varies significantly from region to region, it was essential to modify the first round of estimates of the coefficients, based on United States data, to bring them into conformity with the regional consumption control totals. The estimates of the total regional consumption of each specific resource were obtained from the statistics of regional production,

[20] Irving B. Kravis and others. *A System of International Comparisons of Gross Product and Purchasing Power*, (Baltimore, Johns Hopkins University Press, 1975).

TABLE 4. COEFFICIENT ESTIMATION AND PROJECTION FOR A SINGLE REGION BLOCK

	Agri-culture	Metals	Energy	Input-output	Investment	Inventory	Pollution	Consumption	Urban	Government	Fish	Exports
Agriculture	2	0	0	4	0	4	0	1,2	0		0	4
Metals	0	0	0	2	0	4	0	0	0	0	0	2
Energy	1,2	3	3	2,4	0	4	4	1	2	1	1	2
Industry and services (fertilizer) 2	4 / 4	3	3	1,2	4	4	4	1	2	1	4	1
Capital	1,2	3	3	1	0	0	4	1	2	1	1	0
Pollution	2	0	0	2	0	0	4	0	1,2	0	0	0
Labour	1,2	3	3	1,2	0	0	4	1	2	1	1	0
Imports	2	2	2	1	0	0	0	0	0	0	1	0

Coefficient projection methodology

1. Income dependent
2. Specially projected
3. Changing with resource depletion
4. Held constant

region-specific   other

column-scaled   0 no entry

bench-marked   row-scaled

imports and exports. Each row of the resource-consumption coefficients was then scaled so as to bring the regional consumption of each resource into agreement with the base year resource-consumption statistics.[21] In the diagram, the coefficients which were scaled by region-specific row multipliers are designated by horizontal stripes; those scaled by the column multipliers are indicated by vertical stripes.

The labour coefficients were first estimated on the basis of cross-country regressions. The discrepancies between the regional employment control totals and employment estimates computed from the preliminary labour coefficient estimates resulted in large part from the special characteristics of agriculture in each region. Since the agricultural work force assumes unknown but potentially significant proportions of hidden unemployment in developing countries, we did not attempt to estimate the labour coefficients in agriculture for regions

with *per capita* income below $1000 per annum. The agricultural labour coefficients for the developed countries were scaled so as to reproduce available statistics on the agricultural labour force in the base year. When this was done, the labour requirements computed on the basis of the full set of labour coefficients for each region agreed quite closely with the independent statistics on total regional employment.

The consumption structures for the base year are based on cross-country regressions on income *per capita* for 10 countries, using the price-adjusted consumption data of the Kravis study.[22] The household capital coefficients, representing investment in housing, were estimated from information on the regional rent differentials furnished by Lakshmanan.[23] The consumption of selected agricultural products was estimated from the region-specific consumption functions published by FAO. Food consumption is specified in physical units, with the appropriate food-processing margins and other agriculture

[21] In scaling, a set (a column or row) of coefficients is stepped up or down in the same ratio. The ratio is chosen so as to bring the sum of the scaled coefficients to a given marginal row or column total.

[22] Irving B. Kravis and others, *op. cit.*
[23] T. R. Lakshmanan and others, "Urbanization and environmental quality: a preliminary note", (mimeo), 1 April 1975.

24

expressed in value terms. Urban amenities per urban resident are specified in a vector representing the services of water supply, sewage disposal and solid waste collection. These services are characteristic of urban but not generally of rural life throughout the world. These coefficients were estimated in special studies by Lakshmanan. Household emissions of water pollution and solid-waste loads are tied to the urban amenities column because the abatement of these pollutants is not normally required in a rural setting. Finally, the bench-mark vectors of government-expenditure proportions are based on cross-country regressions of expenditures of *per capita* national income in three broad categories—education, defence and "other".

Returning again to the diagram of table 4, dotted areas identify sectors in which neither the region-specific nor the scaled or bench-mark treatments seemed appropriate. No information exists, for example, on the costs of pollution abatement for medium- or low-income countries; hence, it was necessary to assume that abatement involves the same technology throughout the world as it does in the United States of America. Similarly, the pollution emission coefficients were based primarily on United States data. Pesticides, an area in which emissions are region-specific, and solid-waste emissions, which are bench-marked, are exceptions. Others were weighted on the basis of differences in the detailed process mix in the different geographical regions, but otherwise similar matrices were used for all regions.

Structural projections

The projections of future input and consumption structures must take account of changes in regional *per capita* income, as well as whatever changes in technology and in the resource picture can be anticipated. Methods of projection used for each block are shown in table 4 above. The coefficients representing certain region-specific agricultural inputs—particularly land, pesticide and fertilizer—and regional emissions coefficients for specific pollutants were projected on the basis of special studies. After each decade, the input requirements (input coefficients) for selected mining activities are assumed to increase as cumulative regional output levels pass certain critical values and higher grades of reserves approach exhaustion. Step functions showing the amounts of specific resources expected to be available at various levels of extraction costs formed the basis of projecting increasing input requirements in mining. New discoveries of reserves may well modify these supply functions for resources in the future, but we did not attempt to anticipate these discoveries in quantitative terms. A second set of step functions, based on more generous estimates of reserves, was prepared as a basis for computing alternative scenarios (see Chapter X).

Coefficients representing the consumption of metals by producers of metal products, transportation equipment, housing and the like are scaled down to allow for anticipated increases in recycling in future decades. Most of the other projections of input structures had two components: one for income-dependent changes and another for exogenously estimated changes in technology. Income-dependent changes are plugged in automatically as *per capita* income increases. For each time period, a new set of structural coefficients is selected for each region, in accordance with its approximate new income *per capita*. Thus, as a region becomes richer, it takes on the input-output coefficients characteristic of a higher income region. By 2000, income *per capita* in several regions is expected to rise well above the highest value, $4,625, specified for North America in the 1970 system. Multiplicative adjusters, based on detailed special studies of expected broad changes in technique for the United States of America, are applied to modify these income-dependent values. While region-specific projections were made for the labour and other inputs into agriculture, the scarcity of data for projecting future industrial technology outside of the United States represents a serious limitation for the world projections. The compilation of region-specific information on likely future technological alternatives should be given high priority in future work.

For purposes of projection, it also became necessary to estimate the consumption expenditure patterns for countries with higher *per capita* average income than have yet been observed. These estimates rely heavily on the 1960 United States Consumer Expenditure Survey. Twenty income-specific consumption expenditure patterns from this study were assigned income-class weights derived from simulated income distributions with successively higher mean *per capita* incomes. In this way a weighted average expenditure pattern appropriate to each higher bench-mark income was computed.

Consumption coefficients for specific agricultural products were projected on the basis of estimates of the income elasticity of demand for these products, which were published by FAO. Cross-country regressions of the elasticity estimates on *per capita* income provide a basis for modifying a region's demand elasticities as its income rises. A relation between *per capita* caloric intake and regional *per capita* income was also estimated in order to provide an additional control on estimates of total food intake. The consumption functions for specific agricultural commodities were modified so as to force them into conformity with the income-caloric regression by 2000.

The projections of the import coefficients and export shares for most traded industrial goods were derived from cross-national regression studies using data for 1962 and 1970. The projection of a sector's output that is imported is projected to change with (a) the size of the region's economy and (b) the region's *per capita* income relative to that of the world as a whole. The importance of specific regional endowments makes it more difficult to project the coefficients of trade in agricultural and resource products. In the absence of informed judgements about future interregional trade in agricultural products, their import and export share coefficients at their base-year values were held constant.

The estimates of export shares of individual resources were made judgementally in the light of the present estimates of regional reserves of specific resources. Instead of projecting import coefficients as such, we projected the levels of metal and energy production in non-exporting regions and introduced these levels as exogenous slack variables in the system. The sizes of the regional imports and of the world pools were then determined endogenously. Each region's exports of metal and petroleum refining margins are the sum of observed 1970 margins plus a fixed proportion of the increment over the base year in net exports of the resource in question.

Chapter V

CLASSIFICATION OF SCENARIOS OF FUTURE ECONOMIC GROWTH

The model described above was used to project eight alternative development paths—each based on a more or less different set of factual assumptions—that might be followed by the world economy from the base year 1970 through 1980 and 1990 to 2000.

Table 5 provides a general overview of the eight partially overlapping sets of assumptions. The scenarios are identified by capital letters entered along the top of the table. They differ from each other because of differences in the basic assumptions pertaining to the sets of variables and coefficients listed at the left of each row. The entries in a given column thus summarize the specific assumptions underlying a particular scenario. Some of the differences among the scenarios reflect alternative estimates of the future rates of population growth and the total of still unexplored reserves of various mineral resources. Others examine the implications of various sets of income targets and the alternative means by which they can be effectively attained.

In accordance with the requirements of the International Development Strategy and the priorities arising out of the new international economic order, six of the eight projections are based on three combinations of alternative assumptions concerning future population growth and two alternative sets of prescribed targets (high and low) for the future increase in *per capita* regional GDPs. These three combinations—identified as UN/B, UN/A-1 and UN/A-2—are described in table 6.

TABLE 6. ALTERNATIVE ASSUMPTIONS CONCERNING INCOME TARGETS AND FUTURE POPULATION GROWTH

	Population growth		Per capita GDP targets	
Combinations	Developed regions	Developing regions	Developed regions	Developing regions
UN/B . .	medium	medium	high	high
UN/A-1 . .	low	low	low	high
UN/A-2 . .	high	high	low	high

The income targets for the developing regions are high in all three variants. In UN/B they are, however, combined with the assumption of high rates of income growth in the developed areas as well, and a medium (among the three alternative world-wide United Nations demographic projections) rate of population growth in both the developed and developing areas.[24]

---

[24] The choice of letter symbols to designate alternative projections grew out of a rather complex history of successive steps that led to the final choice of scenarios to be presented in this report.

In UN/A-1 the rates of income growth in the developed areas and the population growth in the developed as well as the developing regions are assumed to be relatively low. UN/A-2 combines a low rate of income growth in the developed areas, with high rates of population growth both in the developing and in the developed regions. UN/B thus imposes a high, UN/A-1 a relatively low, and UN/A-2 an intermediate level of strain on the world's natural and labour resources. According to UN/B, the total world GDP—expressed in 1970 prices—should reach the level of $13,250 billion; according to UN/A-1, $11,999 billion; and according to UN/A-2, $12,651 billion.

With the income targets for 1980, 1990 and 2000 given, the question to be answered is, what would the world economy have to look like in 1980, 1990 and 2000 if it were to attain—while operating within the limits of the given technical and physical constraints—these fixed objectives? In particular, what would the levels of the labour inputs, the volume of investment, and the rate of mineral resource use have to be in each of the 15 regions; and what would the pattern of international trade and payments have to be so as to permit the actual realization of these targets?

As indicated in table 5, regional employment levels (only non-agricultural employment in the developing regions), levels of investment and external balances of payments are endogenous—that is, are unknown variables in all scenarios, except A. In other words, they are assumed to adjust themselves as time goes on to the direct and indirect requirements dictated by the policy objectives of attaining the targets for 1980, 1990 and 2000.

The answer yielded by each solution depends, of course, on the projected sets of structural coefficients that enter into the various equations. Most of these projected coefficients are kept the same across all of the different scenarios. However, alternative sets of coefficients governing resource extraction, import ratios and export shares are introduced in a few scenarios (G, H and M) designed to show the effects of varying specific structural assumptions.

Abatement is described by a set of activities directed towards eliminating some part of the various kinds of pollution generated in the different sectors of each regional economy. Over time, these activities are "operated" with increased intensity on the assumption that the percentages of pollutants abated rises with increases in *per capita* income (see abatement tables in Chapter XI).

As explained in Chapter X, the projection of the input structure of extractive industries is based on the assumption of stepwise diminishing yields. The width of the successive steps for each region depends on the assessment of the quantities and qualities of still unexploited reserves of the mineral in question. The timing of the shift from one step to the next depends in each projection

TABLE 5. ALTERNATIVE SCENARIOS

	X	A	C	D	G	H	R	M
GDP	UN/B	Middle East: UN/B Others: endogenous	UN/A-1	UN/A-2			UN/B	
Employment	Endogenous	DC's equal to estimated labour force Others: endogenous				Endogenous		
Investment	Endogenous	LDC/I (excluding Middle East) and centrally planned Asia: limited by borrowing and saving Others: endogenous				Endogenous		
Balance of payments	Endogenous	LDC/II (excluding centrally planned Asia): set equal to zero Others: endogenous			Endogenous		Aid and capital export coefficient from developed countries are raised; rate of interest on foreign debt is reduced	Endogenous
Foreign trade		Import and export share coefficients change with regional total *per capita* incomes						For LAM, ASL arid Africa: selected import coefficient reduced and export coefficient increased
Abatement		Income dependent (see table 2)						
Food imports	Endogenous				ASL: set to zero Others: endogenous			
Extractive input structure prices		Based on pessimistic estimates of resource endowment				Based on optimistic estimates of resource endowments	Based on pessimistic estimates of resource endowment	

on the cumulative outputs of the resource industries in question. Cumulative outputs—that is, the total extraction of resources since 1970—are among the model's unknown variables: their magnitudes are determined through the solution of the general system of equations.

The available estimates of the total—in contrast to the ascertained—reserves of the various mineral resources vary significantly with the judgement of individual experts; in some instances, the highest figure quoted by an optimistic expert is more than twice as large as the lowest figure coming from the pessimistic side. In the face of such uncertainty, two alternative sets of assumptions concerning the magnitude and the quality of the as yet unexploited reserves of the various natural resources were used, and accordingly, two alternative sets of projected input requirements for extracting these natural resources were introduced into otherwise identical general scenarios (see mineral resource tables in Chapter X). The last line of table 5 calls attention to the fact that the alternative assumptions concerning the input requirements of the mining industries, and the cost and prices of their outputs will be reflected in the relative prices of all internationally traded goods which, in their turn, affect the balances of international trade and payments (see price tables in Annex II).

A very different approach to the exploration of the conditions of future economic growth is delineated in scenario A, described in the second column of table 5. The other seven projections started with fixed income targets, and determined the levels of employment, rates of investment and international transfers required to achieve these targets irrespective of the economic and institutional forces that affect these instruments of growth. In projection A, the institutional factors that up to now have tended to govern the rate of productivity increase and employment in the developed countries, and the rate of investment and the import surplus of the developing countries, are assumed to continue to operate in the future in the same way they did in the past. On the other hand, the levels of income that can be expected to be attained, as time goes on, in different developed and developing regions (except the oil-rich Middle Eastern regions) are now treated as dependent variables. Their values, instead of being fixed in advance, are found through the solution of the world-wide system of simultaneous equations.

The savings and external payments constraints of the developed countries have been accordingly relaxed (as have the other projections) to permit them to secure full (but not more than full) employment of the available labour force. In the developing countries (which can be expected in this case to continue to operate for some time under conditions of latent labour surplus), the future growth of GDP would—in the absence of major institutional changes—tend to be determined either by the projected rates of domestic savings supplemented by funds coming from abroad or by foreign exchange constraints (operating through the balance of payments) which would limit the imports of raw materials and capital goods that these countries cannot yet produce themselves.

Under scenario A, saving constraints—that is, the availability of investable funds—are assumed to dominate the future growth of developing regions well endowed with exportable natural resources. The projected upward trend in the prices of raw materials can be expected to mitigate the balance-of-payments difficulties they have experienced in the past. Centrally planned Asia is included in this group because of its apparent economic self-sufficiency. The growth prospects of the other developing regions depend—under the assumption that the present economic order is maintained—on balance-of-payments constraints.

To recapitulate, scenarios C and D are identical to scenario X in their formal structure and the choice of the exogenously fixed and the endogenously determined variables. Each of them is based, however, on a different combination of assumptions concerning the rate of future population growth, with different choices of prescribed income targets.

Scenario C differs from scenario X in that the populous low-income Asian countries are assumed to expand their agricultural investment and production so as to be able to attain complete self-sufficiency in food by 1980. In scenario H, the relatively conservative estimates of the total reserves of natural resources available for future exploitation as included in scenario X are stepped up to include some portion of "probable" but not certain endowments. That means that the gradual step by step shift to higher and higher extraction costs can be expected to proceed, according to projections based on scenario H, at a slower pace than can be anticipated on the basis of scenario X. Hence, the rise of relative prices of natural resource products, and also of other internationally traded goods whose cost of production depends on them, can be expected to be less pronounced under scenario H than under scenario X.

Scenario R, which appears in the next to the last column in table 5, differs from scenario X in the assumptions regarding international financial flows. In order to reduce the exceedingly large balance-of-payments deficits of some developing regions, capital and aid outflows of developed regions were stepped up and interest rates on foreign lending were reduced.

The last scenario, scenario M, differs from scenario X with respect to the set of structural assumptions pertaining to the future levels of exports and imports of three less developed regions: medium-income Latin America, low-income Asia, and arid Africa. These are the regions which, according to projection X, would experience a particularly rapid deterioration of their foreign trade and payments balances and consequently were shown to accumulate large external debts. Scenario M differs from scenario X in the structural assumptions governing foreign trade. For the three regions involved, (a) the magnitudes of selected import coefficients were lowered and (b) the magnitudes of certain export shares were increased relative to their values in scenario X.

The projection based on scenario M demonstrates to what extent expanded export opportunities and accelerated import substitution could contribute to a reduction in the payments gap. It also shows how such an adjustment would affect the domestic economic balances of these regions and the domestic and foreign balances of all other regions.

Part Two

WORLD ECONOMIC DEVELOPMENT AND ITS IMPLICATIONS

The United Nations world economic model as described briefly in Part One, and in more detail in the annexes of this report, has been used to investigate some of the main problems of economic growth and development in the world as a whole, with special accent on problems encountered by the developing countries. For this purpose a number of alternative scenarios were computed, each scenario differing from others by growth and development targets and by other important influences on development. It will be useful to start with a general description of the scenarios in question.

Chapter VI

BASIC AND ALTERNATIVE SCENARIOS OF
WORLD ECONOMIC DEVELOPMENT

According to the International Development Strategy, approved by the General Assembly in October 1970, the average annual rate of growth of gross product of the developing countries as a whole during the Second United Nations Development Decade should be at least 6 per cent, with the possibility of attaining a higher rate in the second half of the Decade. The International Development Strategy also specified that the average annual growth of *per capita* gross product in developing countries as a whole during the Decade should be about 3.5 per cent. The target for growth in average *per capita* income in the International Development Strategy was calculated on the basis of an average annual increase of 2.5 per cent in the population of the developing countries.[25]

These targets were reaffirmed in the resolution on development and international economic co-operation, adopted at the seventh special session of the General Assembly.[26] As stated in the Declaration on the Establishment of a New International Economic Order, adopted by the General Assembly at the sixth special session, this economic order, based on equity, sovereign equality, interdependence, common interest and co-operation among all States, irrespective of their economic and social systems, is to correct inequalities and redress existing injustices, make it possible to eliminate the widening gap between the developed and the developing countries and ensure steadily accelerating economic and social development, peace and justice for present and future generations.[27]

There are many different kinds of inequalities in the world in which we live. The present report specifically addresses itself to the correction of the existing economic inequalities among countries, and particularly to the conditions necessary for narrowing and eventually eliminating the income gap between developed and developing countries. If the minimum targets of growth for the developing countries, as set by the International Development Strategy, were implemented continuously throughout the remaining decades of the twentieth century, and if the growth rates prevailing in the developed countries during the past two decades were to be retained in the future, then, as can be easily seen from table 7, the gap in *per capita* gross product between these two groups of countries, which in 1970 was 12 to 1 on the average, would not start diminishing even by 2000.

TABLE 7. GROWTH RATES UNDER ASSUMPTIONS OF MINIMUM TARGETS SET BY THE INTERNATIONAL DEVELOPMENT STRATEGY FOR DEVELOPING COUNTRIES, AND EXTRAPOLATION OF LONG-TERM GROWTH RATES IN THE DEVELOPED COUNTRIES

	Gross domestic product	Population	Gross domestic product per capita
Developed countries	4.5	1.0	3.5
Developing countries	6.0	2.5	3.5
Ratio of average *per capita* GDP of developed to developing regions:			
1970	...	...	12:1
2000...............	...	...	12:1

It is true that gross product in the developing countries would continue to expand somewhat faster than in the developed countries, and thus the share of the developing countries in total world product would increase. However, because of the much higher growth rates of population, the expansion of gross product *per capita* would be no faster in the developing countries than in the world as a whole. It is for this reason that the International Development Strategy laid stress on the necessity to accelerate growth starting in the second half of the current decade in order to make at least a modest beginning towards narrowing the income gap between developed and developing countries.[28]

These considerations present a starting point for the basic scenario and some of its variants, which were used for current work with the United Nations model. In these basic scenarios growth rates of gross product *per capita* are set in such a way as to roughly halve the income gap between the developing and the developed countries by 2000, with a view towards closing the income gap completely by the middle of the next century.

The two scenarios compared in table 8 are similar in many respects. Both scenarios assume an average growth rate of 4.9 per cent *per capita* for developing countries, which is substantially higher than the minimum target set by the International Development Strategy (3.5 per cent). Growth rates of population are based on the "medium" (scenario X) and "low" (scenario C) projections made by the Population Division of the United Nations Secretariat. Finally, they assume that growth rates of *per capita* gross product in the

---

[25] *International Development Strategy: Action Programme of the General Assembly for the Second United Nations Development Decade* (United Nations publication, Sales No. E.71.II.A.2), paras. 13-15.

[26] General Assembly resolution 3362 (S-VII) of 19 September 1975, preamble.

[27] General Assembly resolution 3201 (S-VI) of 1 May 1974, preamble.

[28] *International Development Strategy: Action Programme of the General Assembly for the Second United Nations Development Decade* (United Nations publication, Sales No. E.71.II.A.2), para. 14.

TABLE 8. GROWTH RATES AND INCOME GAP UNDER THE ASSUMPTIONS OF THE BASIC SCENARIOS IN THE UNITED NATIONS MODEL[a]

	Scenario	Developed countries	Developing countries
Growth rate			
Gross product (percentage)	X	4.0	7.2
	C	3.6	6.9
Population (percentage) ..	X	0.7	2.3
	C	0.6	2.0
Gross product *per capita* (percentage)	X	3.3	4.9
	C	3.0	4.9
Income gap in the year 2000			
Gross product *per capita* (index, developing countries = 100)	X	769	100
	C	715	100

[a] Scenarios X and C.

developed countries decline when higher absolute levels of *per capita* income are achieved. Thus, a growth rate of 4 per cent *per capita* is assumed at $3,000 to $4,000, 3 per cent at $4,000 to $5,000, 2.5 per cent at $5,000 to $6,000 and so forth. This has the effect of bringing down the average growth rate of gross product in the developed countries to 3.6-4.0 per cent from the long-term trend of 4.5 per cent. This seems realistic in view of the present trends in productivity growth in high-income countries.

Scenario A is quite different from the two basic scenarios. In scenario A, gross product growth rates are determined endogenously by the model in all regions except the Middle East, where the rate is set exogenously at the same level as in scenario X. In order to determine the GDP in each decade, (*a*) employment in the developed countries is set equal to their projected labour force; (*b*) investment in the developing areas which are major resource exporters is limited by the amount of available internal savings generated and possible external borrow-

ings; and (*c*) the balance-of-payments deficits (or surpluses) of all other developing regions are set equal to zero.

TABLE 9. GROWTH RATES AND INCOME GAP IN SCENARIO A

	Developed countries	Developing countries
Growth rate (percentage)		
Gross product	3.9	5.4
Population	0.7	2.3
Gross product *per capita*	3.2	3.1
Income gap in the year 2000		
Gross product *per capita* (index, developing countries = 100)	1120.0	100.0

A comparison of the results of computations based on scenario A as compared with the two basic scenarios shows that development under the assumptions of scenario A is clearly unfavourable for the developing countries. While gross product in the developed countries expands at practically the same rate as in scenarios X and C, growth rates in the developing countries are much lower than the minimum targets set by the International Development Strategy. As a result, the income gap between the developed and the developing areas is hardly reduced at all. The reasons for this unfavourable performance are apparent from the assumptions of scenario A—namely, (*a*) there is no provision for any substantial increases in internal or external investment rates, which would be required in order to accelerate growth in the developing areas; (*b*) except for the extrapolation of current trends, no provision is made for major increases in export shares and import substitution in the developing countries, which would make possible the alleviation of their balance-of-payments problems. Thus, scenario A can be conveniently called an "old economic order" scenario, while scenarios X and C are clearly associated with the goals of the International Development Strategy and the changes in the conditions of development, as envisaged in the new international economic order.

Chapter VII

GENERAL IMPLICATIONS OF THE BASIC SCENARIOS: REGIONAL DIFFERENCES

Additional features become apparent in the basic scenarios, once we go from the general grouping of developed and developing countries to the more detailed regional breakdown represented in the United Nations model.

As can be seen from table 10, the over-all more rapid growth of the developing countries would bring about a significant increase in the share of these countries in total world GDP and, in fact, would double this share, which would reach, by 2000, about 22 per cent for the developing market regions as a whole. According to scenario X, the developed centrally planned economies of Europe would continue their over-all expansion at a rate somewhat higher than the world average, and their share in the world total would also increase. Most of the developed market economies would expand at rates below world averages, and their total share would decrease to about one half as compared with the present two thirds.

TABLE 10. GROWTH RATE AND SHARES OF GDP, BY REGION, 1970-2000 (SCENARIO X)

Region	Average annual growth rate (percentage)	Regional GDP as a percentage of world GDP 1970	Regional GDP as a percentage of world GDP 2000
Developed market . . .		66.1	50.9
North America . . .	3.3	32.9	21.0
Western Europe (high-income).	3.7	22.6	16.7
Japan	4.9	6.2	6.5
Oceania	4.5	1.3	1.2
Southern Africa[a] . . .	7.5	0.5	1.1
Western Europe[a] (medium-income) . .	7.0	2.3	4.4
Developed centrally planned .		18.6	20.7
Soviet Union . . .	5.2	13.5	15.4
East European . . .	4.9	5.1	5.3
Developing market . . .		11.1	22.0
Latin America (medium-income) . .	7.1	3.5	6.9
Latin America (low-income) .	7.2	1.2	2.5
Middle East	9.0	1.1	4.0
Asia (low-income) . . .	6.7	3.8	6.6
Africa (arid) . . .	5.5	0.8	1.0
Africa (tropical) . . .	6.5	0.7	1.0
Developing centrally planned .	6.3	4.2	6.4
Developing as a whole, including Asia (centrally planned) . .	7.2	13.3	28.4

[a] Region classified in developing group II in the print-out of scenario A, which appears in Annex VI.

A note of caution is necessary. In setting the exogenous growth rates no special attempt was made to estimate the relative purchasing power parities of national currencies, and gross products in many cases are compared in terms of official exchange rates. Therefore, the ratios in table 10 should not be taken as representing true comparisons of absolute product volumes but rather as an indication of the direction in which they are expected to change. It should also be noted that figures for the centrally planned economies are not directly comparable with their published figures because of substantial methodological differences in national accounts statistics.

While the gross domestic products of the developing areas on the whole are expected to increase at higher rates than the world average, substantial differences among growth rates of individual regions are indicated in scenario X. The Middle East is expected to grow at average rates of close to 9 per cent, Latin America at 7 per cent, low-income Asia and tropical Africa at about 6.5 per cent and arid Africa at 5.5 per cent. These differences are in part based on disparities in present growth rates, from which development possibilities have to be estimated.

Thus, current growth rates of GDP for the 1970s are estimated to be only 4.5 per cent in arid Africa, 5.0 per cent in tropical Africa and low-income Asia, 5.5 in both Latin American regions and 11.9 per cent in the Middle East. Though growth rates for all developing regions (excluding the Middle East) do increase as they approach 2000, it takes a longer time for arid and tropical Africa to reach significantly higher rates of growth.

TABLE 11. *Per capita* GDP IN DEVELOPING REGIONS, 1970-2000 (SCENARIO X)
(*1970 dollars*)

Region	1970	2000
Middle East	286	1,149
Latin America (low-income) . .	443	1,577
Latin America (medium-income) .	594	2,149
Developing centrally planned . .	167	681
Asia (low-income)	120	401
Africa (arid)	205	436
Africa (tropical)	141	399

It is also important to note that the starting levels of *per capita* GDP are very different in various developing regions. As seen in table 11, this makes it exceedingly difficult for some regions, especially for low-income Asia, arid Africa and tropical Africa, to approach the relatively low-income target of $500 *per capita* by 2000. To achieve this goal low-income Asia would have to increase its GDP at an average annual rate of 7.5 per cent, arid Africa at 6.0 per cent and tropical Africa at 7.3 per cent. While such growth rates are not impossible, provided that special favourable conditions for the development of these areas are created, they would still imply *per capita* incomes in 2000 which are no higher than current average incomes in Latin America. It is obvious that the income situation in low-income Asia, arid Africa and tropical Africa will continue to be acute in the twentieth century, and that attention and concerted international effort favouring development of these regions is necessary.

Chapter VIII

INTERNAL ASPECTS OF DEVELOPMENT: CHANGING ECONOMIC STRUCTURES

Development from low to higher *per capita* income involves changes in economic structure. Increases in *per capita* incomes bring about shifts in the composition of personal consumption and changes in the technologies of production. Higher growth rates lead to an increase of the ratio of investment to gross product and the share of producer goods in total demand.

As shown in table 12, the ratio of gross fixed investment to total final internal use is expected to increase from 20 to 41 per cent in the Middle East and African oil countries, from 17-20 to 31-33 per cent in Latin America, and from 15 to 20-21 per cent in Asia and Africa. The extent of the increase of the investment ratio is largely determined by the growth rate of GDP. Growth

TABLE 12. CHANGE IN THE STRUCTURE OF GROSS DOMESTIC PRODUCT (SCENARIO X)[a]
(*Percentage*)

Region	1970[b]			2000[b]		
	C	I	G	C	I	G
Latin America (medium-income)	68	20	10	55	33	10
Latin America (low-income)	71	17	10	57	31	10
Middle East	61	20	17	48	41	9
Asia (low-income)	69	15	14	63	21	14
Africa (arid)	68	15	15	63	20	15
Africa (tropical)	69	15	14	63	21	14

[a] Final demand components as a share of the sum of personal consumption, government consumption and gross capital investment. Final internal use (sum of personal consumption, government consumption and gross capital formation), rather than GDP, was used for share determination in order to eliminate the effect of imbalances in foreign trade.

[b] C stands for personal consumption, I for gross fixed investment (includes both private and public investment) and G for government final consumption.

rates of 4-6 per cent can be accomplished with an investment ratio of about 20 per cent; growth rates of 7-8 per cent point to investment ratios of about 30 per cent, while sustained growth rates of 10 per cent or more cannot be accomplished unless the investment ratio goes up to 40 per cent.

If the share of government consumption remains constant throughout the period under discussion, then higher investment ratios can be attained only by a relative decrease in the share of personal consumption.

TABLE 13. RATIOS OF NET FOREIGN CAPITAL AND AID INFLOWS TO INTERNAL FIXED INVESTMENT IN PLANT AND EQUIPMENT (SCENARIO X)
(*Percentage*)

Region	1970	2000
Latin America (medium-income) . . .	12.9	6.6
Latin America (low-income) . . .	36.6	20.8
Middle East (oil-producing) . . .	15.1	5.0
Asia (low-income)	51.0	18.8
Africa (arid)	33.3	27.2
Africa (tropical)	52.7	36.3

Personal consumption will probably have to be brought down from about 68-71 per cent in most regions to 63 per cent in Asia and Africa, 55-57 per cent in Latin America and close to 50 per cent in the Middle East.

The share of fixed investment requirements that can be covered by net capital and aid inflow, though still remaining rather high in some regions, is expected to be significantly less than in 1970. Thus, the increased proportion of fixed investment to final use will have to be taken care of predominantly by domestic means.

Such changes in the share of final demand components obviously necessitate relevant measures of taxation, credit and fiscal stimulation of savings, as well as certain institutional changes, facilitating the accumulation of resources for investment and directing them into those areas essential for the process of development. One such change could be an increase in the role of public investment and the public sector in production. It goes without saying that an initial decrease in the share of personal consumption, which may be used to increase investment in production, should alternately lead to higher levels of total personal consumption and personal consumption *per capita*.

Special measures will have to be taken also in order to facilitate a more equal distribution of income in the countries in question, so that the benefits of faster growth of *per capita* incomes are shared fully, as a matter of priority, by the poorest groups in these countries.

Table 14 shows the difference in growth rates of the major sectors of the economies of developing regions. These growth rates tend to vary with the over-all speed of economic expansion characteristic of the region. However, some general tendencies hold true for all regions. The primary industries (agriculture and natural resources) are expected to expand at a slower rate than will total gross product once over-all expansion exceeds 4 per cent. The difference between the over-all growth rate and the growth rate of the primary sector increases from around zero at 4 per cent to about 1 per cent at 6 per cent growth rates, to 1.5-2 per cent at 7-8 per cent growth rates, and to 4 per cent at growth rates close to 11-12 per cent. The secondary industries (manufacturing), on the other hand, tend to lead the economy. Their growth rates exceed over-all growth rates by 1.5 per cent at over-all rates of up to 7 per cent, and by 4 per cent at GDP growth rates of 11-12 per cent. The higher the general rate and level of development, the larger the need for the creation and expansion of manufacturing industries.

The tertiary industries (under the general title of services but including, besides services *per se*, transportation, communication and trade) are also a fast

TABLE 14. AVERAGE ANNUAL GROWTH RATES OF GDP AND OUTPUT OF SECTORS
OF THE ECONOMY, 1970-2000 (SCENARIO X)
(*Percentage*)

Region	GDP	Agriculture and mineral resources	Manufacturing	Services
Latin America (medium-income) . . .	7.1	5.8	8.5	8.0
Latin America (low-income) . . .	7.2	5.6	8.8	8.7
Middle East	9.0	7.7	14.0	12.2
Asia (low-income)	6.7	5.4	7.8	8.7
Africa (arid)	5.5	5.1	6.2	7.4
Africa (tropical)	6.5	5.5	6.6	7.8

TABLE 15. CHANGES IN ECONOMIC STRUCTURE (SCENARIO X)[a]
(*Percentage of total output originating in each sector*)

Region	Agriculture and mineral resources	Manufacturing	Utilities and construction	Services
Developing countries				
Latin America (medium-income)				
1970	21.0	31.5	10.2	37.3
2000	11.4	36.8	14.5	37.3
Latin America (low-income)				
1970	33.5	23.8	9.3	33.4
2000	16.1	28.5	16.2	39.2
Middle East				
1970	63.3	11.3	6.5	18.9
2000	15.0	31.0	17.5	35.6
Asia (low-income)				
1970	33.2	29.9	8.3	28.6
2000	19.4	32.3	11.0	37.3
Africa (arid)				
1970	28.1	33.6	7.1	31.2
2000	23.8	35.9	9.4	35.0
Africa (tropical)				
1970	46.9	17.8	7.9	27.4
2000	39.0	18.6	10.0	32.4
Developed market economies				
North America				
1970	6.6	39.3	11.6	42.5
2000	5.9	38.4	13.4	42.3
Western Europe (high-income)				
1970	8.2	42.5	10.7	38.6
2000	4.1	42.6	12.3	41.0
Japan				
1970	7.0	44.7	13.7	34.6
2000	3.0	46.1	12.7	38.2

[a] Data in this table relate to total output of sectors and are not directly comparable to sectoral shares based on value added.

growing sector of the developing economies. Their expansion rates are more or less in line with manufacturing, tending to exceed those of manufacturing at lower over-all growth rates of GDP and to fall short of them at higher rates. This is understandable, since the creation of an infrastructure is essential as a base for the development of other sectors of the economy.

As their incomes rise the developing regions are expected to approach the economic structure characteristic of highly developed countries (see table 16). This structure is expected to remain relatively stable (3-8 per cent

TABLE 16. AVERAGE ANNUAL GROWTH RATES, OUTPUT OF MANUFACTURING INDUSTRIES, 1970-2000 (SCENARIO X)
(*Percentage*)

Region	Total manufac- turing	Light industry[a]	Machinery and equipment[b]	Materials[c]
Latin America (medium-income)	8.5	7.6	10.6	8.5
Latin America (low-income) .	8.8	7.8	10.5	9.3
Middle East . .	14.0	10.5	16.0	17.5
Asia (low-income) .	7.8	7.1	8.7	8.0
Africa (arid) . .	6.2	5.4	6.4	7.0
Africa (tropical) .	6.6	5.3	8.7	8.3

[a] Consists of food processing, textiles and apparel, furniture and fixtures, paper, printing and "other manufactures".
[b] Consists of motor vehicles, aircraft, other transportation equipment, metal products, machinery, electrical machinery and instruments.
[c] Consists of petroleum refining, primary metals, wood and cork, rubber, industrial chemicals, fertilizers, other chemicals, cement and glass.

in the primary sector, 40-45 per cent in the secondary sector and 38-42 per cent in the tertiary sector). In the developing countries there will be a continuing decline in the share of agriculture and resources, though that share will still remain higher (in some cases, substantially higher) than in the developed countries. The share of manufacturing, while increasing in all developing regions, will in most cases remain significantly lower than in the developed regions. The share of services will increase and come rather close to their share in the developed regions, but their composition will still be quite different.

It is interesting to follow the pattern of industrialization in the developing regions. The most distinctive feature is the generally lower growth rates of light industry as compared to those of heavy industry, including machinery and equipment, and materials. This is a logical consequence of the growth in the share of investment and of the decline in the share of personal consumption in total final use, as well as of an increase in the ratio between the intermediate and final product. The tendency of heavy industry to grow more rapidly than light industry is well pronounced in all developing regions, including those with lower growth rates of GDP.

On the regional, though not necessarily on the country level, an accent on heavy industry is essential for industrialization and economic development. There is special need for priority investment in the growth of machinery- and equipment-producing branches of industry, where faster development is expected. Light industry is, and in some cases will still remain, a larger part of manufacturing than either machinery and equipment or

materials production. But even in instances in which light industry loses its dominant position it cedes its place to "materials" rather than to machinery production. Even in the fastest growing regions the share of machinery and equipment production in total manufacturing does not go much beyond 30 per cent, while its share in the developed regions is close to 40 per cent.

These structural differences reflect differences in mineral resource endowments as well as the relative difficulty of developing machinery and building equipment as compared to the materials industries. However, a much higher share of machinery and equipment would be necessary if the developing regions were to decrease drastically their dependence on imports of machinery and equipment.

TABLE 17. CHANGES IN THE STRUCTURE OF MANUFACTURING (SCENARIO X)
(*Percentage of total output of manufacturing originating in each sector*)

Region	Light industry	Machinery and equipment	Other manufac- turing
Developing countries			
Latin America (medium-income)			
1970	53.2	22.3	24.5
2000	41.1	31.1	27.7
Latin America (low-income)			
1970	56.7	14.4	28.8
2000	43.2	23.3	33.5
Middle East			
1970	65.9	18.2	15.9
2000	22.9	32.6	44.5
Asia (low-income)			
1970	57.5	18.5	24.0
2000	50.7	24.1	25.2
Africa (arid)			
1970	48.1	25.3	26.6
2000	39.4	27.4	33.2
Africa (tropical)			
1970	68.3	7.3	24.4
2000	47.1	13.4	39.5
Developed market economies			
North America			
1970	30.5	40.7	28.7
2000	29.2	40.8	30.0
Western Europe (high-income)			
1970	39.1	34.6	26.3
2000	29.2	42.3	28.5
Japan			
1970	32.2	39.6	28.2
2000	28.2	45.8	26.0

Industrial development along the lines indicated in scenario X would substantially change the position of developing regions in world industrial production (see table 18). Their over-all share of total world manufacturing output is expected to increase from 6 to 18 per cent, while the share of the developed market economies would decline from 70 to 49 per cent. The share of the developing market economies in total world output of light industry would increase from 9 to 22 per cent; in output of materials, from 5 to 19 per cent; and in output of machinery and equipment, from 3 to 13 per cent. Still larger shares would be necessary under conditions of lower imports and higher exports of manufactured goods to the developed countries.

TABLE 18. CHANGES IN REGIONAL SHARES OF WORLD MANUFACTURING OUTPUT (SCENARIO X)
(*Percentage*)

Region	Total manufacturing	Light industry	Machinery and equipment	Materials
Developed market economies				
1970	70	66	73	71
2000	49	45	52	48
North America				
1970	36	30	40	39
2000	21	20	22	22
Western Europe (high-income)				
1970	25	27	24	24
2000	18	17	20	18
Japan				
1970	7	6	8	7
2000	8	7	9	7
Centrally planned economies				
1970	22	23	22	21
2000	29	26	31	28
Soviet Union				
1970	14	14	14	14
2000	17	14	18	17
Eastern Europe				
1970	5.5	5	6	4.5
2000	6.3	5	8	5.4
Asia (centrally planned)				
1970	3	3.5	2	3
2000	6	6	5	6
Developing market economies				
1970	6	9	3	5
2000	17.5	22	13	19
Latin America				
1970	3	4	1.7	3
2000	8	10.6	6	8
Asia and Middle East				
1970	2	4	1	2
2000	8.4	10	6	10
Africa (excluding oil-producing countries)				
1970	0.8	1.2	0.4	0.3
2000	1.1	1.4	0.6	1.3

Chapter IX

FOOD AND AGRICULTURE

Agriculture plays a critical role in economic development. As income and population rise, heavy demands are placed on the agricultural sector to supply more food and materials. According to scenario X, by 2000 total world agricultural production should increase threefold or fourfold, as compared to 1970. This would require substantial investment in opening up new land, in irrigation and in the institution of high-yield techniques. The world model does not include a full assessment of the feasibility of trebling or quadrupling world agricultural production. However, it does project agricultural output and trade and makes estimates of input and capital requirements associated with these levels.

The model identifies five sectors related to agricultural production. Four of these sectors produce specific groups of agricultural commodities: animal products, high-protein crops, grains and roots. The fifth incorporates the remaining agricultural activities. The outputs of the four selected agricultural sectors are measured in physical units—millions of tons of the commodity; the outputs of the fifth sector are measured in millions of dollars. This rather detailed analysis of the agricultural sector emphasizes the importance of food and agriculture in many countries, especially in the developing regions of the world.

In addition to the input-output links of the above agricultural sectors with other sectors, the model computes required increases in acreage planted and the yield of the agricultural sector for each of the regions in the four periods of analysis. *Per capita* consumption levels of two categories of food nutrients—calories and proteins—are also estimated. The study of the levels of the main categories of food nutrients is important in establishing minimal levels of health and development standards in low-income countries.

The model projects the imports and exports of agricultural commodities by the same method used in the case of other commodities. The imports of a given commodity in a given region are assumed to be proportional to the gross domestic output of that commodity. The pool of world imports arising from the aggregation of the individual imports of the different regions of the world are met by exports of pre-defined shares of total exports from each of the regions. The shares of exports of each region are determined exogenously and are projected to change from the base-year values in accordance with recent trends and relative economic levels of the region.

The main pollutants relating to agricultural production are pesticides and fertilizer solid wastes. Agricultural pollution data for this study were available only for pesticides. At present no methods are available for abating pesticide residuals. Study of the relation of the use of pesticides to agricultural output per acre could give useful information relating to environmental protection policies. Such relative estimation could help establish the trade-off between the level of emission of pesticide pollutants and the increase in agricultural output. However, information of this nature is at present restricted to a few experimental studies in the United States of America.

Soil erosion and salinity are undoubtedly serious problems confronting the agricultural sector of most regions of the world. Here again statistical information available on the various regions in which the effect of soil erosion and salinity are serious environmental problems were not available for the present study. It is, however, recognized that soil erosion remains a critical environmental issue seriously affecting the agricultural productivity of developing regions. Salt accumulation presents problems similar to that of soil erosion. But unlike soil losses arising from erosion, salinity problems arise primarily from irrigation through the lack of sufficient water supplies to wash out the excess salts. Salinity can render large irrigation projects useless and could have a substantial impact on future cropland expansion and on the utilization of land under cultivation.

Table 19 shows the projected agricultural output for the world as a whole and its major regions. The world output is expected to increase at an average rate of growth of 3.4 per cent per annum in 1970-2000, starting with the lower rate of 2.7 per cent in the 1970s, which is expected to accelerate to 3.4 per cent in the 1980s and further to 4.0 per cent in the 1990s.

The distribution of growth patterns of world agricultural output among the various regions indicates a much faster rate of growth for the developing regions than for the developed. In the developed regions the average rate of growth for the whole period is 1.6 per cent and the variation among the decades is not large. In developing group I, the average is as high as 6.4 per cent, while in developing group II, it is 5.1 per cent. In most developing regions growth of agricultural output tends to accelerate from decade to decade.

These different rates of growth are reflected in the changing regional shares of world agricultural output. In 1970, 64 per cent of world output was accounted for by the developed countries, with 6 per cent from developing group I and 30 per cent from developing group II. Because of the relatively faster growth in the developing regions by the end of the century, the share of the developed countries is expected to decline to 37.9 per cent, while the two developing regions would account for the remaining 62.1 per cent, with developing group II, at 48.3 per cent, overtaking the total for the developed countries.

The average total growth rate for all developing regions is 5.3 per cent in 1970-2000, with decade averages increasing from 4.7 per cent in the 1970s to 5.8 in the 1980s, and slowing down to 5.4 per cent in the 1990s. These averages are higher, especially in the latter decades, than the 4 per cent growth-rate target indicated in the Inter-

TABLE 19. AGRICULTURAL OUTPUT (SCENARIO X)

	1970	1980	1990	2000
Total agricultural output (billions of 1970 dollars)				
Developed	255.8	296.0	332.2	415.4
Developing group I[a]	23.8	42.1	78.5	151.7
Developing group II	120.1	186.4	322.8	529.9
WORLD	399.7	524.5	733.5	1097.1
Regional share in world output (percentage)				
Developed	64.0	56.4	45.3	37.9
Developing group I	6.0	8.0	10.7	13.8
Developing group II	30.0	35.5	44.0	48.3
WORLD	100.0	100.0	100.0	100.0
Agricultural output per capita (billions of 1970 dollars)				
Developed	0.2615	0.2776	0.2878	0.3381
Developing Group I	0.0665	0.0884	0.1222	0.1770
Developing group II	0.0526	0.0652	0.0910	0.1227
World	0.1104	0.1192	0.1372	0.1713

	1970-1980	1980-1990	1990-2000	1970-2000
Rate of growth of agricultural output[b] (percentage)				
Developed	1.4	1.2	2.2	1.6
Developing group I	5.7	6.2	6.6	6.4
Developing group II	4.3	5.4	5.0	5.1
World	2.7	3.4	4.0	3.4

[a] For definition of developing groups I and II see table 2.
[b] Average annual compound.

national Development Strategy. However, they would only represent a very gradual improvement in *per capita* agricultural output levels.

On a *per capita* basis the average growth rates, as projected, are 3.5 for developing group I and 2.9 for developing group II. This leads to a more than twofold increase in *per capita* agricultural production in the developing countries. The average gap in *per capita* agricultural production between developing group II and the developed countries decreases from 1:5 in 1970 to 1:2.8 in 2000. This is in line with the general progress towards more equality of income assumed in scenario X.

In terms of food consumption, scenario X envisages a general improvement in diet in all regions of the world (see table 20). In developed regions (market and centrally planned alike) there is a clear trend towards equalizing calorie intake at around 3.2 thousand kilo-calories per day and at 100-110 protein grams per day. In developing countries the starting consumption levels are rather low, but it is expected that by 2000 all of them will reach the 2.5 thousand kilo-calories mark and that, at least four regions—namely, both Latin American regions, the Middle East and tropical Africa—will come very close to 3 thousand kilo-calories. It is also expected that in most of the developing regions the average protein intake will be in the 75-90 gram area rather than the 50-60 gram area, where it is today. Only one region—low-income Asia—is expected to lag behind somewhat in protein intake, but even here progress will be obvious.

The agricultural output and food consumption projections are made on the assumption that the extent of self-sufficiency will remain roughly the same as in 1970 (see table 21). In 1970 developing group I imported 17 per cent or less of its requirements of principal agricultural products, and developing group II—6 per cent or less.

TABLE 20. *Per capita* CONSUMPTION OF NUTRIENTS PER DAY (SCENARIO X)

Region	Kilo-calories (thousands)		Proteins (grams)	
	1970	2000	1970	2000
Developed market				
North America	3.2	3.2	96	100
Western Europe (high-income)	3.0	3.2	91	105
Japan	2.4	3.2	71	117
Centrally planned				
Soviet Union	3.2	3.2	92	108
Eastern Europe	3.1	3.2	93	108
Asia (centrally planned)	2.1	2.5	59	79
Developing market				
Latin America (medium-income)	2.4	3.0	60	86
Latin America (low-income)	2.2	2.9	50	74
Middle East	2.0	2.9	53	92
Asia (low-income)	2.0	2.4	52	66
Africa (arid)	2.5	2.5	72	78
Africa (tropical)	2.2	2.8	62	87

TABLE 21. RELATION OF IMPORTS TO OUTPUT OF AGRICULTURAL COMMODITIES IN DEVELOPING COUNTRIES (*Percentage*)

Agricultural commodities	Group I		Group II	
	1970	2000	1970	2000
Livestock products	5.0	5.4	1.6	1.6
High-protein crops	9.2	11.0	5.8	5.5
Grains	17.0	16.6	4.5	4.5
Roots	1.5	1.7	1.2	1.4
Other agricultural products	6.2	10.4	6.9	6.5

39

The assumption that these shares will remain basically the same by 2000 actually means that the significant projected increase in the consumption of agricultural products in the developing countries will have to be achieved predominantly by substantially increasing agricultural output in these regions. Smaller increases in output would lead to much higher dependence on imports and would place an unbearable burden on the balances of payments of the developing countries, interfering with other aspects of their economic growth.

Table 22 (column 1) shows the relative increase of agricultural output in the individual regions. The dif-

ference between the various developed regions is not large; the lowest increase is projected for Western Europe (30 per cent), and the highest for North America and Oceania (96 and 92 per cent respectively).

Among the developing regions the lowest relative increase (projected for tropical Africa) is 338 per cent, which is much larger than the highest increase envisaged for a developed region. The maximum relative increase in the developing world is projected for the Middle East (850 per cent). It seems likely that the rapidly rising food requirements of this region will be met, at least in the short run, by increased import dependence.

TABLE 22. LAND REQUIREMENTS AND LAND PRODUCTIVITY IN 2000 (SCENARIO X)

(Index: 1970 = 100 per cent)

Region	Agricultural output	Land/yield index	Arable land	Land productivity
Developed market				
North America	196	215	111	194
Western Europe (high-income) . . .	130	162	100	162
Japan	176	269	100	269
Oceania	192	296	183	162
Centrally planned				
Soviet Union	164	215	100	215
Eastern Europe	143	186	100	186
Asia (centrally planned)	488	333	120	278
Developing market				
Latin America (medium-income) . . .	495	517	166	311
Latin America (low-income) . . .	532	460	140	328
Middle East	950	612	126	487
Asia (low-income)	506	376	113	331
Africa (arid)	409	371	131	282
Africa (tropical)	438	492	152	324

Column 2 of the same table shows the land/yield index. For each region it measures the changes in land under cultivation, as compared with the base period of 1970, required to achieve the predicted levels of agricultural output, assuming that the productivity of land is unchanged from the 1970 level. This index serves as a basis for estimating requirements for capital stock and investment in agriculture. Large amounts of capital are of course required to open up new land under cultivation, improve available arable land or to increase crop yields and livestock productivity. The requirements for 2000 are estimated to exceed the 1970 levels by a factor of 3.3 to 6, depending on the region in question.

The land/yield index is essentially an index of agricultural production but weighted by land per unit of output rather than by value. Because of this there are significant differences between the respective regional land/yield and the agricultural output indexes wherever substantial shifts in the structure of agricultural output are projected. Exogenous estimates of new land brought into cultivation were made for the individual regions, with the available FAO estimates of their potential arable land borne in mind. Column 3 of table 22 shows the results of these calculations—namely, the arable land index—measuring the total arable land in 2000, as compared to 1970.

In the developed regions the largest relative increase in land under cultivation is projected in Oceania. All developing regions are expected to increase their arable land. The largest relative changes are projected in Latin

America and tropical Africa. In terms of millions of hectares the chunks of newly cultivated land are also expected to be very substantial in centrally planned and low-income Asia. It is estimated that total new additions to arable land in the developing countries may reach 229 million hectares in 1970-2000, which represents an increase of 30 per cent over the total amount of arable land available in these regions in 1970. Assuming agricultural land expansion of this magnitude, the model then shows the increase in land productivity necessary to achieve the estimated increase in agricultural production. The index of land productivity is obtained through dividing the land/yield index by the arable land index (see column 4 of table 22).

The potential for technological change in agriculture in the developing countries is well recognized. Moreover, recent studies relating to the "green revolution" indicate that in an increasing number of developing countries agricultural yields will rise through the use of high-yield varieties of crops, fertilizers and pesticides. Our land productivity index gauges the increases in production that must be sought by these and other means. The results of these calculations show that in the developed regions the productivity of land (combining crop yields and livestock productivity) has to increase roughly twofold before the close of the century in order to keep up with the demand for agricultural production. The estimate for Japan is too high, indicating perhaps that this region will have to depend on imports to a much larger extent than is assumed according to scenario X.

In the developing countries the need for an increase in land productivity is even larger—roughly a threefold increase is needed over the 1970 level. The estimate for the Middle East is also out of line, indicating that this area will have to increase its dependence on imported agricultural goods.

One important way to increase land productivity is investment in irrigation. Estimates made in the course of the present study suggest, as one realistic possibility, the irrigation of a world total of some 80 million hectares over the 1970-2000 period, including 56 million hectares in the developing countries. This newly irrigated area would amount to 5.6 per cent of the total arable land available in the developing countries in 2000.

Self-sufficiency in food is an important national economic policy consideration for many of the developing countries. Developing countries with a rapid increase in population often find that increases in domestic production of food cannot keep pace with the increases in the demand for food brought about by the increases in population. In addition, food production requires foreign fertilizer and pesticides, which also are scarce in these low-income countries and must be imported. Thus, a scenario which exogenously sets a policy of self-sufficiency in food is useful for evaluating the costs in terms of the factors of production, particularly in terms of foreign resources, needed to meet such a desirable policy goal.

Scenario G assumes hypothetical self-sufficiency in food in low-income Asia, where the food situation is a crucial policy consideration. This scenario traces the implications of such a policy for consumption, fertilizer and chemical requirements and the balance of payments. It is computed for a single year, 1980. The results are shown in table 23. To achieve self-sufficiency, it is assumed that the rate of investment in irrigation and in

TABLE 23. COMPARISON OF SCENARIOS X AND G,[a] 1980

Factors related to agricultural production	Scenario X	Scenario G	G − X	Percentage change $\frac{G - X}{X} \times 100$
Agricultural output (millions of dollars)	60.6	62.6	+2.0	+3.3
Land/yield index (percentage)	141.0	147.7	+6.7	+4.8
Land investment (millions of hectares)	1.1	2.3	+1.2	+109.1
Irrigation investment (millions of hectares)	0.4	0.8	+0.4	+100.0
Imports of fertilizer (millions of tons)	1.93	1.99	+0.06	+3.1
Pesticide use (millions of tons)	0.39	0.40	+0.01	+2.6
Capital stock agriculture (millions of dollars)	5.4	5.6	+0.2	+3.7
Net food imports (millions of dollars)	1.7	0.0	−1.7	−100.0
Trade balance (deficit) (millions of dollars)	−10.2	−7.9	+2.3	−22.6

[a] Scenario G assumes hypothetical self-sufficiency in food in low-income Asia.

bringing new land under cultivation will be roughly doubled in the vicinity of 1980. This, along with the increased requirements for plants and equipment needed for higher agricultural production, leads to an increase of roughly 4 per cent in the total capital stock in agriculture.

Net imports of food decline to zero while agricultural production increases to fill the gap. This leads to a marked improvement in the balance of trade (measured in 1980 relative prices). Imports of fertilizers and pesticides would have to increase to support the larger agricultural production. These increases are not so large as to upset the net improvement in the balance of trade that comes with eliminating food imports.

This hypothetical example suggests that self-sufficiency in food is a promising kind of "import substitution" for reducing balance-of-payments deficits in developing countries. The feasibility of such a scenario would depend on whether the increases in food production could indeed be achieved with the levels of investment, fertilizer and chemical inputs specified. The

results of these computations do suggest the importance of anticipating growing food requirements and of increasing agricultural yields for the economies of developing regions. A discussion of specific projections of demand for grain and livestock products follows.

Grain

Under scenario X the world grain output would increase from 1,217 million tons in 1970 to 3,471 million tons in 2000. This implies an average rate of growth of 3.5 per cent per annum. It is lower than the rate of growth of 4.7 per cent indicated for world GDP but larger than the average rate of growth of population of 1.9 per cent per annum.

Table 24 illustrates world and aggregated regional group projections of domestic demand for grain, according to scenario X. Domestic demand is defined as total output plus imports minus exports. If this demand is satisfied by adequate production and imports. it is

TABLE 24. GRAIN: TOTAL DOMESTIC DEMAND

	1970	1980	1990	2000
Total domestic demand (millions of tons)				
Developed countries	565.6	664.4	928.9	1143.4
Developing group I	58.7	85.3	144.9	270.8
Developing group II	593.1	841.5	1330.4	2056.9
WORLD	1217.4	1591.2	2404.2	3471.1
Regional share in world output (percentage)				
Developed countries	0.46	0.42	0.39	0.33
Developing group I	0.048	0.054	0.060	0.078
Developing group II	0.46	0.53	0.55	0.59
WORLD	100.0	100.0	100.0	100.0
Per capita *domestic demand* (millions of tons)				
Developed countries	0.578	0.623	0.805	0.933
Developing group I	0.164	0.179	0.226	0.316
Developing group II	0.260	0.294	0.375	0.476
World	0.336	0.362	0.450	0.534

	1970-1980	1980-1990	1990-2000
Rate of growth[a] (percentage)			
Developed countries	1.6	3.4	2.1
Developing group I	3.7	5.3	6.3
Developing group II	3.6	4.6	4.4
World	2.7	4.1	3.7

[a] Average annual compound.

equivalent to visible consumption. Thus, these demand estimates should be taken as a rough indication of what grain consumption would be like if available resources were in line with other indicators of economic development.

The patterns of increase in grain output among the developed and developing regions of the world show considerable variation. In the less developed countries, because of their low levels of *per capita* consumption in the base period and the relatively more rapid rate of population growth, the growth in the demand for grain is more rapid than in the developed countries. The average rate in the developed countries is 2.3 per cent compared to 5.1 per cent per annum in the developing countries (group II).

The growth in the demand for grain is much smaller when viewed in terms of the levels of *per capita* figures. In the world as a whole, the level of *per capita* output of grain increases from 0.336 tons per person in 1970 to 0.534 tons per person in 2000, indicating an average rate of growth of 1.5 per cent per annum. In the developed countries *per capita* levels of domestic demand increase from 0.578 tons per person in 1970 to 0.933 in 2000— that is, at an implied rate of growth of 1.6 per cent per annum. Much of this increase is due to increased meat consumption. In developing countries (group I), the level of *per capita* demand increases from 0.164 tons per person in 1970 to 0.316 tons in 2000, or at an average annual rate of growth of 2.2 per cent. Although this rate of growth is higher than that of the world as a whole and of the developed countries, the level of *per capita* demand in 2000 remains lower than the average level of *per capita* consumption in the developed countries in 1970. In the developing countries (group II), the *per capita* level of demand in 1970 of 0.260 tons per person, although low by international standards, is considerably higher than that of the other developing regions. This level of *per capita* demand increases to 0.476 tons per

person in the year 2000, indicating an average annual rate of increase of 2.0 per cent. For this region, too, the level of *per capita* demand in 2000 is substantially less than that in the developed countries in the same year and does not reach the 1970 level of the developed countries.

The individual developed regions show variations in their patterns of demand for grain. These regions can be divided into three broad categories. The first category has relatively high levels of *per capita* consumption, in the range of 0.7 tons *per capita* per year, and consists of three regions: North America, the Soviet Union and Eastern Europe. In the next group, *per capita* consumption levels are in the range of 0.4 tons. It includes the two Western European regions of high- and medium-income and Oceania. The other two developed regions, Japan and Southern Africa, belong to the third group with relatively low levels of *per capita* grain consumption.

These interregional differentials are based on traditional differences in the dependence of individual regions on grain as compared with, say, soybeans and root crops. As the income of a region grows, *per capita* consumption of meat increases and there is some tendency for feed grain consumption to rise accordingly. Thus, the gaps between grain consumption in those countries with the highest income and that in all other countries tend to narrow. On the other hand, alternative crops can also serve as a basis for meat production. Thus, while regional differentials of grain consumption *per capita* in developed countries decline a little over time, characteristic differentials tend to remain in 2000.

Within the developing regions there are even wider differentials. The levels of *per capita* consumption of grain in medium-income Latin America and centrally planned Asia are comparable to those of Japan and Southern Africa. At the other end of the spectrum are low-income Latin America and tropical Africa, with levels of consumption of only about half that of the developing regions with high levels of consumption.

Both of these regions consume relatively large quantities of root crops instead of grain. As in the case of the developed regions, the growth rates of *per capita* grain consumption do not show wide variations among individual developing regions, and the traditional preferences with respect to alternative crops tend to persist throughout the forecasted period. Rates of growth for most of the regions tend to accelerate from the 1970s to the 1980s, slowing down somewhat in the final decade.

Since food consumption varies with GDP it is not surprising that the patterns of domestic demand for grain in scenarios X and A show a number of differences. On the whole the growth of demand for grain is more rapid in scenario X than in scenario A. For the world as a whole, the growth of demand projected for 2000 under scenario X is about 15 per cent greater than that projected in scenario A. In *per capita* terms, this amounts to an increase which is 13 per cent greater in X than in A. The differences between the two scenarios for the developed countries are small—on the order of 1 per cent for both total and *per capita* demand.

Animal products

Table 25 gives the projection of total domestic demand for animal products. Total domestic demand is defined in these tables as domestic output plus imports less exports. In the world as a whole it increases at an annual rate of a little over 3 per cent per annum. The rate of growth of the two latter decades is higher than in the 1970s. The regional distribution of growth patterns, as in the case of total agricultural output and of grain, discussed earlier, are weighted towards the two developing groups of regions. In the developed countries the average rate of growth in the 1970s is 2.3 per cent, and is expected to decrease to 1.3 per cent by the final decade of the century. In the developing regions (group I), growth averages 5.5 per cent per annum in the 1970s, and accelerates to 6.6 per cent by the 1990s. In the developing regions (group II) the acceleration is from 4.3 to 4.8 per cent.

In 1970 the developed countries accounted for 63.6 per cent of total world demand. By 2000, the share of the developed countries is expected to decline to 41.8 per cent, while the share of developing countries (group II) will account for 46.2 per cent of the total. Even though these shifts in shares indicate higher levels of demand for the developing countries by the end of the century, the level of *per capita* consumption of these regions remains relatively low. In 1970 the level of *per capita* demand in developed countries was 0.136 units, while it was only 0.028 in developing countries (group II)—approximately one fifth of the level in developed countries. By 2000 the level of *per capita* demand will have increased to 0.077 in the developing countries (group II), while that in the developed countries will have increased to 0.194, a level approximately 2.5 times higher than that in the developing countries.

TABLE 25. ANIMAL PRODUCTS: TOTAL DOMESTIC DEMAND

	1970	1980	1990	2000
Total domestic demand (millions of tons)				
Developed countries	132.6	166.1	208.4	238.3
Developing group I	11.5	20.0	35.5	68.4
Developing group II	64.4	99.3	162.7	263.5
WORLD	208.5	285.4	406.6	570.1
Regional share in world output (percentage)				
Developed countries	63.6	58.2	51.3	41.8
Developing group I	5.5	7.0	8.7	12.0
Developing group II	30.9	34.8	40.0	46.2
WORLD	100.0	100.0	100.0	100.0
Per capita *domestic demand* (millions of tons)				
Developed countries	0.136	0.156	0.181	0.194
Developing group I	0.0321	0.042	0.055	0.0798
Developing group II	0.0281	0.035	0.046	0.077
World	0.0576	0.065	0.076	0.089

	1970-1980	1980-1990	1990-2000
Rate of growth[a] (percentage)			
Developed countries	2.25	2.26	1.34
Developing group I	5.53	5.73	6.55
Developing group II	4.33	4.93	4.82
World	3.13	3.54	3.40

[a] Average annual rate of growth.

Chapter X

MINERAL RESOURCES

In recent years the adequacy of natural resources to meet the demands anticipated by future growth in world income has become a problem of serious concern. The world model projects future production and consumption of six metallic and three energy resources (copper, bauxite, nickel, lead, zinc, iron, coal, petroleum and natural gas). Estimates both of total stocks of resources and of future demands are very uncertain. A few of the important factors responsible for the uncertainties associated with long-run supply-demand balance are that (a) resources already known to exist will be supplemented to an unknown extent by new discoveries in the future, as they were in the past; (b) we do not know the degree to which technological change will affect mining and extraction costs; (c) substitution among resources may result from changes in relative prices and from technological change in industries using these resources.

Since estimates of regional and world resource endowments are highly speculative the strategy of the present study was chosen with an eye towards bracketing the possible consequences of alternative assumptions, some more optimistic than others. We began with estimates of resource endowments that many acknowledge to be very conservative: the unpublished estimates of the Bureau of Mines of the United States of America.[29] These data provided a basis for constructing "step-cost functions", which tell us how much of the various mineral reserves are likely to be available in each region at three levels of extraction costs. Estimates of the supplies of petroleum and natural gas were assembled from a large number of other sources in the current literature. Since the initial estimates of all endowments were considered conservative, a second, more optimistic scenario (scenario H), which assumed more generous resource endowments, was also constructed.

Reserve estimates had three important influences on the results of the computations. First, since extraction costs determine mineral prices in the dual computations, the step-cost functions had an important bearing on the estimates of future prices not only of minerals but also of all other products that incorporate mineral inputs, either directly or indirectly. Second, reserve estimates served as guidelines for projecting the degree of self-sufficiency for mineral inputs and also their future shares of the resource export markets. Third, world endowments determine the ultimate limits on the use of world minerals. Only two of the metallic minerals considered in this study, lead and zinc, are expected to "run out" by the turn of the century, provided that our assumptions about future demand are correct and that proven reserves of mineral resources do not increase from their

current estimates. However, other investigators have expressed concern about the adequacy of the supply of other minerals such as asbestos, fluorine, gold, mercury, phosphorus, silver, sulphur, tin and tungsten. In the future it would be desirable to gather the necessary data for introducing these other critical resources into the world system.

Scenario H differs from the central scenario, X, in that it incorporates alternative, more optimistic estimates of the levels of resource endowments in the various regions of the world. While more optimistic than X, it is still fairly conservative. It does not take account of major new potential sources such as undersea nodules or other new discoveries, which might become economic if resource prices were to rise by an order of magnitude. To construct scenario H, estimated endowments of the relatively scarce metallic resources in scenario X—copper, lead, zinc and nickel—were augmented by "hypothetical" and "speculative" reserves cited in the United States Geological Service Professional Paper 820. World reserves of copper were multiplied by about 2.5, reserves of nickel by 2, reserves of lead by 1.5, and reserves of zinc by 1.2. Additional reserves of zinc and lead were distributed roughly proportionally among all regions. Low-income Asia and centrally planned Asia were assumed to have the largest proportional increases in copper reserves. Additional reserves of nickel were assumed to occur in North America, Latin America, medium-income Western Europe, Southern Africa and Oceania. Additional reserves were added at various cost levels of the step functions.

Of the energy resources, coal is relatively plentiful even under conservative endowment estimates while natural gas endowments furnish only a small proportion of energy for developing countries. In the case of petroleum, United Nations estimates of world reserves are roughly 1.3 times our estimates of cumulative world demand through the year 2000 in the central scenario. However, estimates of reserves are increasing rapidly and it is very difficult to reconcile the various conflicting estimates of possible future changes in the regional distribution of reserves. In scenario H we did not depart from the basic assumption that the Middle East, Latin America and the Soviet Union would be the sole net exporters of petroleum after 1980, though in the light of recent developments it is practically certain that there will be other net exporting regions—for example, centrally planned Asia. Additional scenarios, incorporating these and other developments, may be computed in the future. "Optimism" with respect to petroleum endowments consisted of the assumption that extraction costs would rise less steeply than they did in the central scenario. Thus, in scenario H, the 1990 cost of petroleum in North America is assumed to be a little more than half the cost assumed in scenario X. However, it is assumed that by 2000 the price of petroleum will be the same

[29] United States of America, Bureau of Mines, *Commodity Statement: Summary Tables*, table 14-A.

TABLE 26. ASSUMED RESOURCE ENDOWMENTS FOR METALS AND COAL

(*Millions of tons*)[a]

Resource	Scenario	Developed market	Developed centrally planned	Developing	Total
Copper . . .	X	179	50	215	460
	H	216	147	643	1106
Bauxite . . .	X and H	1207	110	3131	4726
Nickel . . .	X	13774	9141	67649	90871
	H	72856	9141	98949	183263
Zinc . . .	X	159	27	42	235
	H	189	34	53	285
Lead	X	88	11	27	129
	H	131	17	41	193
Iron . . .	X and H	70682	52153	60197	186841
Coal . . .	X and H	755912	2454682	5828805	9078229

[a] Metal content for all metals; nickel in thousands of tons.

TABLE 27. RESOURCE PRICES[a]

(*Thousands of dollars per ton*)

Resource	1990			2000		
	Scenario X	Scenario H	Difference (percentage)	Scenario X	Scenario H	Difference (percentage)
Copper . . .	1.092	1.111	+1.7	2.842	1.239	−56.5
Bauxite . . .	0.011	0.011	—	0.013	0.013	—
Nickel . . .	4.000	4.000	—	7.000	4.000	−42.9
Zinc . . .	0.362	0.367	+1.4	0.635	0.635	—
Lead . . .	0.262	0.267	+1.9	0.597	0.323	−47.6
Iron . . .	0.015	0.015	—	0.015	0.015	—
Crude petroleum .	0.047	0.028	−40.4	0.053	0.053	—
Natural gas .	0.022	0.022	—	0.031	0.031	—
Coal . . .	0.005	0.005	—	0.005	0.005	—

[a] These prices were normalized in accordance with the procedure described in Annex II. Energy prices are per ton of coal equivalent. Metal prices are per ton of metal content.

under both scenarios, that price being equal to the estimated cost per metric ton of extracting petroleum from oil shale.

Table 26 compares the resource endowments under the two alternative scenarios X and H. It is seen that for two of the metals—bauxite and iron—as well as for coal, the estimated endowments of all the regions under the two alternative scenarios are the same. In the case of the other four metals—copper, nickel, zinc and lead—the estimated regional endowments under the two alternative scenarios are different.

Table 27 shows the resource prices under the two alternative scenarios for 1990 and 2000. For 1990, the two scenarios do not indicate significant price differences, except for petroleum. For 2000, however, the differences for three of the metals—copper, nickel and lead—are significant. In the case of copper the price differential exceeds 55 per cent, for nickel it is 43 per cent and for lead close to 48 per cent.

Regional resource consumption

Future consumption of world resources will have an important bearing on the adequacy of world supplies. (In the projections these consumption estimates are very similar for scenarios X and H.) The model provides estimates of the consumption of each of the nine selected resources by the 15 regional economies. These estimates

depend, of course, on the regional growth rates and hence vary with the alternative growth rates assumed in the different scenarios. Future technologies will also exert an important influence on resource consumption. To take such substitutions into account, independent estimates of resource use required by future technologies were introduced to modify the technical input coefficients for specific resource use by individual consuming sectors of each decade. In addition, resource coefficients for each mineral (e.g., tons of virgin copper or iron per unit of automobile production) were scaled down in successive decades to take account of potential savings of primary resources through increased recycling. In the present study it was assumed that all regions would take advantage of the maximum potential for recycling by 2000. In a stationary (that is, not growing) economy the maximum potential for the recycling of many materials might be assumed to be somewhere in excess of 75 per cent over the long run. Because this study assumed continuing economic growth, the maximum potential for recycling is estimated to be much less; below 55 per cent in all regions.[30]

[30] United States of America, *Ad Hoc* Committee on the Domestic and International Monetary Effect of Energy and Other Natural Resource Pricing of the (House) Committee on Banking and Currency, *Meeting America's Resource Needs: Problems and Policies* (Washington, D.C., Government Printing Office, November 1974), table 2.4.

Table 28 shows consumption of specific minerals by various regions of the world in 1970 and projections, according to scenario X, for 2000. Percentage shares of annual world consumption are also listed for each mineral and regional group in table 29.

TABLE 28. RESOURCE CONSUMPTION[a]

Resource	Year	Developed market	Developed centrally planned	Developing
Copper . .	1970	4.5	1.0	6.6
	2000	15.4	5.3	7.5
Bauxite . .	1970	8.4	1.4	1.2
	2000	26.6	7.5	10.3
Nickel . .	1970	429.4	114.7	103.5
	2000	1236.6	562.1	818.0
Zinc . . .	1970	3.6	0.9	0.7
	2000	10.7	4.1	5.9
Lead . . .	1970	2.2	0.7	0.5
	2000	7.3	3.9	5.7
Iron . . .	1970	241.9	116.6	55.1
	2000	792.0	564.3	544.1
Petroleum .	1970	2104.4	409.5	399.8
	2000	7052.5	2447.4	5414.3
Natural gas .	1970	1022.6	312.6	90.2
	2000	2480.8	2141.5	1740.3
Coal . . .	1970	994.2	585.8	500.5
	2000	4245.2	2578.2	3253.6

[a] Tons × 10^6 metal content for all metals except nickel, which is in tons × 10^3. Energy in tons of coal-equivalent.

TABLE 29. RESOURCE CONSUMPTION AS PERCENTAGE OF WORLD CONSUMPTION

Resource	Year	Developed market	Developed centrally planned	Developing
Copper . .	1970	71.0	15.3	9.6
	2000	49.2	16.9	23.9
Bauxite . .	1970	73.5	12.1	10.9
	2000	54.5	15.5	21.0
Nickel . .	1970	64.3	17.2	15.5
	2000	43.6	19.3	28.8
Zinc . . .	1970	67.5	15.9	12.2
	2000	46.6	17.8	25.6
Lead . . .	1970	61.9	20.1	13.6
	2000	37.8	20.3	29.2
Iron . . .	1970	56.9	27.4	13.0
	2000	39.2	27.9	26.9
Petroleum .	1970	70.1	13.6	13.3
	2000	45.0	15.6	34.6
Natural gas .	1970	71.7	21.0	6.3
	2000	38.9	33.6	27.2
Coal . . .	1970	45.9	27.1	23.1
	2000	39.9	24.2	30.6

It is widely known that the high-income regions, particularly North America, Western Europe and Japan, consumed the bulk of world mineral resources in 1970. Their share is particularly high for non-ferrous metals and energy. In the projections, their high share continues but decreases substantially over the period 1970-2000 as developing countries and middle-income countries grow in relative economic importance. In general, the demand for mineral resources is roughly proportional to GDP, but resource consumption tends to increase more than proportionally with rising income in the developing regions as the proportions of agriculture and consumer necessities decline in the region's sectoral output mix. Table 30 gives the rates of growth of GDP and the minerals. It shows that over the period 1970-2000 consumption of petroleum in the developing regions rises at 9.1 per cent per annum while GDP grows at only 7.2 per cent. The increasing relative importance of services in developed regions tends to reinforce the decline in their share of world resource consumption. However, the use of metals and energy in income-elastic housing and in buildings and equipment for service sectors is far from negligible.

TABLE 30. GROWTH RATES OF CONSUMPTION OF MINERALS, 1970-2000

(Percentage)

	Developed market	Developed centrally planned	Developing
GDP growth rate . .	3.6	5.1	7.2
Resource			
Copper . . .	4.2	5.8	8.7
Bauxite . . .	3.9	5.8	7.3
Nickel . . .	3.6	5.4	7.1
Zinc . . .	3.7	5.4	7.6
Lead . . .	4.1	5.9	8.6
Iron . . .	4.0	5.4	7.9
Petroleum . .	4.1	6.1	9.1
Natural gas . .	3.0	6.6	10.4
Coal . . .	5.0	5.1	6.4

Regional resource extraction

Table 31 shows estimates of annual resource extraction in 1970 and 2000, by regional groups for each of the specific resources enumerated. Entries in parentheses represent scenario H; all others represent scenario X. Where no parenthetical entries are supplied, estimated

TABLE 31. RESOURCE PRODUCTION[a]

Resource	Year	Developed market	Developed centrally planned	Developing
Copper . .	1970	2.5	1.0	2.5
	2000	7.2	2.7	20.8
		(6.1)[b]	(5.0)	(19.0)
Bauxite . .	1970	2.9	1.4	6.2
	2000	23.2	3.9	17.2
Nickel . .	1970	326.5	114.7	206.6
	2000	467.2	539.6	1829.2
		(773.6)		(1528.7)
Zinc . .	1970	3.1	0.9	1.3
	2000	10.7	0.1	5.9
Lead . .	1970	1.7	0.8	0.9
	2000	7.3	3.9	5.7
Iron . .	1970	161.3	121.3	129.8
	2000	434.7	653.9	811.7
Petroleum .	1970	770.9	482.4	1741.9
	2000	3165.3	2308.4	10205.1
Natural gas .	1970	1018.4	308.7	98.4
	2000	2473.6	2328.7	1572.1
Coal . .	1970	974.4	615.0	495.3
	2000	4617.5	2578.2	3112.5

[a] Tons × 10^6 metal content for all metals except nickel, which is in tons × 10^3. Energy is in tons of coal-equivalent.
[b] Entries in parentheses represent scenario H.

production under the two scenarios are approximately equal. With the exception of bauxite, developing countries contribute a growing share of world mineral production to the world economy. Thus, the share of copper mined in the developed regions falls from 56 per cent to 32 per cent; the share of iron from 67 to 58 per cent; the share of petroleum from 42 to 35 per cent. Part of the petroleum "extracted" by the developed regions in the year 2000 will be derived from oil shale or liquefied coal.

Adequacy of resource endowments

Tables 32 and 33 show the cumulative production of mineral resources from the base year 1970 through 1980, 1990 and 2000 under the two alternative scenarios X and H, respectively, and tables 34 and 35 compare these cumulative totals with the estimated pessimistic and optimistic endowments, respectively.

For all the enumerated resources except lead and zinc, world endowments are likely to be fully adequate for anticipated demands through the turn of the century. In the case of lead and zinc, and possibly nickel, ways of reducing anticipated rates of consumption will have to be implemented during the last decade of the century, if not earlier. Since it was clear from preliminary work on the world model that world endowments of lead and zinc would be insufficient to satisfy demands with current technological means, it was assumed arbitrarily that all regions would be self-sufficient in these resources between 1990 and 2000. This is tantamount to assuming that regions whose supplies were insufficient to meet

their anticipated requirements would use unspecified substitute materials. Because lead and zinc do not account for a significant volume of world production or trade activity, this assumption does not seriously distort estimates of macro-economic variables.

TABLE 33. AGGREGATE RESOURCES: OPTIMISTIC RESOURCE ESTIMATE
(*Cumulative production from 1970 to 1980, 1990 and 2000*)[a]

Resource	Year	Developed	Developing	Developed centrally planned
Copper	1980	30.3	35.7	13.1
	1990	70.5	109.8	38.3
	2000	124.0	256.1	80.4
Bauxite	1980	35.2	85.1	16.1
	1990	94.4	235.1	37.8
	2000	254.9	420.2	69.6
Nickel	1980	3906.1	2744.0	1601.0
	1990	9405.8	8309.9	4700.9
	2000	16499.9	19808.0	9481.1
Zinc	1980	37.6	17.2	9.6
	1990	108.9	40.1	23.0
	2000	211.6	81.5	51.9
Lead	1980	22.7	13.0	8.3
	1990	90.6	23.5	12.7
	2000	181.2	53.6	32.5
Iron	1980	2221.4	1585.2	1662.4
	1990	5062.1	4777.8	4906.4
	2000	8661.4	11121.1	10384.5
Petroleum	1980	10341.5	24203.1	6438.5
	1990	26183.5	70965.2	19021.7
	2000	51362.9	153234.7	39113.8
Natural gas	1980	11890.8	2225.6	4978.7
	1990	28555.8	7972.8	15850.2
	2000	50781.7	19832.9	34968.9
Coal	1980	12457.0	6460.9	8613.7
	1990	31777.8	18535.2	23580.9
	2000	66578.2	42344.6	45964.1

[a] Tons × 10⁶ metal content for all metals except nickel which is in tons × 10³. Energy is in tons of coal-equivalent.

TABLE 34. PERCENTAGE OF BASE-YEAR ENDOWMENTS USED BY 1980, 1990 AND 2000: PESSIMISTIC RESOURCE ESTIMATE

Resource	Year	Developed	Developing	Developed centrally planned
Copper	1980	16.9	16.6	26.2
	1990	41.2	53.6	61.8
	2000	76.1	128.1[a]	108.2[a]
Bauxite	1980	2.9	2.7	14.6
	1990	7.8	7.5	34.4
	2000	20.6	13.3	63.3
Nickel	1980	28.4	4.1	17.5
	1990	68.4	12.3	51.4
	2000	108.9[a]	31.5	103.6[a]
Zinc	1980	23.6	41.0	35.6
	1990	68.5	95.5	85.2
	2000	132.8[a]	193.8[a]	191.5[a]
Lead	1980	25.8	48.1	75.5
	1990	103.0[a]	87.0	115.5[a]
	2000	205.7[a]	199.3[a]	294.5[a]
Iron	1980	3.1	2.6	3.2
	1990	7.2	7.9	9.4
	2000	12.3	18.4	19.9
Coal	1980	1.6	1.1	0.4
	1990	4.2	3.2	1.0
	2000	8.8	7.2	1.9

[a] Cumulative production exceeds pessimistic resource endowment.

TABLE 32. AGGREGATE RESOURCES: PESSIMISTIC RESOURCE ESTIMATE
(*Cumulative production from 1970 to 1980, 1990 and 2000*)[a]

Resource	Year	Developed	Developing	Developed centrally planned
Copper	1980	30.3	35.7	13.1
	1990	73.8	115.3	30.8
	2000	136.2	275.4	54.1
Bauxite	1980	35.2	85.1	16.1
	1990	94.4	235.1	37.8
	2000	248.9	417.3	69.6
Nickel	1980	3906.1	2744.0	1601.0
	1990	9418.6	8294.9	4702.0
	2000	14993.6	21280.4	9473.5
Zinc	1980	37.6	17.2	9.6
	1990	108.9	40.1	23.0
	2000	211.2	81.4	51.7
Lead	1980	22.7	13.0	8.3
	1990	90.6	23.5	12.7
	2000	181.0	53.8	32.4
Iron	1980	2221.4	1585.2	1662.4
	1990	5061.8	4776.9	4906.9
	2000	8660.7	11090.8	10365.3
Petroleum	1980	10341.5	24203.1	6438.5
	1990	26183.5	70959.0	19029.1
	2000	51364.8	153253.3	39135.3
Natural gas	1980	11690.8	2225.6	4978.7
	1990	28560.1	7972.7	15640.4
	2000	50798.9	19851.1	34910.4
Coal	1980	12457.2	6460.9	8613.7
	1990	31783.8	18513.8	23558.6
	2000	66613.2	42144.6	45855.8

[a] Tons × 10⁶ metal content for all metals except nickel, which is in tons × 10³. Energy is in tons of coal-equivalent.

47

TABLE 35. PERCENTAGE OF BASE-YEAR ENDOWMENTS USED BY 1980, 1990 AND 2000: OPTIMISTIC RESOURCE ESTIMATE

Resource	Year	Developed	Developing	Developed centrally planned
Copper . .	1980	12.0	5.5	8.9
	1990	28.0	17.0	26.1
	2000	49.2	39.7	54.7
Bauxite . .	1980	2.9	2.7	14.6
	1990	7.8	7.5	34.4
	2000	21.1	13.4	63.3
Nickel . .	1980	5.4	2.8	17.5
	1990	12.9	8.4	51.4
	2000	22.6	20.0	103.7[a]
Zinc . . .	1980	19.9	32.5	28.3
	1990	57.6	75.7	67.8
	2000	111.8[a]	153.8[a]	153.1[a]
Lead . . .	1980	17.3	32.0	50.3
	1990	69.1	57.9	77.0
	2000	138.2[a]	132.0[a]	197.0[a]
Iron . . .	1980	3.1	2.6	3.2
	1990	7.2	7.9	9.4
	2000	12.3	18.5	19.9
Coal . . .	1980	1.6	1.1	0.4
	1990	4.2	3.2	1.0
	2000	8.8	7.3	1.9

[a] Cumulative production exceeds optimistic resource endowment.

Effects of alternative petroleum prices on the balance of payments

There is general agreement that world supplies of petroleum are of an order of magnitude which is at least sufficient to supply world requirements through the 1990s, and probably into the early part of the next century as well. Adequate world endowment does not necessarily ensure against regional shortages and high prices; nor does it guarantee smooth economic transition to dependence on shale oil, gasified coal and other "new" energy sources. In both scenarios X and H it is assumed that the world price of petroleum reaches the expected cost of producing petroleum by currently known processes of shale-oil extraction by 2000. Under scenario H it is assumed that this petroleum price is not reached until the latter half of the 1990-2000 decade. Thus, the principal economic effect of switching from scenario X to scenario H is an improvement in the balances of payments of the net importers of petroleum and a corresponding deterioration in the balances of payments of petroleum exporters in 1990. This is shown in table 36.

Developing countries (exclusive of the Middle East) fare better in 1990 but worse in 2000 under the generous

TABLE 36. COMPARISON OF REGIONAL BALANCES OF PAYMENTS[a] IN SCENARIOS X AND H, 1990 AND 2000

(*Billions of 1970 dollars*)

Region	1990X	1990H	2000X	2000H
Developed market .	−73.8	−22.8	−7.2	−4.7
Developed centrally planned . .	24.1	27.9	66.4	79.9
Middle East . .	111.4	49.5	119.8	118.8
All other developing	−37.1	−34.9	−114.6	−128.3

[a] Payments surplus less interest on foreign debt.

endowment scenario. Some developing regions are net exporters and others net importers of specific resources. Changes in the shares of resource exports and of resource prices have very different effects on individual regions depending on their individual endowments and trade dependence. The payments deficit for centrally planned Asia in 2000 is $24 billion under scenario X and only $8 billion under scenario H. On the other hand, switching from scenario X to H reduces the payments surplus of tropical Africa from $73 to $60 billion and of low-income Latin America from $10 billion to a deficit of $16 billion.

Share of capital stock devoted to resource extraction

Table 37 shows the proportion of the stock of investment capital devoted to resource extraction in the nine specific extractive industries in each successive decade according to scenario X. Investment in extraction is estimated by multiplying the output level for each resource by a capital coefficient representing the value of equipment and construction required to deliver a unit of output per year of the mineral in question. As the richer levels of ores are exhausted, requirements per unit of output for all inputs, including capital goods, must be stepped up. Resource grade in each region is treated as a function of the region's cumulative resource output. Capital coefficients for 1980, 1990 and 2000 were derived by the application of "step multipliers" representing crude estimates of the relative costs of extracting the resource in each decade as compared with the base year. The step multipliers in turn are dependent on the approximate resource grades to be mined during the decade.

TABLE 37. CAPITAL STOCK USED IN RESOURCE EXTRACTION (SCENARIO X)

(*Percentage of total capital stock*)

Region	1970	1980	1990	2000
Developed market . .	1.05	1.56	2.31	2.88
Developed centrally planned	2.45	5.37	5.36	6.63
Developing countries . .	3.67	5.02	4.69	8.36

Investment in extractive industries per unit of production tends to increase in successive decades, although some of this increase is offset by improvements in productivity and methods of extraction. As might be expected, the proportion of investment that is devoted to extraction tends to increase in most regions between 1970 and 1980. Exceptions occur for regions such as the Middle East, where economic growth is so rapid that requirements for industrial capital outpace growth in extractive investment. After 1980 the proportion of capital in the extractive industries tapers off in those regions whose resource endowments are nearing exhaustion. Others whose remaining reserves are more plentiful pick up a larger share. Over the three decades, investment in extraction becomes a progressively larger proportion of total capital in the slowly growing industrialized regions but often fails to keep pace with over-all capital formation in the developing regions. By 2000, increased costs of extraction result in a larger proportion of extractive investment than previously in virtually all regions.

Chapter XI

POLLUTION AND ABATEMENT

The model estimates emissions of some but not all major pollutants: particulate air pollution, biological oxygen demand, nitrogen water pollution, phosphates, suspended solids, dissolved solids, urban solid wastes and pesticides. Abatement activities represented in the model consist only of the commonly recognized treatment for particulate air pollution, primary, secondary and tertiary treatment of water pollution and the landfilling or incineration of urban solid wastes. These abatement activities comprised the bulk of investment in pollution abatement in North America in 1970.

Five of these pollutants are water-borne (biological oxygen demand, suspended solids, dissolved solids, phosphates and nitrogen); one is airborne (particulates); and one is a solid waste. The study also includes information on the emission of pesticides by the agricultural sector. Pesticide residuals are essentially a pollutant, but none of this pollutant is abated under 1970 standards of abatement in the United States of America, and no information on the costs of abatement in this case is available.

The levels of pollutant emissions are measured in physical units: millions of tons of the pollutant generated within the region in the years of the study. The coefficients of emission in the model specify the physical quantity of the pollutant generated within the agricultural or industrial sectors per unit of output of the sector. Emission coefficients for water pollution and urban solid waste are also associated with the level of consumption.

Since statistics on pollution and abatement are very scarce, estimates of coefficients in this field are necessarily rough and assumptions about abatement levels are somewhat arbitrary. Gross emissions (before abatement) per unit of output for each industrial sector in the various regions under study are based on coefficients of industries in the United States of America, with some adjustments for differences in intrasectoral product mix among regions. Urban solid waste generation and urban water wasteloads for the different regions are based on cross-national regressions. Region specific estimates of pesticide application are taken from a special study. In the absence of region-specific data, input requirements per unit of each abatement process are assumed to be uniform throughout the world.

A proportion of the gross levels of pollutants generated by these sectors is treated by the abatement sector. Some pollutants, such as pesticides, as noted earlier, are not abated at all because at the present level of technical progress no technique for their abatement is commercially available. Among abatable pollutants not all the emissions are treated; not all the pollutants that are treated by the abatement processes are completely abated. A proportion of the pollutant treated, negligible in the case of some pollutants and significant in the case of others, is left unabated at the end of an abatement process. For example, abatement processes in the elimina-tion of airborne waste—particulates—eliminates more than 99 per cent of the pollutants treated, leaving unabated only 1 per cent of the pollution in the treated pollutants. In the case of the abatement processes for water pollution, the primary water treatment eliminates 80 per cent of the suspended solids, leaving 20 per cent of the suspended solid unabated.

The total of pollutants left in the environment after abatement consists of two categories: first, the part of the pollutants that was untreated by the abatement processes; second, the proportion of pollutants that are left over after they are treated by the abatement processes. The sum of these two constitutes the net total emission of the pollutants. Although concern for the impact of pollution on the environment has led to rapid technological progress in the abatement processes, knowledge of abatement processes is still limited, and even this is assumed only in the case of a few of the pollutants. For many pollutants, such as sulphur, the nitrogen oxides, carbon monoxide and the hydrocarbons in the case of airborne waste, pesticides and manure waste dumping, agricultural pollutants and such pollutants as radioactive waste, no abatement processes are available. For the pollutants for which no abatement process is available, the level of total net emissions is equal to the level of gross emissions. The levels of emission of these pollutants should be monitored in the future and studied in order to evaluate their impact on the environment. The present study, however, has not attempted to measure the levels of these pollutants, with the exception of pesticide residuals.

Most of the pollution and abatement data used in the study are those available for the United States of America. Quantitative estimates of emissions, abatement technologies and environmental standards are available for only a few of the developing countries. In the case of other regions, because of the absence of specific information, the data for the United States or countries in which similar environments exist had to be used. Estimates of pollution and abatement coefficients were made by reweighing the available coefficients for individual processes in accordance with product-mix information.

Since there is no comprehensive information for worldwide abatement practices we assume that abatement will be implemented more intensively at high rather than low levels of GDP. Four abatement standards or scenarios are applied in the model. The standards are developed on the basis of *per capita* gross domestic product of the region for each year in question and the standards of abatement relating to the levels of *per capita* product are made by weighing the available abatement coefficients based on the 1970 United States standards of abatement. For regions with a *per capita* product of less than $700, no abatement standards are applied. In regions with a *per capita* product of less than $2,000 but more than

$700, the standard applied is half the proportion abated in the United States of America in 1970. In regions in which the *per capita* product is currently more than $2,000 but was less than $2,000 in the previous periods, the 1970 United States abatement standards are applied. Finally, in the category of countries in which the *per capita* product was greater than $2,000 in the previous period and is also greater than $2,000 in the present period, the level of emission is held at the level of the first period when full abatement was applied. Table 38 gives the abatement standards applied in the model.

TABLE 38. ASSIGNMENT OF REGIONAL ABATEMENT SCENARIOS[a]

Region	1970	1980	1990	2000
North America	3	4	4	4
Latin America (medium-income)	1	2	2	3
Latin America (low-income)	1	1	1	2
Western Europe (high-income)	3	4	4	4
Western Europe (medium-income)	2	2	2	3
Soviet Union	2	3	4	4
Eastern Europe	2	3	4	4
Asia (centrally planned)	1	1	1	1
Japan	3	4	4	4
Asia (low-income)	1	1	1	1
Middle East	1	2	2	3
Africa (arid)	1	1	1	1
Africa (tropical)	1	1	1	1
Southern Africa	2	2	2	2
Oceania	3	4	4	4

[a] *Abatement scenarios* / *GDP* per capita (y)

1. Zero abatement — y_t less than $700
2. Half the proportion abated in the United States of America in 1970 — y_t is more than $700 but less than $2,000
3. Same proportion as abated in the United States of America — y_t more than $2,000; and y_{t-1} less than $2,000
4. Net emissions held at the level of the first year that full abatement was applied — y_t more than $2,000; and y_{t-1} more than $2,000

Thus, in the base year, 1970, high-income regions (North America, high-income Western Europe, Japan and Oceania) were assigned percentage abatement levels equal to those of the United States of America for each pollution abatement process (abatement scenario 3). In successive decades, net emissions of particulates, suspended solids and urban solid waste were held constant for these regions (abatement scenario 4). Four other regions—medium-income Western Europe, Eastern Europe, the Soviet Union and Southern Africa—were assumed to abate only half the proportion of gross emissions abated by high-income regions in 1970 (abatement scenario 2). Low-income regions were assigned zero abatement levels (abatement scenario 1). As income *per capita* rises over successive decades, regions are assumed to progress from zero to the 50 per cent level and from the 50 per cent level to the full abatement category. These scenarios are of course highly speculative; they serve only to illustrate one of the many possible development patterns.

Interregional comparisons of emissions in physical units are difficult to interpret because the regions vary in size, population and capacity of the environment to absorb pollutants. For this reason, net total emissions, while measured in physical units, should be interpreted as indexes in relation to base-year net emissions. For a given region, changes in net total emissions over time give some rough indication of changes in environmental quality.

Solid waste

Solid waste generated by the industrial and agricultural sectors was not estimated in the study since information relating to solid waste generated within these sectors is difficult to obtain. The estimated solid waste loading is related only to the urban sector (see table 39). In the

TABLE 39. NET TOTAL EMISSION OF SOLID WASTE

(*Millions of tons*)

Region	1970	1980	1990	2000
North America	0.00	0.00	0.00	0.00
Latin America (medium-income)	59.46	48.07	78.65	0.00
Latin America (low-income)	19.51	34.35	60.08	53.05
Western Europe (high-income)	0.00	0.00	0.00	0.00
Western Europe (medium-income)	13.79	21.92	36.00	0.00
Soviet Union	54.20	0.00	0.00	0.00
Eastern Europe	20.97	0.00	0.00	0.00
Asia (centrally planned)	54.51	96.62	165.29	276.71
Japan	0.00	0.00	0.00	0.00
Asia (low-income)	56.72	92.86	167.17	295.07
Middle East	13.44	17.13	75.32	0.00
Africa (arid)	11.66	26.26	41.18	65.52
Africa (tropical)	5.19	11.41	20.81	37.16
Southern Africa	2.96	4.82	8.49	0.00
Oceania	0.00	0.00	0.00	0.00

United States of America, under the 1970 standard virtually all urban solid waste generated is treated by landfilling or incinerating. Thus, under abatement scenarios 3 and 4 (when the full standards are applied) the net total emissions of solid waste are zero. In those developed regions in which either scenario 3 or 4 was applied, at least for the last period, the net emissions of solid waste decreased to zero by the end of the century. However, in the low-income regions of Asia and Africa, where scenario 1 is applied for all four periods, the generation of solid waste increased rapidly (see table 40).

TABLE 40. RATES OF GROWTH OF SOLID WASTE FOR SELECTED REGIONS

(*Percentage per annum*)

Region	1970-1980	1980-1990	1990-2000
Asia (low-income)	4.9	5.9	5.7
Asia (centrally planned)	5.7	5.4	5.1
Latin America (low-income)	5.6	5.6	−1.2
Western Europe (medium-income)	4.6	4.9	—
Middle East	2.9	14.8	—
Africa (arid)	8.1	4.5	4.6
Africa (tropical)	7.9	6.0	5.8
Southern Africa	4.8	5.7	—

NOTE: Solid waste is fully abated in 2000 in Western Europe (medium-income), Middle East and Southern Africa.

In low-income Asia, for example, the solid waste generated increases from 56.7 million tons in 1970 to 295 million tons by 2000, and in centrally planned Asia, from 54.5 to 276.7 million tons (at the rate of about 5 per cent per annum). In tropical Africa, the generation of solid waste is even more rapid, although the quantity generated is relatively small. In the Middle East, an increase of more than 10 per cent per annum is estimated during the 1980 to 1990 period.

Air pollution

In the abatement of particulate air pollution, the United States of America's standard for abatement in 1970 is 90.94 per cent of gross emissions. Particulates are the only category of air pollution considered in the study. The total net emission in North America for 1970, under full United States standards, is 4.21 million tons of particulates. This quantity remains constant, as defined by scenario 4, for the remaining four periods. It is significant that even with this standard fully applied, total net emission in North America is the highest among all regions, comparing even with the regions in which abatement of particulates is considered to be absent (see table 41). In the Soviet Union, where scenario 2 is applied for 1970 the net emission of particulates is 3.72 million tons, but this level drops to 0.70 million tons in

TABLE 41. NET TOTAL EMISSION OF PARTICULATES: AIR POLLUTION

(*Millions of tons*)

Region	1970	1980	1990	2000
North America . . .	4.21	4.21	4.21	4.21
Latin America (medium-income) . .	1.09	1.23	2.51	0.78
Latin America (low-income).	0.34	0.75	1.76	1.74
Western Europe (high-income) . . .	1.22	1.22	1.22	1.22
Western Europe (medium-income) .	0.45	0.82	1.53	0.55
Soviet Union . .	3.72	0.70	1.17	1.17
Eastern Europe . .	1.41	0.12	0.53	0.53
Asia (centrally planned) .	0.96	2.13	3.74	6.02
Japan . . .	0.23	0.23	0.23	0.23
Asia (low-income) .	0.64	1.04	2.47	3.44
Middle East . .	0.15	1.02	6.63	1.25
Africa (arid) . .	0.19	0.26	0.56	0.67
Africa (tropical) .	0.12	0.22	0.47	0.45
Southern Africa . .	0.11	0.17	0.32	0.15
Oceania . . .	0.05	0.05	0.05	0.05

TABLE 42. RATE OF GROWTH OF THE PARTICULATE AIR POLLUTION GENERATED IN SELECTED REGIONS

Region	1970-1980	1980-1990	1990-2000
Asia (low-income) . .	4.8	8.6	3.3
Asia (centrally planned) .	7.9	5.6	4.8
Latin America (low-income).	7.9	8.5	0.0
Western Europe (medium-income) . .	6.0	6.2	−9.7
Middle East . . .	19.0	18.7	−15.4
Africa (arid) . . .	3.1	7.6	−1.8
Africa (tropical) . .	6.0	7.5	0.0
Southern Africa . .	4.3	6.3	7.3

1980, when full abatement standards are applied. In the East European countries the emission of particulates drops from 1.41 to 0.53 million tons in the same interval.

The level of particulate air pollution in the oil-producing Middle East starts with a low 0.15 million tons in 1970 under scenario 1 with no abatement but increases rapidly to 1.02 and 6.63 million tons in the following two periods under the limited abatement standard and in 2000, when full standards are applied, the level drops to 1.25 million tons. In those regions of Asia and Africa in which no abatement is applied the level of total net emission, which in this case is also the gross pollution, increases at a rather high rate. The level of pollutants generated in low-income Asia is 3.44 million tons. In the case of the two African regions with no abatement, the quantity of air pollutants generated remains relatively low.

Water pollution

Three water pollution abatement processes—primary, secondary and tertiary—are discussed in the present study. Five water pollutants—biological oxygen demand, nitrogen water pollution, phosphates, suspended solids and dissoved solids—are identified and the quantities of these pollutants generated for each of the regions are estimated. When the polluted water is treated in each of the three water abatement processes—primary, secondary and tertiary—some of each of the five water pollutants are abated. The level of abatement of water pollution is measured by the quantities of suspended solids that are abated. The quantities of the other pollutants abated are in direct proportion to the suspended solids and are determined once the quantity of suspended solids abated is determined. Under 1970 abatement standards in the United States of America, 44.31 per cent of suspended solids are abated. The secondary treatment of water abates 5.7 per cent of the primary water pollutants abated, and the tertiary water treatment procedure abates 2.2 per cent of the secondary treatment.

The total net emissions of suspended solids for North America of 6.82 million tons are assumed to remain unchanged in the period under observation (see table 43).

TABLE 43. NET TOTAL EMISSION OF POLLUTANTS: SUSPENDED SOLIDS

(*Millions of tons*)

Region	1970	1980	1990	2000
North America . . .	6.82	6.82	6.82	6.82
Latin America (medium-income) . .	0.76	1.25	2.68	4.86
Latin America (low-income).	0.19	0.43	0.87	1.90
Western Europe (high-income) . . .	3.84	3.84	3.84	3.84
Western Europe (medium-income) . .	0.34	0.66	1.51	2.60
Soviet Union . . .	2.98	3.67	3.99	3.99
Eastern Europe . .	1.09	1.27	1.52	1.52
Asia (centrally planned) .	0.60	1.38	2.43	4.96
Japan . . .	0.95	0.95	0.95	0.95
Asia (low-income) . .	0.35	0.63	1.64	3.00
Middle East . . .	0.05	0.39	2.44	4.63
Africa (arid) . .	0.12	0.18	0.40	0.65
Africa (tropical) . .	0.08	0.20	0.60	0.68
Southern Africa . .	0.09	0.13	0.32	0.71
Oceania . . .	0.18	0.18	0.18	0.18

For the Soviet Union 2.98 million tons of suspended solids are estimated to have been generated in 1970. This level increases to 3.67 million tons in 1980 and to 3.99 million tons in the two final periods. For high-income Western Europe, the level of suspended solids generated is maintained at 3.84 million tons at maximum 1970 United States abatement standards. In Eastern Europe, the quantity of suspended solids generated increases from 1.09 million tons under abatement scenario 2, to 1.52 million tons in 1990 under full abatement standards.

Again, the regions of Asia and Africa which are under scenario 1 (no abatement) show rapid growth in the emission of suspended solids. For centrally planned Asia the quantity of suspended solids emitted grows from a low of 0.60 million tons in 1970 to 4.96 million tons by 2000, more than an eightfold increase in the 30-year period. The rates of growth within the three decades are 8.3 per cent in the 1970s, a somewhat lower rate of growth of 5.7 per cent in the 1980s and an increase of 7.1 per cent in the final decade of the century (see table 44).

TABLE 44. RATE OF GROWTH OF SUSPENDED SOLIDS IN WATER,
FOR SELECTED REGIONS

(*Percentage*)

Region	1970-1980	1980-1990	1990-2000
Asia (low-income)	5.9	9.6	6.0
Asia (centrally planned)	8.3	5.7	7.1
Latin America (low-income)	8.2	7.0	7.8
Western Europe (medium-income)	6.6	8.3	5.4
Middle East	20.5	18.3	6.4
Africa (arid)	4.1	10.9	4.8
Africa (tropical)	3.7	10.9	1.2
Southern Africa	3.7	9.0	8.0

Low-income Asia shows rapid growth in the pollutants of suspended solids emitted. The quantity increases from 0.35 million tons in 1970 to 3 million tons by the end of the century. In that region, all three decades show rapid

growth; in the 1970s, water pollution grows by 5.9 per cent; in the next decade by 9.6 per cent; and in the final decade of the century by 6.0 per cent. In the Middle East, the quantity of suspended solids emitted increases from a very low 0.05 million tons in 1970 to 4.63 million tons by 2000. The magnitude of this growth should be evaluated against the fact that in 1970, under scenario 1, none of the pollutants emitted is abated, while in 2000, under scenario 3 (under full standards), 44.31 per cent of the suspended solids are abated. In spite of the maximum abatement standards applicable in the final period, the rate of growth of the emission of pollutants increases by 20.5 per cent in the 1970s, by 18.3 per cent in the 1980s and by 6.4 per cent in the final decade of the century. As noted earlier, arid and tropical Africa are under abatement standard 1 (no abatement). The net total emission indicated for these regions is also their gross emission. Pollution growth is most marked in the 1980s, when both of these regions have an annual rate of growth of 10.9 per cent.

Cost of abatement

Table 45 shows the abatement capital stock by region in the four successive decades. Comparisons of patterns of intertemporal change in net emissions with the corresponding changes in abatement capital stock suggest strong trade-offs between levels of net emission on the one hand and levels of investment in abatement capital on the other. In high-income regions, net emission is held constant for three pollutants (particulates, urban solid waste and suspended solids) and increases very moderately over time for all other abatable pollutants. In lower-income regions, net total emission rises much more dramatically over time. This is due in part to the fact that the rates of growth of industry are most rapid in developing regions, but primarily to the fact that low-income regions do not undertake costly abatement activities until their *per capita* income levels rise sufficiently to warrant the necessary capital outlays.

Developed regions are assumed to stabilize their net total emission at the cost of relatively large and steadily growing investment in abatement facilities. Developing

TABLE 45. CAPITAL STOCK OF ABATEMENT SECTOR (CAB) AND ITS SHARE IN TOTAL CAPITAL STOCK (PERCENTAGE OF CT)

Region	1970		1980		1990		2000	
	CAB (billions of dollars)	Percentage of CT	CAB (billions of dollars)	Percentage of CT	CAB (billions of dollars)	Percentage of CT	CAB (billions of dollars)	Percentage of CT
North America	77.5	3.4	121.9	3.4	156.0	3.0	191.7	2.5
Latin America (medium-income)	—	—	4.3	1.5	8.8	1.3	38.4	2.3
Latin America (low-income)	—	—	—	—	—	—	6.0	1.0
Western Europe (high-income)	35.9	2.7	67.2	3.2	107.9	3.1	160.6	3.2
Western Europe (medium-income)	1.2	1.1	2.4	1.1	5.6	1.1	21.3	1.8
Soviet Union	9.9	1.3	38.9	2.8	87.4	3.1	125.3	2.6
Eastern Europe	3.5	1.2	13.8	2.7	28.8	3.1	40.8	2.9
Asia (centrally planned)	—	—	—	—	—	—	—	—
Japan	8.6	2.8	23.7	3.6	45.9	3.9	70.0	3.9
Asia (low-income)	—	—	—	—	—	—	—	—
Middle East	—	—	1.9	1.2	7.1	1.1	39.8	1.9
Africa (arid)	—	—	—	—	—	—	—	—
Africa (tropical)	—	—	—	—	—	—	—	—
Southern Africa	0.3	0.9	0.6	1.2	1.3	1.1	5.8	2.0
Oceania	1.7	2.1	4.0	3.1	8.9	3.6	10.4	2.5

regions experience rapidly growing net emission until they reach a stage at which they start investing in the abatement capital necessary to cut pollution. At that point, levels of pollution are apt to level off or even fall. In medium-income Latin America, for example, net total emission of particulates tends to rise until 1990, despite the fact that the region advances from abatement scenario 1 (zero abatement) to abatement scenario 2 (half of the 1970 United States standard) in 1980. Between 1990 and 2000 medium-income Latin America advances from half to full abatement and net total emission of particulates falls, despite rapid industrial growth.

As shown in table 45, in the regions in which full abatement standards are applied throughout 1970-2000, the stock of capital in the abatement sector increases in line with the over-all rates of economic growth, or somewhat faster. For example, in North America it increases from $77.5 billion in 1970 to $191.7 billion by 2000 (or at an annual rate of 3.1 per cent). In Japan it increases from $8.6 billion in 1970 to $70 billion by 2000 (or at the rate of 7.2 per cent); in high-income Western Europe, from $35.9 billion to $160.6 billion (5.1 per cent per annum); and in Oceania, from $1.7 billion to $10.4 billion (6.2 per cent per annum).

In regions which pass from lower to higher standards of abatement, the rate of increase of the capital stock employed in abatement activities tends to grow substantially faster than gross domestic product. Thus, in medium-income Western Europe the stock of capital in the abatement sector increases from $1.2 billion in 1970 to $21.3 billion in 2000 (or at an annual rate of 10 per cent), in the Soviet Union from $9.9 billion in 1970 to $125.3 billion in 2000 (an annual rate of 8.9 per cent), and in Eastern Europe from $3.5 billion to $40.8 billion in 2000 (at 8.5 per cent per annum).

As stated earlier, in four developing regions—centrally planned Asia, low-income Asia, arid Africa and tropical Africa—no pollutants are assumed to be abated, and consequently no capital investment in the abatement sector is indicated. Two developing regions—Latin America and the Middle East—both starting from zero abatement in 1970, move to full abatement by 2000. As such, these two regions, starting from no capital invest-

ment in 1970, show substantial abatement capital by 2000; medium-income Latin America accumulates a capital stock of $38.4 billion and the Middle East a stock of $39.8 billion by 2000. Low-income Latin America, which is assumed to be under 50 per cent of the 1970 United States abatement standards by 2000, accumulates a capital stock of $6.0 billion by that year.

Table 45 also shows the proportion of estimated capital in abatement to total capital stock in the economy as a whole. Since capital goods constitute the principal inputs into pollution abatement, the value of the stock of investment goods provides a good index of abatement costs. As regions take on the abatement levels of high-income countries, their proportion of abatement capital jumps. Within a given abatement class, however, investment in pollution control rises in absolute terms but constitutes a declining proportion of the economy's gross capital stock in successive decades. Our present estimates suggest that pollution abatement will tend to absorb somewhere between 2 and 4 per cent of total investment in moderate- and high-income countries over the next 20 years. For lower-income countries, the proportion is smaller.

In North America for example, the share of capital in abatement in 1970 is 3.4 per cent, which decreases somewhat to 2.5 per cent by 2000. In Japan the share increases from 2.8 per cent in 1970 to 3.9 per cent by 2000. In the Soviet Union because of the shift in abatement standards the share rises from 1.3 per cent in 1970 to 2.6 per cent by 2000. Similar change is indicated for Eastern Europe. In developing regions the share is between 1 and 2.3 per cent in the regions in which abatement exists.

The economic costs of abatement can be measured, alternatively, in terms of the percentage of current plus annualized capital costs of abatement to GDP. Table 46 shows the estimated annual abatement expenditure as a per cent of GDP in the various regions. For those abatement activities covered in this study, computed costs constitute less than 1 per cent of GDP even in the developed regions.

As expected, the cost of abatement in regions with full abatement standards is relatively high. For such regions, the share of these costs as a proportion of GDP amounts

TABLE 46. CURRENT COSTS OF ABATEMENT AND THEIR SHARE OF GDP

Region	1970		1980		1990		2000	
	Cost (billions of dollars)	Share of GDP (percentage)	Cost (billions of dollars)	Share of GDP (percentage)	Cost (billions of dollars)	Share of GDP (percentage)	Cost (billions of dollars)	Share of GDP (percentage)
North America	8.5	0.80	13.5	0.877	17.2	0.829	21.2	0.780
Latin America (medium-income)	—	—	0.05	0.244	1.0	0.245	4.1	0.461
Latin America (low-income)	—	—	—	—	—	—	0.6	0.198
Western Europe (high-income)	3.9	0.533	7.2	0.690	11.5	0.709	17.2	0.793
Western Europe (medium-income)	0.1	0.179	0.3	0.194	0.6	0.216	2.3	0.399
Soviet Union	1.1	0.247	4.2	0.554	9.4	0.683	13.4	0.670
Eastern Europe	0.4	0.229	1.5	0.538	3.1	0.641	4.3	0.635
Asia (centrally planned)	—	—	—	—	—	—	—	—
Japan	0.9	0.465	2.5	0.678	4.9	0.830	7.5	0.895
Asia (low-income)	—	—	—	—	—	—	—	—
Middle East	—	—	0.2	0.149	—	—	4.3	0.436
Africa (arid)	—	—	—	—	—	—	—	—
Africa (tropical)	—	—	—	—	—	—	—	—
Southern Africa	—	0.164	0.1	0.222	0.1	0.219	0.6	0.418
Oceania	0.2	0.421	0.4	0.671	0.9	0.858	1.1	0.689

53

Type of pollution		Included in both studies	Not included in United Nations study but included in United States estimates	Estimated percentage of United States abatement costs covered by United Nations study (1970)
Air pollution (particulates) . . .		Urban residual Commercial Industrial	Rural residual Mobile sources	63
Water pollution[b]	BOD COD SS DS NN P	Urban residual Commercial Industrial Industrial	Non-sewered population Urban run-off Agriculture (partial) Residential Urban run-off Agriculture (partial)	39
Solid waste	Collection	Urban residential Commercial	Industrial Mining Agriculture	45 (included in urban amenities)
	Disposal: Land-fill Incineration	Urban residential Commercial	Industrial Mining Agriculture	45 (included in solid waste abatement)[c]

[a] *Fourth Annual Report of the Council on Environmental Quality* (Washington, D.C., Government Printing Office, 1973); R. G. Ridker (ed.), *Population, Resources and the Environment* (Washington, D.C., Government Printing Office, 1972).
[b] BOD = biochemical oxygen demand, COD = chemical oxygen demand, SS = suspended solids, DS = dissolved solids, NN = nitrogen, P = phosphates.
[c] Solid waste collection plus disposal costs; therefore, only about 10 per cent are included in the United Nations study's abatement sector.

to about 0.8 per cent. In those regions which turn from zero abatement or from 50 per cent of the 1970 United States abatement standards in the early periods to full abatement in the latter periods, the cost of abatement, as expected, shows very significant increases. In the Soviet Union for example, these costs increase from $1.1 billion in 1970 to $13.4 billion in 2000; and in Eastern Europe from $0.4 billion to $4.3 billion within the same two periods. The share of abatement costs in these regions increases from 0.2 to 0.65 per cent in GDP. The only developing regions with prospective high costs are the Middle East and medium-income Latin America. In these two regions, over 0.4 per cent of GDP would be attributed to the abatement of pollutants in 2000, with a much lower share in 1980 and 1990. The projections of the present study have to be interpreted carefully, since they account for only a limited subset of known pollutants and abatement activities.

As mentioned earlier, some forms of pollution were not covered (e.g., heavy metals and toxic chemical residuals) because data are not available on the corresponding abatement technologies or because such technologies do not yet exist. Even for the pollutants that are covered, certain emission sources were not included because the data from the United States of America seemed to be especially unrepresentative from the viewpoint of cross-regional generalizations.

When weighted by their importance relative to total abatement expenditures, the abatement activities covered by the present study account for about 45 per cent of the abatement activities regularly included in recent United States estimates.[31] Moreover, since the collection of solid waste (as opposed to its final disposal) is not treated as an abatement activity but rather as an urban service, the pollution abatement sectors cover only about

35 per cent of the activities typically included elsewhere. Table 47 shows a more detailed view of the differences in coverage between this study and the more comprehensive estimates available for the United States of America in 1970.

In the future, the abatement of pollutants other than those covered in the world model may assume growing relative importance. For example, the model keeps track of the level of pesticide application in the light of its potentially harmful effects but does not incorporate any estimates for the costs of removing the harmful effects of pesticides, except, of course, in the reduction of agricultural output levels. Table 48 shows steady

TABLE 48. NET TOTAL EMISSION OF PESTICIDE[a]

(*Millions of tons*)

Region	1970	1980	1990	2000
North America . . .	0.98	2.03	2.41	2.56
Latin America (medium-income) . .	0.04	0.20	0.54	0.95
Latin America (low-income).	0.11	0.22	0.47	1.20
Western Europe (high-income). . .	0.38	0.52	0.68	0.84
Western Europe (medium-income) . .	0.21	0.40	0.78	1.05
Soviet Union . . .	0.16	0.38	0.70	0.84
Eastern Europe . . .	0.25	0.44	0.51	0.53
Asia (centrally planned) .	—	0.02	0.21	0.70
Japan	0.12	0.28	0.72	1.25
Asia (low-income) . .	0.16	0.39	1.95	3.77
Middle East . . .	0.05	0.36	1.57	3.35
Africa (arid) . . .	0.05	0.17	0.59	1.00
Africa (tropical) . . .	0.02	0.04	0.08	0.42
Southern Africa . . .	0.01	0.01	0.02	0.05
Oceania	0.02	0.02	0.03	0.04

[a] In the case of pesticide, the net total emission corresponds to the total application of pesticide.

[31] *Fourth Annual Report of the Council on Environmental Quality* (Washington, D.C., Government Printing Office, 1973); R. G. Ridker (ed.), *Population, Resources and the Environment* (Washington, D.C., Government Printing Office, 1972).

increases in pesticide applications over time. The environment is threatened by rising levels of such pollutant emissions as pesticides, heavy metals and radioactive wastes, for which no abatement processes are yet known. The present model does not take account of all pollutants known today. Moreover, many additional substances may some day be classed as pollutants. Thus, the fact that our estimated cost of applying conventional abatement processes in higher-income countries is moderate should not be interpreted to mean that the world can avert all environmental disruption at moderate cost. Furthermore, even modest levels of investment in abatement processes may not be negligible, particularly for countries that are just entering the intermediate stages of industrialization and are already burdened by large indebtedness.

Chapter XII

CHANGES IN THE STRUCTURE OF INTERNATIONAL TRADE

High rates of world economic growth lead to a brisk expansion of international trade. In scenario X the total physical volume of trade is expected to increase 5.5 times in 1970-2000—that is, at an annual rate of 5.9 per cent. This is subsequently higher than the growth rate of world gross product, 4.8 per cent. A fast increase in world trade is clearly a necessary condition of fast and balanced world economic development. In fact, in 2000, 14.5 per cent of world gross product will cross national borders as compared to 10.6 per cent in 1970. This growth is expected to be characterized by a particularly rapid expansion of trade in manufactured goods. The average annual growth of the physical volume of trade in light industry products is projected at 6.8 per cent, of machinery and equipment at 6.7 per cent and of industrial materials at 7.2 per cent. On the other hand, growth in agricultural trade—2.5 per cent per annum—and in mineral resources—2.6 per cent—is projected to be substantially less than the average for all trade.

The composition of trade would change, as would the composition of total world output, in favour of products from manufacturing industries. Estimated in 1970 relative prices, the share of these products would increase from 65.4 per cent in 1970 to 86.4 per cent in 2000, while the share of agricultural goods and mineral resources would decline from 34.6 to 13.6 per cent. This reflects greater international division of labour, leading to expanded exchange in a diversified range of manufactured products.

Paralleling the shift in the relative size of their total outputs, the share of developed countries in most categories of world exports of goods is expected to fall, and the share of developing countries, to increase. As can be seen from table 49 developing countries manage to increase their already quite large combined export share of mineral resources and light industry and raise even more their still modest shares in both machinery and industrial materials, but their shares in agricultural exports are actually reduced. The over-all export share for all traded goods is not substantially different in 2000 than it was in 1970.

The aggregate export share of the centrally planned economies increases with gains in materials, light industry and machinery and equipment, but there is a reduction in natural resources and agriculture; and the share of the developed market economies decreases in all categories except agriculture and invisibles (comprising services and transportation), with their total share in exports declining from 68.7 to 64.7 per cent.

Primary commodities are expected to continue to dominate the export structure of most developed regions, though the shares of these commodities tend to decline

TABLE 49. SHARES OF REGIONS IN WORLD EXPORTS OF GOODS

(*Percentage in 1970 prices*)

Region	Year	Scenario[a]	Agriculture	Mineral resources	Light industry	Machinery and equipment	Materials	Invisibles[b]	Total exports
Developed market economies[c]	1970		46.0	43.5	75.2	83.9	85.0	75.0	68.7
	2000	X	47.5	16.4	69.6	73.2	77.4	76.3	64.7
	2000	M	41.4	16.4	66.7	73.2	77.6	74.1	63.2
Centrally planned economies .	1970		10.5	12.4	7.5	13.0	6.4	0	9.3
	2000	X	9.8	6.2	9.1	20.2	8.6	0	12.0
	2000	M	8.5	6.2	8.6	20.1	8.5	0	11.7
Developing market economies.	1970		32.7	39.3	12.8	1.5	5.1	12.3	16.2
	2000	X	31.6	75.0	13.8	2.7	7.1	11.9	17.2
	2000	M	40.5	75.0	17.4	2.7	7.1	14.4	19.1
Latin America . . .	1970		12.7	10.8	1.2	0.4	1.7	6.2	5.1
	2000	X	12.9	15.6	1.9	0.9	2.7	5.7	4.6
	2000	M	24.0	15.6	2.2	0.9	2.7	7.0	5.5
Asia and the Middle East .	1970		12.9	23.8	9.9	1.0	2.6	4.5	8.5
	2000	X	12.1	51.9	11.2	1.7	3.9	4.6	11.0
	2000	M	10.7	52.1	14.4	1.8	3.9	5.6	11.9
Africa (non-oil) . . .	1970		7.1	4.8	1.7	0.1	0.8	1.6	2.5
	2000	X	6.6	7.5	0.7	0.1	0.5	1.6	1.8
	2000	M	5.8	7.4	0.8	0.1	0.5	1.8	1.8

[a] For 2000, X and M indicate names of two scenarios with different assumptions. Scenario M is analysed in the balance-of-payments section.

[b] Including services and transportation.

[c] Not including medium-income regions.

(see table 50). This is mainly due to substantial decreases in the shares of agricultural exports, while the shares of mineral resources are expanding in most areas. It should be remembered that in this case petroleum refining products and primary metals are counted as exports of "resources" rather than as "industrial materials". However, their inclusion in the latter category would not substantially change the above conclusion.

Products of light industry continue to dominate the export of manufactured goods in developing regions. As a rule, industrial materials come next, followed by machinery and equipment, which fare better in medium-income Latin America and low-income Asia than in other regions. Though the role of industrial exports from the developing countries will increase, it is expected that

a number of difficulties will be encountered. Thus, it is expected that by the end of the century, the developing countries will be supplying 13.8 per cent of the world exports of products of light industry and 7 per cent of the world exports of industrial materials but still only 2.7 per cent of the world exports of machinery and equipment.

The increase in the role of imports to the developing countries is due to the large and rapidly growing requirements caused by accelerated development. The total share of developing countries out of world imports of goods is expected to reach, under scenario X, 31.4 per cent in 2000, as compared with 16.4 per cent in 1970. This increase is substantial in all the categories but especially in agricultural goods, industrial materials, and machinery and equipment (see table 51).

TABLE 50. REGIONAL STRUCTURE OF EXPORTS OF DEVELOPING REGIONS

(*Percentage of total exports from each region, based on 1970 prices*)

Region	Agriculture	Resources[a]	Light industry	Machinery and equipment	Materials[b]	Invisibles[c]	Agriculture and resources	Manufacturing
Latin America (medium-income)								
1970	49.4	18.1	3.8	3.4	4.0	21.4	67.5	11.2
2000	21.6	34.9	9.0	11.1	8.6	14.7	56.5	28.7
Latin America (low-income)								
1970	31.6	52.0	2.3	0.7	2.4	10.9	83.6	5.4
2000	17.0	56.0	6.5	2.2	7.6	10.7	73.0	16.3
Middle East								
1970	8.6	84.7	1.2	0.5	0.7	4.3	93.8	2.4
2000	1.9	88.0	4.4	1.6	2.3	1.8	89.9	8.3
Asia (low-income)								
1970	40.3	11.2	26.9	6.5	5.3	9.9	51.5	38.7
2000	16.6	9.3	44.0	13.2	8.7	8.2	25.9	63.9
Africa (arid)								
1970	47.2	14.2	17.2	3.4	5.4	12.6	61.4	26.0
2000	36.3	9.8	23.2	4.0	8.8	17.9	46.1	36.0
Africa (tropical)								
1970	46.7	37.5	5.3	1.0	2.4	7.1	84.2	8.7
2000	23.2	62.8	3.7	0.7	2.3	7.3	86.0	6.7

a Resources in this and other tables relating to foreign trade include exports of petroleum, refining products and primary metals.
b Materials (manufactured) in this and other tables relating to foreign trade exclude exports of petroleum-refining products and primary metals.
c Including services and transportation.

TABLE 51. SHARES OF REGIONS IN WORLD IMPORTS[a]

(*Percentage in 1970 prices*)

Region	Year	Scenario[a]	Agriculture	Mineral resources	Light industry	Machinery and equipment	Materials	Invisibles[b]
Developed market economies[c]	1970		63.5	70.6	70.5	63.2	63.8	79.0
	2000	X	43.1	56.0	59.4	45.8	44.5	62.5
	2000	M	43.0	55.8	60.1	47.2	45.8	62.4
Developing market economies	1970		15.3	10.7	16.2	18.8	20.4	13.9
	2000	X	39.4	19.3	22.2	34.0	39.6	27.0
	2000	M	39.4	19.4	20.9	33.5	37.8	27.0
Latin America	1970		3.5	3.5	3.7	6.4	7.0	7.0
	2000	X	7.5	8.2	4.4	12.0	8.9	12.5
	2000	M	8.0	8.2	4.1	10.7	8.1	12.7
Asia and the Middle East	1970		9.3	5.7	9.4	9.3	10.0	5.0
	2000	X	28.6	10.3	15.1	22.0	28.4	12.7
	2000	M	28.3	10.3	14.3	21.3	27.6	12.6
Africa (non-oil)	1970		2.4	1.5	3.1	3.0	3.4	2.0
	2000	X	3.2	0.9	2.7	1.7	2.3	1.8
	2000	M	3.2	0.9	2.5	1.6	2.1	1.7

a X and M indicate names of two scenarios with different assumptions. Scenario M is analysed in the balance-of-payments section.
b Including services and transportation.
c Not including medium-income regions.

The dependence of the developing countries on imports, as described in table 52, is largest in the area of machinery and equipment, ranging in 1970 from 27 to 80 per cent of the total requirements (domestic consumption plus exports) in the different regions. Under scenario X this dependence would be reduced by 2000 to not more than 50 per cent and not less than 24 per cent for all of these regions.

The dependence on imported industrial materials and mineral resources is next in importance, and current rates vary respectively in the ranges of 15-64 and 7-34 per cent. The low dependence of the oil-rich Middle East on imported mineral resources (7 per cent) is the exception rather than the rule. The dependence on imported industrial materials is expected to decrease substantially by 2000, owing to the rapid expansion of internal production, but the dependence on mineral resource imports is projected to be reduced only moderately and will even increase in two regions—medium-income Latin America and low-income Asia. The same is true of imported light-industry products and agricultural goods, where the dependence ratios are relatively low.

In spite of these changes, the structure of imports of the developing countries is expected to remain relatively stable with 60 to 85 per cent accounted for by manufactured goods, and 8 to 28 per cent by primary commodities (see table 53). Machinery and equipment will be

TABLE 52. IMPORT DEPENDENCE OF DEVELOPING REGIONS

(*Ratio of import to total requirements, percentage based on 1970 prices*)[a]

Region	Year	Scenario	Agriculture	Mineral resources	Light industry	Machinery and equipment	Materials
Latin America (medium-income) .	1970		3.0	24.0	4.0	27.0	15.0
	2000	X	3.0	30.0	5.0	24.0	13.0
	2000	M	3.0	28.0	4.0	18.0	9.0
Latin America (low-income) . .	1970		8.0	12.0	17.0	61.0	37.0
	2000	X	7.0	3.0	19.0	50.0	32.0
	2000	M	7.0	3.0	19.0	50.0	32.0
Middle East	1970		15.0	7.0	27.0	80.0	64.0
	2000	X	12.0	3.0	23.0	36.0	44.0
	2000	M	12.0	3.0	23.0	36.0	44.0
Asia (low-income)	1970		9.0	34.0	16.0	50.0	29.0
	2000	X	10.0	49.0	15.0	40.0	27.0
	2000	M	10.0	47.0	11.0	30.0	20.0
Africa (arid)	1970		8.0	26.0	11.0	31.0	22.0
	2000	X	8.0	15.0	28.0	33.0	26.0
	2000	M	8.0	15.0	21.0	24.0	19.0
Africa (tropical). . . .	1970		7.0	19.0	28.0	80.0	50.0
	2000	X	7.0	13.0	55.0	47.0	59.0
	2000	M	7.0	13.0	55.0	47.0	59.0

[a] Total requirements are the sum of internal consumption and exports.

TABLE 53. REGIONAL STRUCTURE OF IMPORTS OF DEVELOPING REGIONS

(*Percentage of total imports of goods into each region, based on 1970 prices*)

Region	Agriculture	Resources[a]	Light industry	Machinery and equipment	Materials	Invisibles	Subtotals Agriculture and resources	Subtotals Manufacturing
Latin America (medium-income)								
1970	10.6	13.1	6.7	37.2	13.6	18.1	23.7	57.5
2000	5.0	17.1	6.4	46.6	11.3	13.5	22.1	64.4
Latin America (low-income)								
1970	11.7	8.4	11.9	37.0	13.2	17.6	20.1	62.1
2000	6.1	1.5	12.6	51.3	14.5	14.0	7.6	78.4
Middle East								
1970	13.9	11.8	12.2	40.0	12.8	9.3	25.7	65.0
2000	7.3	2.1	14.2	47.5	22.7	6.2	9.4	84.4
Asia (low-income)								
1970	21.1	11.6	15.6	31.8	12.2	7.9	32.7	59.6
2000	14.6	13.7	15.6	35.4	13.8	6.9	28.3	64.8
Africa (arid)								
1970	21.0	9.0	15.0	31.3	13.3	10.6	30.0	59.6
2000	13.1	3.1	26.8	30.1	18.2	18.7	16.2	75.1
Africa (tropical)								
1970	13.4	9.7	15.6	37.8	13.2	10.2	23.1	66.6
2000	9.9	7.4	25.3	33.2	14.1	10.1	17.3	72.6

[a] Including services and transportation.

the major import group in all the regions, and its share will increase in the fastest developing regions. In some regions—medium-income Latin America and low-income Asia—mineral resource imports may become the second most important category if special measures are not taken to expand the exploration of their domestic reserves. Under the basic assumptions of scenario X, all the developing regions would continue to be large net importers of both machinery and equipment, and industrial materials (see table 54). Most of them would also

remain net importers of light-industry products. However, low-income Asia (and under favourable circumstances, Latin America) will become net exporters of these products. Under scenario M (discussed in detail on p. 85) it was assumed that in three developing regions not richly endowed with mineral resources—medium-income Latin America, low-income Asia and arid Africa—special measures are taken to improve the export performance in certain agricultural and industrial commodities and to reduce their extremely high dependence

TABLE 54. NET EXPORTS OF REGIONS (SCENARIO X)

(*Billions of 1970 dollars*)

Region	Year	Agriculture	Mineral resources	Light industry	Machinery and equipment	Materials
Developed Market Economies						
North America . .	1970	1.5	−7.2	−3.4	2.5	2.1
	2000	8.6	27.9	−6.4	10.1	16.5
Western Europe and Japan	1970	−11.1	−15.4	5.5	18.8	6.2
	2000	−10.5	−76.1	8.8	172.7	67.0
Developing Market Economies						
Latin America . .	1970	4.0	4.0	0.1	−6.3	−1.8
	2000	2.7	11.2	−7.2	−80.0	−15.8
Asia (low-income) . .	1970	2.5	−0.7	0.9	−5.3	−1.6
	2000	−2.5	−17.0	9.1	−34.7	−12.3
Middle East . . .	1970	0.3	10.6	−1.1	−2.3	−0.9
	2000	−8.9	97.0	−32.5	−101.0	−49.9
Africa (non-oil producing)	1970	2.7	1.7	−0.6	−4.1	−0.9
	2000	5.1	9.0	−9.6	−21.7	−6.4

on the imports of certain industrial goods. The effects of this alternative computation on the shares of the developing countries in world exports and imports are shown in tables 49 and 51.

The net effect of these changes on total world trade is not large, but they have a definite significance for the trade of the regions in question. Thus, under scenario M, medium-income Latin America increases its share of world exports of agricultural commodities and products of light industry. The share of exports of light industry products increases also for Africa, and especially for low-income Asia. At the same time these regions manage to reduce their combined shares in world imports of all three groups of manufactured goods: products of light industry from 22.2 to 20.9 per cent; machinery and

equipment from 35.9 to 33.5 per cent; industrial materials from 39.6 to 37.8 per cent. Again the changes in the shares are modest, but they involve substantial savings for the balances of payments of these regions.

The question arises as to whether these changes will seriously affect the structure of the agricultural and mineral resource world markets, which have a special significance for the developing regions. The model provides the means for a further detailed investigation of this problem by providing data on gross and net regional exports and imports of livestock products, high-protein crops, grains, roots, "residual" agriculture (including a large volume of cash crops), petroleum, coal, natural gas, iron ore, copper, nickel, lead, zinc and bauxite.

Chapter XIII

INTERNATIONAL SERVICE, AID AND CAPITAL FLOWS

In the framework of the model, international service payments include payments for transportation and for other non-factor services entering international markets. A significant proportion of "other" service payments consists of tourist outlays. Income from foreign investment was not included in service payments and thus was treated separately.

In the first computations the current shares of services sold by the developed and the developing market regions were left basically unchanged. Developed market economies supplied three quarters of total world services in 1970. Ratios of regional dependence on foreign transportation were also kept close to their 1970 levels. By 2000, the share of services bought by developing market regions would increase significantly from 14 to 26 per cent (see table 55). This leads to a substantial imbalance in net service payments for the developing regions, amounting to a total deficit of $30 billion.

TABLE 55. INTERNATIONAL TRANSPORTATION AND OTHER SERVICE PAYMENTS (SCENARIO X)

(*Billions of 1970 dollars*)[a]

Region	1970			2000		
	Inflows	Outflows	Net	Inflows	Outflows	Net
Three developed market regions	34.9	36.8	−1.9	154.0	126.2	23.8
	(75)	(80)		(76)	(63)	
Six developing market regions	5.8	6.5	−0.7	23.9	53.4	−29.5
	(12)	(14)		(12)	(26)	
World total	46.6	46.6		201.9	201.9	

[a] Figures in parentheses indicate percentage of world payments.

Aid flows

Comprehensive information on "aid" combines all intergovernmental loans and grants, and debt repayment. For this reason even developed regions have relatively large aid inflows, which are really intergovernmental short-term loans and the repayment of debts by other countries. For the same reason developing regions have substantial aid outflows. However, aid outflows from developed and aid inflows into developing regions are mainly public aid and credit movements and net outflows and inflows of aid tend to reflect closely real net foreign assistance.

Aid flows are influenced to a certain extent by political considerations and hence are very difficult to predict. The basic scenario depicts the present pattern of aid flows in terms of (*a*) an unchanging ratio of gross aid outflows to GDP of each exporting region and (*b*) essentially unchanging regional shares of the total aid pool.[32] Later we discuss modifications of this pattern.

---

[32] Some of the "aid" flows among developed countries are short-term intergovernmental loans made to countries with payments deficits. In 1970, unusually large inflows were received by North America from Western Europe and Japan. Since the model's results indicate reversals in the direction of payment imbalances among the developed regions, aid inflow shares were reallocated in all subsequent years. Specifically, the shares of developing regions were left unchanged, the North American share was halved, and the remaining half of the North American share was redistributed to other developed market economies in proportion to their 1970 shares.

In 1970 the ratio of gross aid outflow to GDP was 0.85 per cent for North America, 1.5 per cent for high-income Western Europe, 0.45 per cent for Japan and 2.32 per cent for the Middle East. These rates were assumed to continue with rising GDP. Because of the much faster rate of economic growth in the Middle East, as compared to the three developed market regions, the role of the latter as the principal suppliers of aid tends to decline in scenario X from 78 per cent in 1970 to 53 per cent in 2000.

Total aid outflow increases more than fourfold, from $27 billion to $114 billion. However, the share of the developing countries in the total aid pool is assumed to remain unchanged at 45 per cent, while their GDPs increase relative to world GDP. Thus, their aid inflows actually tend to decrease relative to their GDPs. They decline from 1.5 to 0.8 per cent in medium-income Latin America, from 3.3 to 1.7 per cent in low-income Latin America, and from 4.9 to 3.3 per cent in low-income Asia. It is only in the two African regions, which have slower than average GDP growth, that these ratios do increase.

Since both its growth rate and its base-year share of aid are very high, the Middle East gains rapidly as a supplier of net aid. By 2000 in scenario X, its share of net aid and short-term credit exceeds that of the three principal developed market regions. This position is reinforced in part by a very favourable balance-of-payments position. On the other hand, it is not reasonable to expect that such a large part of the developing countries' net aid inflows would be taken care of by the "rich poor" regions—notably, the Middle East, as opposed to the developed countries.

Because the shares of developed regions in total aid inflows are also constant in this scenario, there is an even more apparent stagnation in the net aid outflows of these regions. Their total net aid outflows increase very slowly by 1990 and decline afterwards.

TABLE 56. AID AND SHORT-TERM INTERGOVERNMENTAL LOANS[a]
(SCENARIO X, VARIANT 1)

(*Billions of 1970 dollars*)[b]

	1970	1980	1990	2000
Outflow				
North America	9.0	13.1	17.6	23.1
Western Europe (high-income)	11.1	16.0	24.7	32.9
Japan	0.9	1.6	2.6	3.6
Three developed market regions	21.0	30.7	44.9	59.6
	(77.9)	(72.6)	(63.6)	(52.5)
Middle East	0.8	3.2	9.5	23.1
World total[a]	27.0	42.3	70.5	113.8
Inflow				
Latin America (medium-income and low-income, combined)	3.0	4.8	8.0	12.3
Middle East	1.1	1.7	2.9	4.5
Asia (low-income)	6.0	9.8	16.3	25.2
Africa (arid and tropical, combined)	1.9	3.3	5.4	8.3
Six developing market regions	12.0	19.6	32.6	50.3
Three developed market regions	11.4	16.9	28.1	43.4
Net outflows				
North America	3.9	8.8	10.6	12.2
Western Europe (high-income)	4.9	3.7	4.3	1.4
Japan	0.7	1.3	2.0	2.7
Three developed market regions	9.5	13.8	16.9	16.3
Middle East	−0.2	1.5	6.6	18.6
Net inflows				
Latin America (medium-income and low-income, combined)	1.7	2.6	3.5	2.1
Asia (low-income)	4.9	7.9	12.6	18.2
Africa (arid and tropical, combined)	1.1	2.0	3.5	5.2
Five developing market regions	7.7	12.5	19.6	25.5

[a] Including a provision for aid outflows from centrally planned regions to the extent of $0.73, 1.28, 2.30 and 3.54 billion for the respective years in the table. Official annual estimates of such aid are not available. According to estimates made by the Centre for Development Planning, Projections and Policies of the United Nations, total average annual bilateral aid commitment from these countries in 1971-1973 amounted to $1,994 million, including $944 million from the Soviet Union, $603 million from Eastern Europe and $446 million from China (*World Economic Survey, 1974. Part One. Mid-term Review and Appraisal of Progress in the Implementation of the International Development Strategy* (United Nations publication, Sales No. E.75.II.C.1, p. 195).
[b] Figures in parentheses indicate percentage of world total.

This is, of course, something like an "old order" aid scenario built into a "new order" growth scenario, and they do not seem to live well with one another.

TABLE 57. AID MOVEMENTS (SCENARIO X, VARIANT 2 WITH ASSUMPTION OF LARGER AID FROM DEVELOPED COUNTRIES)

(*Billions of 1970 dollars*)[a]

	1970	1980	1990	2000
Outflow				
North America	9.0	15.4	31.1	54.4
Western Europe (high-income)	11.1	16.0	24.7	42.4
Japan	0.9	2.8	5.9	12.6
Three developed market regions	21.0	34.2	61.7	109.4
	(77.9)	(74.7)	(70.8)	(67.0)
Middle East	0.8	3.2	9.5	23.1
World total	27.0	45.8	87.3	163.6
Inflow				
Latin America (medium-income and low-income, combined)	3.0	5.4	11.3	21.3
Asia (low-income)	6.0	11.7	24.4	50.7
Africa (arid and tropical, combined)	1.9	3.9	8.7	19.6
Middle East	1.1	1.8	3.5	6.5
Six developing market regions	12.0	22.8	47.9	98.1
	(44.5)	(50.0)	(55.0)	(60.0)
Three developed market regions	11.4	16.0	26.2	40.9
Net outflows				
North America	3.9	11.2	24.0	43.5
Western Europe (high-income)	4.9	4.6	6.2	13.3
Japan	0.7	2.4	5.3	11.7
Three developed market regions	9.5	18.2	35.5	68.5
Middle East	−0.2	1.4	6.0	16.6
Net inflows				
Latin America (medium-income and low-income, combined)	1.7	3.2	6.8	11.1
Asia (low-income)	4.9	9.8	20.7	43.7
Africa (arid and tropical, combined)	1.1	2.7	6.8	16.6
Five developing market regions	7.7	15.7	34.3	71.3

[a] Figures in parentheses indicate percentage of world total.

The second variant (see table 57) was developed on the basis of different assumptions—namely, that (*a*) the ratio of gross aid outflows to GDP remains unchanged only for developing countries, including the relatively high ratio for the Middle East, and that for the developed regions they are increased decade by decade; (*b*) the shares of most developing countries in the total aid pool are increased from 45 to 60 per cent and the share of developed regions is reduced.[33] Both assumptions would

[33] Under the assumptions of scenario X changes in the magnitudes of aid flows can affect payments balances but not any of the other (real) variables of the system. Hence, the elaboration of the second variant of X did not require a new solution of the entire system of equations.

reflect special measures taken nationally and internationally to help economic development within the framework of a new world economic order. Specifically, it would mean an increase in total aid to developing countries without an increase in their repayment obligations. This would be effected by raising the grant as compared with the loan component of foreign assistance.

In variant 2, gross aid outflows from North America are assumed to increase from 0.85 per cent in 1970 to 1.0 per cent in 1980, to 1.5 per cent in 1990 and to 2.0 per cent in 2000. Similar schedules in percentage terms for high-income Western Europe are 1.5 in 1970, 1.5 in 1980, 1.5 in 1990 and 2.0 in 2000; and for Japan, 0.45 in 1970, 0.75 in 1980, 1.0 in 1990 and 1.5 in 2000. This would lead to a 50 billion dollar increase in total gross aid outflows from the three principal developed market regions in 2000, as compared to the basic scenario. The absolute change in net and gross aid outflows would be approximately the same size, owing to the stabilization of repayments. In relation to GDP, net outflows from North America would be, in the respective years of the forecast, 0.37, 0.74, 1.16 and 1.64 per cent; from high-income Western Europe, 0.67, 0.44, 0.39 and 0.61 per cent; and from Japan, 0.35, 0.64, 0.89 and 1.39 per cent. This is only an illustration, and other presumably better schedules could be tested. An increase of aid outflows from the countries with centrally planned economies to 0.5 per cent of their gross products by 1980, to 0.7 per cent by 1990 and to 2.0 per cent by 2000 would render absolute increments of $5.1, $13.7 and $31.6 billion respectively, as compared to aid estimates contained in scenario X (see foot-note to table 56).

In relation to their GDPs the net aid inflows into the five developing market regions (excluding the Middle East) would be 3.3 per cent in 2000, as compared to 2.4 per cent in 1970. In the central scenario, X, there was a reduction to 1.2 per cent. The extent to which this is adequate from the point of view of the balance of payments is discussed in chapter XIV.

Long-term private capital flows

Scenario X assumes that long-term inflows of capital are proportional to investment in a region. Each region continues to lend a constant share of the total loan pool. Thus, gross capital outflows from North America will increase from 1 to 2 per cent of its gross product, and from both high-income Western Europe and Japan, from the current 1.4 to 3 per cent in 2000. The total outward movement of long-term capital from developed market countries would increase from $23 billion in 1970 to $148 billion in 2000, or at an annual average rate of 6.4 per cent (see table 58). Because of their much larger investment potential, these countries would remain the predominant source of long-term capital flows. However, capital outflows from developing market countries are also expected to increase to 1.5 per cent of their GDP in 2000, as compared to 0.7 per cent in 1970. This would lead to an increase in the share of developing countries in total world long-term capital outflows (from 9.4 per cent in 1970 to 22.7 per cent in 2000). However, the principal developed market regions would still account for much more than this—87.3 per cent in 1970 and 70.3 per cent in 2000.

At present a relatively small share of capital movements actually reaches the developing countries (only 19.3 per cent of world inflows), while developed market

TABLE 58. LONG-TERM CAPITAL FLOWS (SCENARIO X)
(*Billions of 1970 dollars*)[a]

	1970	1980	1990	2000
Capital outflows				
Three developed regions .	23.1	41.8	85.1	148.1
	(87.2)	(84.9)	(79.2)	(70.3)
Six developing regions .	2.5	5.5	16.7	47.9
	(9.4)	(11.2)	(15.5)	(22.7)
World total . . .	26.5	49.3	107.4	210.6
Capital inflows				
Six developing regions .	5.2	14.1	44.1	119.7
	(19.3)	(28.6)	(41.0)	(56.9)
Three developed regions .	19.8	28.3	45.0	54.1
	(74.7)	(57.5)	(41.9)	(25.7)

[a] Figures in parentheses indicate percentage of world total.

countries account for three quarters of the world inflows. It is expected that the share of developing market regions in total world capital inflows would increase to 57 per cent in 2000. Part of these inflows would come from other developing countries. However, not less than 40 per cent of total world inflows would represent capital exported from developed to developing countries. Net capital inflows to developing from developed countries (inflows minus outflows) should amount to $72 billion, or 34 per cent of the total world movement.

A number of conditions would have to prevail to bring about this large redirection of international capital investment. These include the solution of such problems as the exercise of sovereignty over natural and other economic resources, as well as national and international regulation of transnational corporations.

Foreign income

One condition for the continued international lending of capital is a sustained flow of income from foreign investment in the opposite direction. On the other hand, an increasing outflow of income on foreign investment can create severe balance-of-payments problems for the importers of capital.

Scenario X includes a simple assumption that income from private foreign investment (over and above income on investment already made by 1970) amounts to 8.0 per cent per annum on net long-term capital investment accumulated. This income includes the generally much lower income from short-term capital as well as the higher returns from direct investment abroad. It is assumed that interest payments are not made on accumulated aid, even though this category includes some long-term intergovernmental loans.[34]

For the six developing regions cited in table 59 net payment of income on foreign investments is expected to increase steadily—from $8 billion in 1970 to $65 billion in 2000. Most of these payments are scheduled to come from Latin America and the Middle East, which are assumed to be the major net importers of foreign capital.

---

[34] Net foreign income figures discussed in this section apply only to net foreign capital accumulated through regular capital flows, discussed in the previous section. These figures may differ from foreign income presented in scenario tabulations in Annex VI, which also includes income on foreign capital flows resulting from the investment (disinvestment) of balance-of-payments surpluses (deficits).

TABLE 59. NET LONG-TERM CAPITAL INFLOW AND PAYMENTS OF
INCOME ON FOREIGN INVESTMENT, DEVELOPING COUNTRIES

(*Billions of 1970 dollars*)

	1970	1980	1990	2000
Latin America (*medium-income*)				
Net capital inflow .	0.8	2.1	5.2	13.6
Net income on investment .	− 1.3[a]	− 2.4	− 5.3	− 12.8
Difference .	− 0.5	− 0.3	− 0.1	0.8
Latin America (*low-income*)				
Net capital inflow .	0.7	1.6	5.5	17.4
Net income on investment	− 1.3	− 2.2	− 5.0	− 14.1
Difference .	− 0.6	− 0.6	0.5	3.3
Middle East				
Net capital inflow .	0.3	4.1	12.9	35.6
Net income on investment .	− 3.9	− 5.7	− 12.5	− 31.9
Difference .	− 3.6	− 1.6	0.4	3.7
Asia (*low-income*)				
Net capital inflow .	0.6	0.8	3.5	4.9
Net income on investment .	− 0.8	− 1.4	− 3.0	− 5.6
Difference .	− 0.2	− 0.6	0.5	− 0.7
Africa (*tropical*)				
Net capital inflow .	0.12	0.03	0.19	0.36
Net income on investment .	− 0.4	− 0.5	− 0.6	− 0.7
Difference .	− 0.3	− 0.5	− 0.4	− 0.3
Africa (*arid*)				
Net capital inflow .	0.04	0.03	0.09	0.17
Net income on investment .	− 0.2	− 0.2	− 0.3	− 0.4
Difference .	− 0.2	− 0.2	− 0.2	− 0.2
Total: six developing regions				
Net capital inflow .	2.6	8.7	27.4	72.0
Net income on investment .	− 7.9	− 12.4	− 26.7	− 65.5
Difference .	− 5.3	− 3.7	0.7	6.5

[a] A minus sign indicates net outflow.

When compared to long-term capital inflows, it turns out that the developing regions are currently paying out substantially more in income on foreign investment than they receive in net new inflows of capital. Since net capital outflows are scheduled to grow somewhat faster than net income payments, this adverse balance tends to diminish from more than $5 billion in 1970 to less than $4 billion in 1980, to disappear by 1990 and to change into a surplus of $6.5 billion in 2000. What this projection really means is that in the coming decades the net effect of foreign investment on the balance of payments of the developing countries may be close to zero—that is, any addition to the investment capacity of these countries or transfer of modern technology implied in long-term capital movements would have to be completely paid for by a transfer of other real resources from the developing to the developed countries. Table 59 shows that areas with more development problems (Asia and Africa) will be relatively worse off as far as real benefits of foreign investments are concerned, while regions expanding at a faster rate will be in a relatively better position.

The reason for this described general trend and the specific regional differences arises from simple algebra. Regions are assumed to pay 8 per cent on accumulated debt. If the volume of their loans is increasing by less than 8 per cent a year, then interest payments will exceed additional borrowing.

The ratio of the net increment in foreign assets to fixed capital stock in 1970-2000 is 16.8 per cent for the Middle East,[35] 12.3 per cent for low-income Latin America, 9.6 per cent for medium-income Latin America, 6.2 per cent for low-income Asia, 3.3 per cent for tropical Africa and 2.1 per cent for arid Africa. Thus, the larger the extent of foreign capital participation in economic development the better the relation of net capital inflows to income paid on foreign investment. Dependence on past foreign capital inflows breeds an even larger dependence on such inflows in the future.

Transfer of technology

Computations in scenario X and the others involve substantial changes in production technologies. The basic assumption is that regions would turn from their current technologies to those that are in conformity with higher levels of *per capita* gross product and, thus, to those technologies necessary for higher levels of productivity. At the same time, projected changes in the technology of developed countries are introduced. All these changes are reflected in changing the technical coefficients (the "A matrix").

For agriculture this generally involves the increase of all material and service inputs per unit of output, and of the degree of specialization inside agriculture itself. In mineral resources technological advancement would involve increased mechanization and significant increases in services (including transportation and other distribution margins). Changes in the costs of mineral extraction are also related to differences in grades of ore and geological conditions. In both heavy and light manufacturing the adoption of more modern technologies often means a substitution of synthetic for agricultural products and a reduction in the relative importance of materials inputs.

Capital-output coefficients are also expected to change, increasing in some cases and decreasing in others, as the developing countries proceed with rapid industrialization. Changes in design and product quality are important factors in changing input and capital requirements. These and other technological changes, which are treated within the model in much more detail, involve substantial transfers of technology from developed to developing regions. Such transfers in fact are implicitly assumed in the model. However, no explicit forms of technological transfers, or of payments for such transfer, are specified in the model, other than importing products (machinery, materials and the like), capital and aid flows, and income on investments. No attempt was made to quantify the extent to which technological changes are contingent on transfers of technology from abroad.

[35] The assumption of high rates of foreign investment in the Middle East is based on its high growth rate and the attractiveness of investment opportunities in a rapidly growing economy. Presumably foreign investment in the Middle East would take place simultaneously with Middle Eastern investment in other developed and developing regions of the world.

Chapter XIV

BALANCE-OF-PAYMENTS PROBLEMS

Balance-of-payments position: unchanged relative prices

Summing up the various international flows discussed in the preceding sections, the model shows the balance-of-payments position of various regions under different conditions of development and international economic relations. It is what might be called a basic balance of payments, since it does not include short-term capital movements, changes in monetary reserves, and some other details often present in the balance-of-payments statistics. But it does include the principal elements that make up a balance of payments—namely, the net balance of goods and services, net income from foreign investment and net capital and aid flows.

While all other quantities in the model are measured in constant 1970 prices, traded goods are valued in current prices in the balance-of-payments accounts. Projects of relative prices for 1980, 1990 and 2000 were computed with the system's simplified price dual described in the following section. Balance-of-payments results that are obtained when these relative prices are used to value international transactions are shown in tables 62 and 67 and in the complete solution tables included at the end of the volume. The balance of payments are quite sensitive to changes in relative product prices. For this reason, the model's balance-of-payments accounts will be presented here in several alternative forms, differing only in terms of the assumptions made about relative product prices. To begin with, table 60 provides a summary of the balance-of-payments results under the assumption that all prices remain at 1970 levels.

One should observe the important difference in the structure of the balance of payments of the developed and developing countries in 1970. In the developed market regions a big surplus of net income from foreign investments, together with a smaller surplus on goods and services, served as a basis for large net capital and aid outflows. Quite the opposite is true of the developing market regions, where new net inflows of capital and aid were used to pay out debts and income on foreign investment.

Moving on to 1980 one observes that with relative prices unchanged there are small but significant shifts in the over-all picture. The trade surplus of the two oil-exporting developing regions, the Middle East and low-income Latin America, becomes quite large, and there is also a big surplus in tropical Africa.

At the same time substantial deficits appear in medium-income Latin America, low-income Asia and arid Africa. These deficits are not caused by any extraordinary events such as crop failures or drastic price changes but are a logical result of the acceleration of internal development which leads to much larger import requirements, while

TABLE 60. BALANCE OF PAYMENTS (SCENARIO X)

(Billions of 1970 dollars)

	1970	1980	1990	2000
Three developed market regions . . .	−3.4	−7.7	42.5	202.3
(including goods and services by region) .	2.7	3.0	60.6	219.1
North America	0.2	1.1	27.6	39.1
Western Europe (high-income) . .	−0.1	−0.9	18.5	124.0
Japan	2.6	2.8	14.5	56.0
Net income on investment[a] . .	8.7	16.6	38.8	93.4
Net capital outflows . . .	−5.3	−13.5	−40.0	−93.9
Net aid outflows . . .	−9.5	−13.8	−16.9	−16.3
Six developing market regions . . .	3.1	9.1	−32.0	−189.2
(including goods and services by region) .	0.6	1.9	−45.7	−202.7
Latin America (medium-income) . .	−0.5	−7.1	−21.6	−57.2
Latin America (low-income) . . .	0.2	1.5	−9.8	−41.9
Middle East	5.3	18.4	27.6	4.5
Asia (low-income)	−4.2	−10.3	−36.0	−81.0
Africa (arid)	−0.6	−1.8	−7.3	−16.2
Africa (tropical)	0.4	1.2	1.4	−16.9
Net income on investment[a] . .	−7.9	−12.4	−26.7	−65.5
Net capital inflows	2.5	8.6	27.4	72.1
Net aid inflows	7.9	11.0	13.0	6.9

[a] Net income on investment is limited to income on foreign capital investment accumulated as a result of regular capital flows. As a result, foreign income and the balance-of-payments surplus (or deficit) figures discussed in this section as a rule differ from figures presented in the tabulations of the annexes.

export shares of these regions do not significantly increase. In fact, the deficits on the goods and services account of these two regions in 1980 are $10 billion and $7 billion respectively. Developing regions with more exportable mineral resources and/or agricultural products fare much better in this period.

However, during the 1980s much larger imbalances start to appear. It is estimated that by 1990, given constant 1970 relative prices, all developed market regions would have surpluses and their total will exceed $60 billion, while all developing market regions, with the exception of the Middle East and tropical Africa, will end up with substantial deficits, the largest of them in low-income Asia and medium-income Latin America.

In the absence of remedial action in the 1970s and 1980s, by the 1990s the balance-of-payments gap would increase tremendously with the total deficit of the developing regions reaching $190 billion. Only the Middle East is able to retain a payments surplus under these assumptions. Gaps of such proportions would make it impossible for developing regions to grow at rates assumed in the basic scenario and would cause a sharp slowdown in their rates of growth beginning in the 1980s, which would make fast growth impossible in the 1990s.

All of the discussion thus far is based on the hypothetical assumption of fixed 1970 prices. It is now necessary to see how this picture is modified by price changes occurring in the 1970s and beyond.

Effect of price changes

To compute a more realistic balance of trade and the associated balance of payments, the various component import and export items valued in 1970 prices for the bulk of the analysis, are repriced to reflect expected relative prices of different goods in each of the years in question: 1980, 1990 and 2000. Relative prices of commodities are measured against average prices of final consumption. The changes in prices are "normalized" so that this average would remain the same in all years as it was in 1970. Thus, the average absolute level of prices remains unchanged, but relative prices of various products and groups of products do change in relation to each other.

The technique of determining such prices involves the solution of the "dual" of the input-output system, given the technologies and the value-added proportions of the respective years. The changes in relative prices thus reflect the expected shifts in the techniques of production, in labour productivity and also in the cost of resource extraction expected to occur between 1970 and the years in question. This technique was applied for one region only (North America) and it was assumed that the relative prices obtained would be representative of price changes prevailing in world trade. Considering that this area produces and absorbs a substantial part of the world's total marketable output, this can be considered a reasonable first approximation to the actual situation. Additional computations would have to be made later to study relative price changes in other regions and to see how they differ. Many alternative price projections should be evaluated.

The over-all result of this computation is that the average relative price of mineral resources increases 2.67 times between 1970 and 2000; the average price for agricultural goods increases by 14 per cent; and the average price for manufactured goods declines by 6.8 per cent. On the average, mineral resources would be 2.9 times as costly in 2000 in relation to manufactured goods, and agricultural commodities would be 1.2 times as expensive.

TABLE 61. CHANGE OF RELATIVE PRICES OF MINERAL RESOURCES
(SCENARIO X)[a]

(1970 = 1.00)

Resource					1980	1990	2000
Copper	.	.	.	.	1.01	0.99	2.59
Bauxite	.	.	.	.	1.00	0.98	1.17
Nickel	.	.	.	.	1.02	1.39	2.32
Zinc .	.	.	.	.	1.00	1.32	2.32
Lead .	.	.	.	.	1.00	0.98	2.22
Iron ore	.	.	.	.	1.02	1.02	1.02
Petroleum	.	.	.	.	1.33	2.89	3.25
Natural gas	.	.	.	.	1.54	5.45	7.56
Coal	.	.	.	.	0.95	0.87	0.86
Other resources	.	.	.	.	0.98	0.97	0.98

[a] This scenario assumes a pessimistic estimate of mineral reserves (see chapter X).

Let us examine the changes of mineral resource prices in some detail (see table 61). The price changes in the 1970s, as determined by technological shifts and resource scarcity, are relatively small, with only petroleum and natural gas showing some increases (33 and 54 per cent, respectively). In the 1980s, as less productive and more costly sources of minerals are brought into operation, relative prices start to change rapidly, and in the 1990s there is a further broad upturn.

Though the model at this stage assumes autonomous substitution of materials with changing technology and supply conditions, no attempt has been made to measure the effect of price changes on the choice of competing technologies or to link the prices of competing materials directly. Thus, the price of coal does not necessarily follow the prices of petroleum and natural gas.

The surge of inflation in the first half of the 1970s has in fact brought about drastic changes in absolute and relative prices very much in advance of what would be expected from the predictions of this model. However, these movements have not been uniform. While the price of petroleum in 1975 was 4.7 times higher than in 1970 in relation to the average prices of final consumption in the United States of America, the price of copper fell by 35 per cent after first increasing by 9 per cent in 1974 (the absolute swing was much sharper). In a bad crop year the price of wheat (in the same terms) increased some 90 per cent, which is much more than the model considers likely by the year 2000 (31 per cent). Because prices fluctuate widely in the short run, it was difficult to reprice trade with confidence in current relative prices. However, other computations were made to show the extent of changes involved.

It was first assumed that prices in world trade would change in accordance with relative price movements computed within the model. These changes are gradual and take place mostly in the 1980s and the 1990s. As shown in table 62, the net difference for the trade balances in 1980 are not large. Moreover, by 1990 substantial deficits emerge in high-income Western Europe and Japan, which become even larger by 2000.

65

TABLE 62. CHANGE IN THE BALANCE OF TRADE DUE TO
PROJECTED RELATIVE PRICE CHANGES IN 1980, 1990 AND 2000

(*Billions of 1970 dollars*)

Region	1980	1990	2000
North America . . .	−0.9	−1.1	6.1
Western Europe (high-income)	−5.7	−64.7	−102.1
Japan	−2.2	−31.5	−62.6
Three developed market regions . . .	−8.8	−97.3	−158.6
Latin America (medium-income)	0.0	−13.8	−29.2
Latin America (low-income) .	1.3	14.0	27.3
Middle East . . .	6.2	100.6	210.2
Asia (low-income) . . .	0.0	−7.6	−21.8
Africa (arid)	0.1	0.5	1.0
Africa (tropical) . . .	0.0	0.3	14.1
Six developing market regions	7.6	94.0	201.6

In the developing regions the trade balances of medium-income Latin America and low-income Asia are adversely affected, while substantial additional net export earnings are achieved in the mineral-exporting regions—the Middle East, low-income Latin America and tropical Africa.

In another computation it was assumed that 1970 prices would generally prevail, but that there would be a 3.5-fold increase in the price of petroleum. This alternative would lead to a net improvement in the balance of trade of the developing regions as a whole but the balances of trade of the petroleum-importing developing regions would deteriorate significantly, resulting in very large deficits. The net loss to the oil-importing developing regions resulting from this increase in the price of petroleum is shown in table 63. Some kind of scheme

TABLE 63. NET LOSS IN THE BALANCE OF TRADE DUE TO A
3.5-FOLD INCREASE IN PETROLEUM PRICES

(*Billions of 1970 dollars*)

Region	1980	1990	2000
Latin America (medium-income) .	6.6	11.6	30.8
Asia (low-income) . . .	3.4	9.5	25.3
Africa (tropical) . . .	0.6	0.8	2.0
Three developing market regions .	10.6	21.9	58.1

providing financial compensation to these regions would have to be devised in order to alleviate these losses, so that their economic development would not be adversely affected.

As another hypothetical alternative one can examine the situation that would result from the implementation of international commodity schemes, through which the prices of some of the other mineral resources and agricultural goods of which developing countries are substantial net exporters would be increased starting in 1980. Apart from the prices of copper and nickel, which were raised to their 2000 level in the model, the prices of bauxite, iron ore and coal were increased by 200 per cent so as to maintain their 1970 relation to the price of copper. In this computation the relative price of natural gas was assumed to remain unchanged, since the main impact of its change would be a redistribution of re-

sources among the developing countries themselves. Prices of "other agricultural products" were, on the other hand, raised twofold (see table 64).

TABLE 64. CHANGE IN THE BALANCE OF TRADE DUE TO INCREASED
PRICES OF SOME MINERAL RESOURCES AND AGRICULTURAL GOODS

(*Billions of 1970 dollars*)

	1980	1990	2000
North America	0.7	3.0	1.5
Western Europe (high-income) .	−8.5	−16.6	−6.3
Japan	−12.4	−15.8	−14.8
Three developed market regions .	−20.2	−29.4	−19.6
Latin America (medium-income) .	4.0	7.4	5.5
Latin America (low-income) . .	3.2	5.8	3.5
Middle East	—	—	—
Asia (low-income) . . .	5.0	5.5	4.9
Africa (arid)	0.8	0.7	0.8
Africa (tropical)	6.4	13.0	5.0
Six developing market regions .	19.4	32.2	19.7
Changes due to preferential pricing of			
Copper	6.0	14.3	—
Bauxite	0.2	0.3	0.2
Nickel	1.0	2.0	3.0
Iron ore	2.8	8.3	12.0
Coal	−0.2	−0.6	−1.6
"Other agriculture" . . .	9.6	7.9	6.1

The over-all effect would be a reduction in the total deficit in the balance of payments of the developing regions by $20 to $30 billion. A substantial part of the reduction would come from higher earnings for copper, iron ore and "other" agricultural goods. The two Latin American regions, tropical Africa and low-income Asia, would be the largest beneficiaries. Arid Africa would be a small net exporter and the Middle East would have to pay an additional bill amounting to $9 billion in the year 2000. The effect of all these additional price changes is much smaller than that of the petroleum price increase.

The total changes in the balance of trade of the developing countries which are due to these price shifts and provide for financial compensation to oil-importing regions are illustrated in table 65. The main beneficiaries are still the oil-exporting region and tropical

TABLE 65. TOTAL CHANGES IN BALANCE OF TRADE DUE TO
PRICE CHANGES

(*Billions of 1970 dollars*)

Region	1980	1990	2000
Latin America (medium-income) .	8.9	3.7	8.4
Latin America (low-income) . .	10.6	19.4	24.0
Middle East . . .	40.4	114.2	151.5
Asia (low-income) . .	6.5	4.4	8.3
Africa (arid)	1.1	1.2	2.1
Africa (tropical) . . .	8.5	17.6	23.8
Six developing market regions .	76.0	160.5	218.1

Africa, but the position of all the other developing regions is also somewhat improved as compared with the variant in 1970 relative prices.

The reader should bear in mind that the tables present only the "first round" effects of price changes on the balance of payments. To the extent that the balance of trade is more favourable to a region in any given year, the future foreign debt and interest payments associated with it will be lower than originally computed. Hence, improvements in the balance of payments are likely to be appreciably greater than these estimates, which deal only with trade rather than payments balances.

Effect of different growth rates in developed countries

The balances of payments of the developing regions are affected directly and indirectly by economic conditions prevailing in the developed countries. A faster growth rate in the developed countries tends to increase world imports and thus expand the export opportunities for the developing regions. However, in view of the persistently small share of developing countries in world exports, the significance of these factors should not be overrated.

Consider table 66, which compares world trade in scenarios X and D. The shift from one scenario to another has a small effect on the GDPs of most regions, except North America and high-income Western Europe, where gross product is substantially larger in scenario X than in scenario D (for North America by $487 billion and for high-income Western Europe by $100 billion).

As expected, in variant X world trade is larger than in variant D by some $74 billion, most of which is accounted for by the higher imports of North America and Western Europe.[36] However, total exports from developing countries gain only $10 billion because their share in world exports is low. Even under alternative assumptions of an increase in their total export share to about 24 per cent, the gain would only be about $18 billion—that is, only 3 per cent of the total increment of gross product in the two developed regions.

For these reasons the absolute improvement in the balance-of-trade deficit of the developing countries would be very modest, ranging between $8 billion and $16 billion under various assumptions. This is only 3-6 per cent of the combined trade deficit of the develop-

ing countries measured in 2000 prices. A much higher growth rate in the developed countries would be required to close the trade deficit of the developing countries. In fact, it would take a doubling of the total gross product of the developed regions in 2000 to produce such a result, and would imply an average annual growth rate of more than 6 per cent in the developed areas as a whole, rather than the average 4 per cent envisaged in scenario X. It is doubtful that such high growth rates for developed countries would be realistic.

Faster economic growth in the developed countries would increase their potential for exporting capital to the developing countries. The net increase in capital outflow from the three developed market regions (in scenario X as compared to scenario D) amounts to some $8 billion. However, most of this increase would represent movements from one developed region to another without directly benefiting the developing countries. A major shift in the directions of international capital movements would be necessary to direct more net capital inflows into the developing areas.

Means for reducing the balance-of-payments deficit of less developed regions

One of the consequences, or rather pre-conditions, of rapid economic growth in many less developed market economies is a persistent excess of imports over exports. These import surpluses have to be financed by a combination of net capital inflow—that is long-term borrowing, official aid and annual short-term borrowing referred to in our tabulation as the (negative) balance of payments. Moreover, interest payments on total foreign obligations ("debt") are carried over from one year to the next, accelerating the rate of their accumulation. In the section on the effect of price changes, above, we have already seen how the flow of international payments would be affected by changes in the relative prices of various internationally traded goods.

The most direct attack on the balance-of-payments difficulties of developing countries would consist of raising capital and official inflows while reducing the annual rate of interest charged on their outstanding

---

[36] Price effects of such shifts were not considered.

TABLE 66. COMPARISON OF WORLD TRADE IN SCENARIOS X AND D IN 2000

(*Billions of 1970 dollars*)

Region	Difference in exports	Difference in imports	Difference in balance of trade
North America	10.5	35.4	− 24.9
Western Europe (high-income)	32.6	32.5	0.1
Japan	7.0	0.9	6.1
Subtotal, three developed market regions	50.1	68.8	− 18.7
Latin America (medium-income)	1.8	0.1	1.7
Latin America (low-income)	1.0	0.2	0.8
Middle East	2.7	0.5	2.2
Asia (low-income)	3.4	1.0	2.4
Africa (arid)	0.3	0.0	0.3
Africa (tropical)	0.9	0.1	0.8
Subtotal, six developed market regions	10.1	1.9	8.2
Developed centrally planned	10.9	0.9	10.0
Other regions	14.1	3.7	10.4
World total	74.4	74.4	—

TABLE 67. INTERNATIONAL FINANCIAL FLOWS: COMPARISON OF SCENARIOS X AND R

(*Billions of 1970 dollars*)

Region	Year	Balance of trade[a] X and R	Net capital inflows[b] X	R	Net aid inflows X	R	Foreign income or interest[b] X	R	Balance of payments[b] X	R
Latin America (middle-income) .	1970	−0.4	0.84	0.84	0.88	0.88	−1.3	−1.3	0.0	0.0
	2000	−84.7	13.60	17.80	0.80	8.90	−172.7	−87.5	−243.0	−145.0
Latin America (low-income) .	1970	0.3	0.71	0.71	0.79	0.79	−1.3	−1.3	0.5	0.5
	2000	−14.1	17.40	20.70	1.30	4.70	6.1	3.7	11.0	15.0
Asia (low-income) . . .	1970	−4.2	9.25	9.25	−3.75	−3.75	−0.8	−0.8	0.5	0.5
	2000	−81.7	4.90	7.10	18.20	47.60	−128.8	−40.6	−187.0	−67.0
Middle East . . .	1970	5.3	0.25	0.25	0.23	0.23	−3.9	−3.9	1.8	1.8
	2000	102.9	35.60	42.40	−18.60	−15.80	298.6	165.2	418.0	295.0
Africa (arid) . . .	1970	−0.6	0.04	0.04	0.76	0.76	−0.2	−0.2	0.0	0.0
	2000	−7.9	0.20	0.20	3.50	9.00	−7.9	1.5	−12.0	3.0
Africa (tropical). . .	1970	0.4	0.12	0.12	0.32	0.32	−0.4	−0.4	0.4	0.4
	2000	18.8	0.40	0.60	1.70	3.90	52.6	29.7	73.0	53.0

[a] Balance-of-trade figures in this table may differ from those shown in other tables of chapter XIV, owing to the different relative prices used.
[b] Net capital inflows in these computations include additional

capital movements which are necessary to balance the payments deficits; foreign income or interest payments are calculated on total foreign capital and debt accumulated as a result of such net capital inflows; balance-of-payments totals are calculated on the same basis.

foreign obligations. A particular combination of such changes is incorporated in scenario R, presented below (see table 67).

The capital export coefficients of the large developed regions used in scenario X (annual capital exports) are stepped up by 20 per cent in order to increase the magnitude of the world pool of capital exports. The shares drawn by the capital receiving countries remain the same as under scenario X, which means that the amounts received by each increases by 20 per cent. The interest rate charged on foreign borrowing is 6 per cent in scenario R, reduced from 8 per cent in scenario X. The foreign aid export coefficient of the developed regions is assumed to increase gradually to 2000, as can be seen from table 68, while the shares of the aid pool assigned to the developing regions were stepped up to 1.33 of the 1970 base-year share.

TABLE 68. INCREASED CONTRIBUTIONS OF FOREIGN AID BY DEVELOPED REGION[a]

(*Percentage*)

Year	North America	Western Europe (high-income)	Soviet Union	Eastern Europe	Japan
1970[b] (original share)	0.0085	0.0152	—	—	0.0043
1980 .	0.0100	0.0152	0.0050	0.0050	0.0075
1990 .	0.0150	0.0152	0.0070	0.0070	0.0100
2000 .	0.0200	0.0200	0.0200	0.0200	0.0150

[a] Gross aid outflow as a proportion of GDP.
[b] Including a provision for aid outflows from centrally planned regions to the extent of $0.73, 1.28, 2.30 and 3.54 billion for the respective years in the table. Official annual estimates of such aid are not available. According to estimates made by the Centre for Development Planning, Projections and Policies of the United Nations, total average annual bilateral aid commitment from these countries in 1971-1973 amounted to $1,994 million, including $944 million from the Soviet Union, $603 million from Eastern Europe and $446 million from China (*World Economic Survey, 1974. Part One. Mid-term Review and Appraisal of Progress in the Implementation of the International Development Strategy* (United Nations publication, Sales No. E.75.II.C.1), p. 195).

The role of the interest to be paid on the accumulated foreign debt is enhanced by the fact that it is being compounded from one year to the next. It has to be paid, however, both on accumulated long-term capital imports and the cumulative amount of negative "foreign balances"—that is, aggregate short-term foreign debt, to the extent that stepped up capital imports relieve the pressure on the payments imbalance by reducing the short-term borrowing by an equal amount. Such shifts cannot affect the aggregate amount of interest payments, provided that the same rate of interest is applied to the entire foreign debt.

The situation is different in the case in which the magnitude of the negative annual foreign balance is reduced by the amount of additional official foreign aid—the reason being that such aid is not subject to an interest charge. A lowering of the rate of interest reduces, in either case, the rate of cumulative growth of external debt. Every increase in official aid at the same time reduces the size of the accumulated obligation to which the given rate of interest has to be applied.

In table 67 the separate components of the financial positions of the developing regions, as projected to 2000 on the basis of the revised set of financial assumptions (described above), are compared with the corresponding figures derived from the original scenario, X. The hypothetical change in the means by which these less developed regions are expected to finance their projected import surpluses can indeed slow down the growth of their external short-term debt. The balance of payments of some of the areas would necessarily shift in the opposite direction. Other contributions of such purely financial measures could of course have brought about similar results.

It is the question of the practicality of this type of arrangement that prompts proposals to attack the problem of the increasing external indebtedness of less developed countries by reducing the annual deficits in their balance of trade, in expanding their foreign earnings by promulgating measures that would increase the share of their principal exports on the world markets, and by cutting down imports through import substitution—that is, by stepping up the domestic output of goods, the demand for which has up to now been covered to a large extent by imports.

Scenario M was especially designed to demonstrate the effectiveness of such double-pronged action as a means of cutting down the rise in the foreign indebtedness of developing areas and its indirect influence on the economic growth of these regions and on the payments balance and growth paths of other countries. Scenario M deviates from scenario X only to the extent that low-income Asia, medium-income Latin America and arid Africa are assigned higher world market shares for their agricultural exports (the share of medium-income Latin

America for instance, is increased by 3 per cent per annum) and for their manufacturing exports (the shares of all three regions are increased by 1 per cent per annum), while at the same time the import coefficients—that is, the share of imports out of total domestic supply (domestic output and exports) of light industry, materials and chemicals, and machinery and equipment in these regions were reduced by 1 per cent per annum. The domestic output of each of these products was, to a certain extent, substituted for imports. The old and the new export shares and import coefficients are shown on table 69. The effects of these postulated changes on the balance of payments in these three selected regions are

TABLE 69. IMPORT COEFFICIENTS[a] AND EXPORT SHARES[b] (SCENARIOS X AND M)

	Latin America (medium-income)				Asia (low-income)				Africa (arid)			
	Import coefficient		Export shares		Import coefficient		Export shares		Import coefficient		Export shares	
Sector	X	M	X	M (percentage)	X	M	X	M (percentage)	X	M	X	M (percentage)
Agriculture	0.03	0.03	8.5	20.2	0.10	0.10	10.2	9.0	0.08	0.08	1.8	1.6
Resources	0.30	0.28	7.6	7.5	0.49	0.47	3.2	3.2	0.15	0.15	0.3	0.3
Materials	0.13	0.09	1.7	1.7	0.27	0.20	2.7	2.8	0.26	0.19	0.2	0.2
Light industry	0.05	0.04	1.3	1.7	0.15	0.11	9.7	12.9	0.28	0.21	0.4	0.5
Machinery and equipment	0.24	0.18	0.8	0.8	0.40	0.30	1.5	1.5	0.33	0.24	—	—
Invisibles	0.05	0.05	3.8	5.1	0.04	0.04	3.3	4.4	0.04	0.04	0.6	0.8

$$^a\ m = \frac{imports}{imports + output}$$
$$^b\ \text{For each commodity in question, export share} = \frac{regional\ export}{total\ world\ export}$$

shown in table 70. The negative balance of payments of medium-income Latin America, low-income Asia and arid Africa are seen—as could have been expected—as being reduced drastically; the same is true of their negative net foreign income.

TABLE 70. THE BALANCE OF PAYMENTS IN 2000 (SCENARIOS X AND M)

(Billions of 1970 dollars)

Region	Scenario X	Scenario M
Latin America (medium-income)	− 242.77	− 109.11
Asia (low-income)	− 187.40	− 89.07
Africa (arid)	− 12.18	− 0.99
North America	97.31	48.89
Western Europe (high-income)	− 17.95	− 120.59
Middle East	418.44	417.53

An improvement in the balance of payments of these countries must, of course, necessarily be accompanied by a deterioration in the balance of payments of some other regions. The payments surplus of North America is seen as being reduced by 50 per cent, the payments deficit of high-income Western Europe is drastically increased, while in the oil-exporting Middle East it remains practically unaffected.

Comparing the two sets of figures for 2000 entered in tables 69 and 70, we can see how the particular combination of an export drive and import substitution in the three developing regions would affect the export and import structure of some other parts of the world. In

examining these figures it is necessary to remember that both scenarios X and M imply the assumption that the same prescribed set of gross product targets will actually be attained. A quite different picture would have emerged if the same export drives and import substitution measures were promulgated in the same three less developed regions under the general conditions corresponding to the set of alternative assumptions incorporated in scenario A.

Concluding observations

The comparative analysis of the alternative paths—each based on a different set of structural and policy assumptions—along which the world economy might advance from now to 2000 provides a deep and systematic insight into various aspects of mutual interdependence between the economic prospects of the more and the less developed parts of the world. Problems concerning the availability of natural resources and environmental conditions are shown to be inextricably imbedded in the complex network of these interrelations.

In compiling the data base used in these projections, a great effort was made to mobilize the best available sources of information and authoritative expert judgement. Some parts of the data base may prove to be relatively unreliable. To a certain extent this is of course inevitable, since we are attempting to look into the distant future. It is hoped that this report can facilitate concrete and close delineation of the areas of greatest weakness in the available statistics and provide a logical basis for establishing the order of priorities for future efforts to eliminate these areas of weakness.

TECHNICAL ANNEXES

Annex I

REGIONAL CLASSIFICATION

TABLE 71. THE GEOGRAPHICAL CLASSIFICATION SCHEME

No.	Region	Country or territory	No.	Region	Country or territory
I.	*North America* (1970 population, 229.1 million)[a] (1970 *per capita* income, $4,625)[b]	1. Canada 2. Canal Zone 3. Greenland 4. Puerto Rico 5. United States of America 6. Virgin Islands			7. Germany, Federal Republic of 8. Greenland 9. Iceland 10. Ireland 11. Italy 12. Luxembourg 13. Netherlands 14. Norway 15. Sweden 16. Switzerland 17. United Kingdom of Great Britain and Northern Ireland (including the Channel Islands and Isle of Man)
II.	*Latin America* (medium-income) (1970 population, 191.4 million) (1970 *per capita* income, $594)	1. Argentina 2. Bahamas 3. Bermuda 4. Brazil 5. Chile 6. Cuba 7. Mexico 8. St. Lucia/Grenada/St. Vincent/Dominica/St. Kitts/Nevis/Anguilla/ Netherlands Antilles/ Turks and Caicos Islands/Montserrat 9. Uruguay	V.	*Europe* (medium-income) (1970 population, 108.1 million) (1970 *per capita* income, $698)	1. Cyprus 2. Gibraltar 3. Greece 4. Malta 5. Portugal 6. Spain 7. Turkey 8. Yugoslavia
III.	*Latin America* (low-income) (1970 population, 90 million) (1970 *per capita* income, $443)	1. Barbados 2. Bolivia 3. British Honduras 4. Colombia 5. Costa Rica 6. Dominican Republic 7. Ecuador 8. El Salvador 9. French Guiana 10. Guadeloupe 11. Guatemala 12. Guyana 13. Haiti 14. Honduras 15. Jamaica 16. Martinique 17. Nicaragua 18. Panama 19. Paraguay 20. Peru 21. Surinam 22. Trinidad and Tobago 23. Venezuela	VI.	*Soviet Union* (1970 population, 242.8 million) (1970 *per capita* income, $1,791)	1. Union of Soviet Socialist Republics
			VII.	*Eastern Europe* (1970 population, 105.1 million) (1970 *per capita* income, $1,564)	1. Albania 2. Bulgaria 3. Czechoslovakia 4. German Democratic Republic 5. Hungary 6. Poland 7. Romania
			VIII.	*Asia* (centrally planned) (1970 population, 808.4 million) (1970 *per capita* income, $167)	1. China 2. Democratic People's Republic of Korea 3. Democratic Republic of Viet-Nam 4. Mongolia
IV.	*Europe* (high-income) (1970 population, 282.0 million) (1970 *per capita* income, $2,574)	1. Austria 2. Belgium 3. Denmark 4. Faeroe Islands 5. Finland 6. France	IX.	*Asia* (high-income) (1970 population, 104.3 million) (1970 *per capita* income, $1,916)	1. Japan 2. Ryukyu Islands

[a] According to the Demographic Division of the United Nations Secretariat.

[b] World Bank, *Atlas* (Washington, D.C., 1970). GDP data converted at official exchange rates.

71

TABLE 71 (continued)

No.	Region	Country or territory	No.	Region	Country or territory
X.	*Asia* (low-income) (1970 population, 1023.2 million) (1970 *per capita* income, $121)	1. Afghanistan 2. Bangladesh 3. British Solomon Islands 4. Brunei 5. Bhutan 6. Burma 7. Democratic Kampuchea 8. Fiji Islands 9. Hong Kong 10. India 11. Indonesia 12. Republic of Korea 13. Laos 14. Malaysia 15. Maldive Islands 16. Macao 17. Nepal 18. New Hebrides 19. Pacific territories and islands, n.e.s. 20. Pakistan 21. Papua New Guinea 22. Philippines 23. Republic of South Viet-Nam 24. Sikkim 25. Singapore 26. Sri Lanka 27. Thailand			10. Mauritania 11. Morocco 12. Niger 13. Somalia 14. Sudan 15. Syrian Arab Republic 16. Tunisia 17. Upper Volta 18. Western Sahara
			XIII.	*Africa* (tropical) (1970 population, 141.4 million) (1970 *per capita* income, $168)	1. Angola 2. Benin 3. Botswana 4. Burundi 5. Cape Verde 6. Central African Republic 7. Congo 8. Equatorial Guinea 9. Gambia 10. Ghana 11. Guinea-Bissau 12. Ivory Coast 13. Kenya 14. Lesotho 15. Liberia 16. Madagascar 17. Malawi 18. Mauritius 19. Mozambique 20. Rwanda 21. Sao Tome and Principe 22. Senegal 23. Seychelles Islands 24. Sierra Leone 25. Southern Rhodesia 26. Swaziland 27. Togo 28. United Republic of Tanzania 29. Uganda 30. Zaire 31. Zambia
XI.	*Middle East — Africa* (oil producers) (1970 population, 126.5 million) (1970 *per capita* income, $286)	1. Algeria 2. Bahrain 3. Democratic Yemen 4. Gabon 5. Iran 6. Iraq 7. Kuwait 8. Libyan Arab Republic 9. Muscat/Trucial/Oman 10. Nigeria 11. Qatar 12. Saudi Arabia 13. United Arab Emirates 14. Yemen			
			XIV.	*Africa* (medium-income) (1970 population, 21.5 million) (1970 *per capita* income, $786)	1. South Africa, including Namibia
XII.	*Africa* (arid) (1970 population, 131.2 million) (1970 *per capita* income, $205)	1. Chad 2. Comoro Islands 3. Egypt 4. Ethiopia 5. French Territory of the Afars and the Issas 6. Israel 7. Jordan 8. Lebanon 9. Mali	XV.	*Oceania* (1970 population, 15.4 million) (1970 *per capita* income $2,799)	1. Australia 2. New Zealand

TABLE 72. AGGREGATED REGIONAL CLASSIFICATION

Classification	Region	Classification	Region
I. Developed country	A. North America B. Western Europe (high-income) C. Soviet Union D. Eastern Europe E. Western Europe (medium-income)[a] F. Japan G. Oceania H. Africa (medium-income)[a]	II. Developing group I (resource rich)	A. Latin America (low-income) B. Middle East — Africa C. Africa (tropical)
		III. Developing group II (resource poor)	A. Africa (arid) B. Asia (low-income) C. Asia (centrally planned) D. Latin America (medium-income)

[a] Classified in developing group II in the print-out of scenario A, which appears in annex VI.

PRICES IN THE WORLD MODEL

In the present version of the world system most of the variables are expressed either in physical units or in value units measured in 1970 United States prices. To estimate the balance-of-payments positions of the various regions in future decades, however, it was necessary to estimate changes in the relative prices of the various traded goods that enter the regional trade balances. To compute the balance of trade, the various component import and export items valued in 1970 prices were repriced to reflect relative prices of the year of the balance: 1980, 1990 and 2000. The following procedure was used to revalue exports and imports:

1. The dual of the input-output structure for North America was used to compute 1970 prices, given the input-output structure and value-added proportions of the base year, 1970. To facilitate subsequent projections, the non-wage portion of value added was treated as endogenous and proportional to the size of the required capital stock, as determined by the capital coefficients in the system. In the base-year price computations, prices of commodities measured in value units were equal to one and prices of commodities measured in physical units were equal to the actual 1970 prices of these products (except for minor statistical discrepancies).

2. Prices for subsequent years were computed by "up-dating" the base year interindustry structure to incorporate expected changes in the input-output coefficients, and particularly in the costs of resource extraction expected to occur between 1970 and the years in question,

and by modifying the value-added proportions in terms of expected changes in labour productivity. The input-output dual equations were then solved for new prices. The prices obtained were "normalized" so that the average price of all goods consumed would remain the same as it was in 1970. Normalized prices for the years 1970, 1980, 1990 and 2000 are shown in the attached tables.

3. The normalized prices computed for any given year were expressed as ratios to the corresponding prices for each good in the base year. The relative price ratios, computed in step three, were in turn used to revalue each region's balance of trade so as to express it in prices appropriate for the year in question.

4. A second set of prices was computed incorporating the assumptions of the generous resource endowment scenario (H) for 1990 and 2000. In scenario H some of the high-grade mineral deposits are assumed to be larger than under the central solution. Availability of larger high-grade deposits postpones the increases in extraction costs with cumulative output along the step functions. Thus, at any given time, an assumption of more generous resource endowments implies lower prices for resources and for commodities that use resources as direct or indirect inputs. Scaled prices based on the generous resource endowment are labelled "H".

TABLE 73. SECTORAL ALIGNMENT FOR PRICES

1. Livestock	23. Industrial chemicals
2. Oil-crops	24. Fertilizer
3. Grains	25. Miscellaneous chemicals
4. Root-crops	26. Petroleum-refining margins
5. Residual agriculture	27. Cement
6. Copper	28. Glass
7. Bauxite	29. Primary metal-processing
8. Nickel	margins
9. Zinc	30. Motor vehicles
10. Lead	31. Shipbuilding
11. Iron	32. Aircraft
12. Crude petroleum	33. Metal products
13. Natural gas	34. Machinery
14. Coal	35. Electric machinery
15. Mining	36. Scientific instruments
16. Food-processing margins	37. Watches, clocks
17. Textiles	38. Electricity, water
18. Wood and cork	39. Construction
19. Furniture	40. Trade
20. Paper	41. Transport
21. Publishing	42. Communication
22. Rubber	43. Services

TABLE 74. 1970 PRICE VECTOR ACTUALLY USED IN THE MODEL

Sector number	Value	Sector number	Value
1.	0.48848	23.	1.00000
2.	0.08900	24.	0.22100
3.	0.05000	25.	1.00000
4.	0.04100	26.	1.00000
5.	1.00000	27.	1.00000
6.	1.27238	28.	1.00000
7.	0.01422	29.	1.00000
8.	0.00382	30.	1.00000
9.	0.33780	31.	1.00000
10.	0.34441	32.	1.00000
11.	0.01802	33.	1.00000
12.	0.01704	34.	1.00000
13.	0.00453	35.	1.00000
14.	0.00698	36.	1.00000
15.	1.00000	37.	1.00000
16.	1.00000	38.	1.00000
17.	1.00000	39.	1.00000
18.	1.00000	40.	1.00000
19.	1.00000	41.	1.00000
20.	1.00000	42.	1.00000
21.	1.00000	43.	1.00000
22.	1.00000		

TABLE 75. SCALED PRICES (PROJECTED)

Sector number	1980	1990	2000	1990/H	2000/H
1.	0.4715846	0.5295061	0.5453332	0.5281837	0.5455642
2.	0.0868334	0.1055473	0.1117671	0.1051411	0.1118123
3.	0.0453746	0.0566079	0.0602279	0.5629880	0.0602604
4.	0.0375510	0.0425566	0.0442620	0.0424734	0.0442750
5.	0.8772329	0.9986162	1.0395646	0.9952492	1.0399174
6.	1.1050879	1.0923001	2.8421391	1.1110338	1.2390527
7.	0.0114891	0.0111874	0.0133492	0.0114022	0.0133609
8.	0.0031274	0.0042938	0.0071451	0.0043325	0.0042946
9.	0.2750834	0.3619504	0.6352571	0.3669327	0.6351027
10.	0.2691138	0.2620593	0.5969119	0.2670918	0.3232007
11.	0.0146771	0.0147815	0.0147724	0.0148711	0.0147924
12.	0.0216991	0.0472089	0.0532312	0.0278083	0.0531880
13.	0.0063502	0.0224777	0.0312232	0.0224534	0.0312038
14.	0.0055782	0.0051086	0.0050595	0.0051855	0.0050615
15.	1.0074278	0.9986765	1.0067435	0.9975552	1.0071116
16.	0.9992462	0.9445345	0.9307430	0.9561735	0.9315816
17.	1.0096960	0.9376241	0.9272148	0.9561967	0.9287697
18.	1.0929318	1.0337282	1.0229519	1.0509006	1.0243069
19.	0.9832604	0.9032276	0.8936343	0.9215217	0.8948109
20.	1.0301242	1.0131584	1.0031029	1.0206484	1.0045383
21.	0.9500254	0.8520805	0.8418933	0.8715975	0.8432532
22.	0.9871731	0.9418864	0.9347672	0.9514013	0.9354331
23.	0.9339276	0.9440165	0.9685875	0.9264448	0.9669437
24.	0.2172055	0.2298784	0.2384396	0.2167759	0.2383829
25.	1.0010214	0.9852384	0.9839447	0.9772471	0.9824860
26.	1.0880460	1.2827419	1.3549678	1.1438156	1.3524839
27.	1.0670523	1.2232508	1.2832669	1.2038879	1.2843502
28.	0.9377331	0.9010825	0.9092962	0.9065813	0.9101426
29.	1.0546318	1.0486861	1.0459825	1.0637076	1.0467682
30.	1.0113723	0.9640184	0.9510717	0.9838466	0.9443461
31.	0.9387604	0.8194656	0.7974871	0.8380671	0.7911729
32.	0.9769343	0.8899747	0.8876152	0.9199070	0.8821940
33.	1.0684172	1.0320851	1.0342894	1.0557805	1.0244944
34.	0.9527988	0.8686999	0.8644319	0.8874994	0.8564546
35.	0.9829555	0.8944727	0.9241938	0.9165773	0.8905787
36.	0.9269948	0.8174579	0.8121823	0.8362862	0.8104644
37.	0.9559097	0.8703210	0.8764019	0.8638885	0.8640103
38.	1.0489761	1.0196147	0.9502457	1.0170158	0.9507198
39.	1.0069287	0.9666024	0.9584614	0.9852380	0.9583886
40.	1.0225525	0.9883455	0.9776941	1.0072847	0.9794355
41.	0.9638541	0.9253741	0.9356127	0.8965181	0.9366090
42.	0.9706932	0.9020645	0.8962053	0.9124895	0.8969694
43.	1.0393891	1.0291504	1.0195703	1.0460086	1.0207281

Annex III

THE SECTORAL CLASSIFICATION SCHEME AND A DETAILED LIST OF VARIABLES

AB	Abatement	EE	Exports
CA	Calibration	EM	Emissions
CU	Cumulative resource use	FS	Fishing
DU	Dummy and constant variables	IN	Investment and capital

MA	Macro-economic variables
MM	Imports
MS	Imports slacks for resources

SE	Physicals: agriculture, resources
WW	World pools
XS	Output slacks
XX	Outputs

A. Column variables

Type of variable and variable symbol				Full name of variable	Unit of measurement
Level of abatement activities					
AB	1	ABATE	23.1	Air pollution control	T(M)
AB	2	ABATE	23.2	Primary water treatment	T(M)
AB	3	ABATE	23.3	Secondary water treatment	T(M)
AB	4	ABATE	23.4	Tertiary water treatment	T(M)
AB	5	ABATE	23.5	Solid waste disposal	T(M)
Abatement equations slacks					
AB	6	ABSLK	93.1	Air pollution control	T(M)
AB	7	ABSLK	93.2	Primary water treatment	T(M)
AB	8	ABSLK	93.3	Secondary water treatment	T(M)
AB	9	ABSLK	93.4	Tertiary water treatment	T(M)
AB	10	ABSLK	93.5	Solid waste disposal	T(M)
Calibration slack for resources (shortage)					
CA	1	RSSLK	86.1	Copper	T(M)
CA	2	RSSLK	86.2	Bauxite	T(M)
CA	3	RSSLK	86.3	Nickel	T(000s)
CA	4	RSSLK	86.4	Zinc	T(M)
CA	5	RSSLK	86.5	Lead	T(M)
CA	6	RSSLK	86.6	Iron	T(M)
CA	7	RSSLK	86.7	Petroleum	T(M coal equivalent)
CA	8	RSSLK	86.8	Natural gas	T(M coal equivalent)
CA	9	RSSLK	86.9	Coal	T(M coal equivalent)
Historical selected resource output					
CU	1	HRSS	90.1	Copper	T(M)
CU	2	HRSS	90.2	Bauxite	T(M)
CU	3	HRSS	90.3	Nickel	T(000s)
CU	4	HRSS	90.4	Zinc	T(M)
CU	5	HRSS	90.5	Lead	T(M)
CU	6	HRSS	90.6	Iron	T(M)
CU	7	HRSS	90.7	Petroleum	T(M coal equivalent)
CU	8	HRSS	90.8	Natural gas	T(M coal equivalent)
CU	9	HRSS	90.9	Coal	T(M coal equivalent)
Cumulative resource output at end of period					
CU	10	ECUMR	74.1	Copper	T(M)
CU	11	ECUMR	74.2	Bauxite	T(M)
CU	12	ECUMR	74.3	Nickel	T(000s)
CU	13	ECUMR	74.4	Zinc	T(M)
CU	14	ECUMR	74.5	Lead	T(M)
CU	15	ECUMR	74.6	Iron	T(M)
CU	16	ECUMR	74.7	Petroleum	T(M coal equivalent)
CU	17	ECUMR	74.8	Natural gas	T(M coal equivalent)
CU	18	ECUMR	74.9	Coal	T(M coal equivalent)
Cumulative resource output at start of period					
CU	19	SCUMR	75.1	Copper	T(M)
CU	20	SCUMR	75.2	Bauxite	T(M)
CU	21	SCUMR	75.3	Nickel	T(000s)
CU	22	SCUMR	75.4	Zinc	T(M)
CU	23	SCUMR	75.5	Lead	T(M)
CU	24	SCUMR	75.6	Iron	T(M)
CU	25	SCUMR	75.7	Petroleum	T(M coal equivalent)
CU	26	SCUMR	75.8	Natural gas	T(M coal equivalent)
CU	27	SCUMR	75.9	Coal	T(M coal equivalent)

Type of variable and variable symbol				Full name of variable	Unit of measurement
Dummy and constant variables					
DU	1	GMSUR	82.1	Grain substituted for meat	T(M)
DU	2	CONST	61.1	Constant vector	
Dummy variables					
DU	3	DUMA	62.1	Dummy	
DU	4	DUMA	62.2	Dummy	
DU	5	DUMMY	73.1	Dummy	
DU	6	DUMMY	73.2	Dummy	
Exports of selected agriculture					
EE	1	EAGS	50.1	Livestock	T(M)
EE	2	EAGS	50.2	Oil-crops	T(M)
EE	3	EAGS	50.3	Grains	T(M)
EE	4	EAGS	50.4	Roots	T(M)
EE	5	EAGR	51.1	Exports of residual agriculture	$(B)
Exports of selected resources					
EE	6	ERSS	52.1	Copper	T(M)
EE	7	ERSS	52.2	Bauxite	T(M)
EE	8	ERSS	52.3	Nickel	T(000s)
EE	9	ERSS	52.4	Zinc	T(M)
EE	10	ERSS	52.5	Lead	T(M)
EE	11	ERSS	52.6	Iron	T(M)
EE	12	ERSS	52.7	Petroleum	T(M coal equivalent)
EE	13	ERSS	52.8	Natural gas	T(M coal equivalent)
EE	14	ERSS	52.9	Coal	T(M coal equivalent)
EE	15	ERSR	53.1	Exports of residual resources	$(B)
EE	16	EAGM	54.1	Exports of agricultural margins	$(B)
Exports of resource margins					
EE	17	ERSM	55.1	Petroleum refining	$(B)
EE	18	ERSM	55.2	Primary metal processing	$(B)
Exports of traded goods					
EE	19	EXT	56.1	Textiles, apparel	$(B)
EE	20	EXT	56.2	Wood and cork	$(B)
EE	21	EXT	56.3	Furniture, fixtures	$(B)
EE	22	EXT	56.4	Paper	$(B)
EE	23	EXT	56.5	Printing	$(B)
EE	24	EXT	56.6	Rubber	$(B)
EE	25	EXT	56.7	Industrial chemicals	$(B)
EE	26	EXT	56.8	Fertilizer	T(M)
EE	27	EXT	56.9	Miscellaneous chemical products	$(B)
EE	28	EXT	56.10	Cement	$(B)
EE	29	EXT	56.11	Glass	$(B)
EE	30	EXT	56.12	Motor vehicles	$(B)
EE	31	EXT	56.13	Shipbuilding	$(B)
EE	32	EXT	56.14	Aircraft	$(B)
EE	33	EXT	56.15	Metal products	$(B)
EE	34	EXT	56.16	Machinery	$(B)
EE	35	EXT	56.17	Electric machinery	$(B)
EE	36	EXT	56.18	Professional instruments	$(B)
EE	37	EXT	56.19	Watches, clocks	$(B)
EE	38	ESER	57.1	Exports of services	$(B)
EE	39	ETR	80.1	Exports of transport	$(B)
EE	40	EAID	59.1	Aid (inflow)	$(B)
EE	41	ESLK	60.1	Export slack	$(B)
EE	42	ECAP	58.1	Foreign capital (inflow)	$(B)
Net emissions of abatable pollutants					
EM	1	EMA	12.1	Pesticides	T(M)
EM	2	EMA	12.2	Particulates	T(M)
EM	3	EMA	12.3	Biological oxygen demand	T(M)
EM	4	EMA	12.4	Nitrogen water pollution	T(M)
EM	5	EMA	12.5	Phosphates	T(M)
EM	6	EMA	12.6	Suspended solids	T(M)
EM	7	EMA	12.7	Dissolved solids	T(M)
EM	8	EMA	12.8	Solid waste	T(M)
Net total emissions					
EM	9	EMTOT	13.1	Pesticides	T(M)
EM	10	EMTOT	13.2	Particulates	T(M)
EM	11	EMTOT	13.3	Biological oxygen demand	T(M)

Type of variable and variable symbol			Full name of variable	Unit of measurement
EM	12 EMTOT	13.4	Nitrogen water pollution	T (M)
EM	13 EMTOT	13.5	Phosphates	T (M)
EM	14 EMTOT	13.6	Suspended solids	T (M)
EM	15 EMTOT	13.7	Dissolved solids	T (M)
EM	16 EMTOT	13.8	Solid waste	T (M)
Fishing variables				
FS	1 XFISH	76.1	Fish catch	T (M)
FS	2 NFISH	94.1	Non-human consumption of fish	T (M)
FS	3 MFISH	77.1	Fish imports	T (M)
FS	4 EFISH	78.1	Fish exports	T (M)
Investment and capital variables				
IN	1 IEQP	26.1	Equipment investment	$ (B)
IN	2 IPLT	25.1	Plant investment	$ (B)
IN	3 INVCH	96.1	Inventory change investment	$ (B)
IN	4 IIRR	27.1	Irrigation investment	H (M)
IN	5 ILAND	28.1	Land development	H (M)
IN	6 SEQP	30.1	Equipment capital stock	$ (B)
IN	7 SPLT	29.1	Plant capital stock	$ (B)
IN	8 SINVY	95.1	Inventory stocks	$ (B)
IN	9 SFAS	31.1	Stock of foreign assets	$ (B)
IN	10 SLAND	33.1	Cultivated land area	H (M)
IN	11 HEQP	35.1	Historical equipment capital stock	$ (B)
IN	12 HPLT	34.1	Historical plant capital stock	$ (B)
IN	13 HINVY	97.1	Historical inventory stock	$ (B)
IN	14 HFAS	36.1	Historical stock of foreign assets	$ (B)
IN	15 HRFAS	91.1	Historical net inward capital flow	$ (B)
IN	16 INICF	92.1	1970 net foreign investment income	$ (B)
Macro-economic variables				
MA	1 GDP	1.1	Gross domestic product	$ (B)
MA	2 CONS	2.1	Consumption level	$ (B)
MA	3 DSAVE	8.1	Excess savings potential	$ (B)
MA	4 INV	3.1	Investment level	$ (B)
MA	5 GOV	4.1	Government expenditures	$ (B)
MA	6 BAL	5.1	Balance of payments	$ (B)
MA	7 IMPRT	6.1	Total imports	$ (B)
MA	8 EXPRT	7.1	Total exports	$ (B)
MA	9 POP	8.1	Population	(M)
MA	10 URBAN	9.1	Urban population	(M)
MA	11 LABOR	10.1	Employment	MY (M)
Consumption of food nutrition units				
MA	12 NUTRN	11.1	Calories	(KCAL/DAY) (B)
MA	13 NUTRN	11.2	Proteins	(GRAMS/DAY)
Imports of selected agriculture				
MM	1 MAGS	39.1	Livestock	T (M)
MM	2 MAGS	39.2	Oil-crops	T (M)
MM	3 MAGS	39.3	Grains	T (M)
MM	4 MAGS	39.4	Roots	T (M)
MM	5 MAGR	40.1	Imports of residual agriculture	$ (B)
Imports of selected resources				
MM	6 MRSS	41.1	Copper	T (M)
MM	7 MRSS	41.2	Bauxite	T (M)
MM	8 MRSS	41.3	Nickel	T (000s)
MM	9 MRSS	41.4	Zinc	T (M)
MM	10 MRSS	41.5	Lead	T (M)
MM	11 MRSS	41.6	Iron	T (M)
MM	12 MRSS	41.7	Petroleum	T (M coal equivalent)
MM	13 MRSS	41.8	Natural gas	T (M coal equivalent)
Imports of selected resources				
MM	14 MRSS	41.9	Coal	T (M coal equivalent)
MM	15 MRSR	42.1	Imports of residual resources	$ (B)
MM	16 MAGM	43.1	Imports of agricultural margins	$ (B)
Imports of resource margins				
MM	17 MRSM	44.1	Petroleum refining	$ (B)
MM	18 MRSM	44.2	Primary metal processing	$ (B)
Imports of traded goods				
MM	19 MXT	45.1	Textiles, apparel	$ (B)
MM	20 MXT	45.2	Wood and cork	$ (B)

Type of variable and variable symbol			Full name of variable	Unit of measurement
MM	21 MXT	45.3	Furniture, fixtures	$(B)
MM	22 MXT	45.4	Paper	$(B)
MM	23 MXT	45.5	Printing	$(B)
MM	24 MXT	45.6	Rubber	$(B)
MM	25 MXT	45.7	Industrial chemicals	$(B)
MM	26 MXT	45.8	Fertilizer	T(M)
MM	27 MXT	45.9	Miscellaneous chemical products	$(B)
MM	28 MXT	45.10	Cement	$(B)
MM	29 MXT	45.11	Glass	$(B)
MM	30 MXT	45.12	Motor vehicles	$(B)
MM	31 MXT	45.13	Shipbuilding	$(B)
MM	32 MXT	45.14	Aircraft	$(B)
MM	33 MXT	45.15	Metal products	$(B)
MM	34 MXT	45.16	Machinery	$(B)
MM	35 MXT	45.17	Electric machinery	$(B)
MM	36 MXT	45.18	Professional instruments	$(B)
MM	37 MXT	45.19	Watches, clocks	$(B)
MM	38 MSER	46.1	Imports of service	$(B)
MM	39 MTR	79.1	Imports of transport	$(B)
MM	40 MAID	48.1	Aid (inflow)	$(B)
MM	41 MSLK	49.1	Import slack	$(B)
MM	42 MCAP	47.1	Foreign capital (outflow)	$(B)

Resource import slacks

MS	1 MRSLK	99.1	Copper	T(M)
MS	2 MRSLK	99.2	Bauxite	T(M)
MS	3 MRSLK	99.3	Nickel	T(000s)
MS	4 MRSLK	99.4	Zinc	T(M)
MS	5 MRSLK	99.5	Lead	T(M)
MS	6 MRSLK	99.6	Iron	T(M)
MS	7 MRSLK	99.7	Petroleum	T(M coal equivalent)
MS	8 MRSLK	99.8	Natural gas	T(M coal equivalent)
MS	9 MRSLK	99.9	Coal	T(M coal equivalent)

Selected agricultural activities

SE	1 AGS	14.1	Livestock	T(M)
SE	2 AGS	14.2	Oil-crops	T(M)
SE	3 AGS	14.3	Grains	T(M)
SE	4 AGS	14.4	Roots	T(M)

Selected resource activities

SE	5 RSS	16.1	Copper	T(M)
SE	6 RSS	16.2	Bauxite	T(M)
SE	7 RSS	16.3	Nickel	T(000s)
SE	8 RSS	16.4	Zinc	T(M)
SE	9 RSS	16.5	Lead	T(M)
SE	10 RSS	16.6	Iron	T(M)
SE	11 RSS	16.7	Petroleum	T(M coal equivalent)
SE	12 RSS	16.8	Natural gas	T(M coal equivalent)
SE	13 RSS	16.9	Coal	T(M coal equivalent)

Export pool of selected agriculture

WW	1 PAGS	63.1	Livestock	T(M)
WW	2 PAGS	63.2	Oil-crops	T(M)
WW	3 PAGS	63.3	Grains	T(M)
WW	4 PAGS	63.4	Roots	T(M)
WW	5 PAGR	64.1	Export pool of residual agriculture	$(B)

Export pool of selected resources

WW	6 PRSS	65.1	Copper	T(M)
WW	7 PRSS	65.2	Bauxite	T(M)
WW	8 PRSS	65.3	Nickel	T(000s)
WW	9 PRSS	65.4	Zinc	T(M)
WW	10 PRSS	65.5	Lead	T(M)
WW	11 PRSS	65.6	Iron	T(M)
WW	12 PRSS	65.7	Petroleum	T(M coal equivalent)
WW	13 PRSS	65.8	Natural gas	T(M coal equivalent)
WW	14 PRSS	65.9	Coal	T(M coal equivalent)
WW	15 PRSR	66.1	Export pool of residual resources	$(B)
WW	16 PAGM	67.1	Export pools of agricultural margins	$(B)

Export pool of resource margins

WW	17 PRSM	68.1	Petroleum refining	$(B)
WW	18 PRSM	68.2	Primary metal processing	$(B)

Type of variable and variable symbol			Full name of variable	Unit of measurement
Export pool of traded goods				
WW	19 PXT	69.1	Textiles, apparel	$(B)
WW	20 PXT	69.2	Wood and cork	$(B)
WW	21 PXT	69.3	Furniture, fixtures	$(B)
WW	22 PXT	69.4	Paper	$(B)
WW	23 PXT	69.5	Printing	$(B)
WW	24 PXT	69.6	Rubber	$(B)
WW	25 PXT	69.7	Industrial chemicals	$(B)
WW	26 PXT	69.8	Fertilizer	T(M)
WW	27 PXT	69.9	Miscellaneous chemical products	$(B)
WW	28 PXT	69.10	Cement	$(B)
WW	29 PXT	69.11	Glass	$(B)
WW	30 PXT	69.12	Motor vehicles	$(B)
WW	31 PXT	69.13	Shipbuilding	$(B)
WW	32 PXT	69.14	Aircraft	$(B)
WW	33 PXT	69.15	Metal products	$(B)
WW	34 PXT	69.16	Machinery	$(B)
WW	35 PXT	69.17	Electric machinery	$(B)
WW	36 PXT	69.18	Professional instruments	$(B)
WW	37 PXT	69.19	Watches, clocks	$(B)
WW	38 PSER	70.1	Export pool of services	$(B)
WW	39 PTR	81.1	Export pool of transport	$(B)
WW	40 PAID	72.1	Pool of aid (inflow)	$(B)
WW	41 PCAP	71.1	Pool of foreign capital (inflow)	$(B)
Output slacks				
XS	1 XSLK	98.1	Primary metal	$(B)
XS	2 XSLK	98.2	Rubber	$(B)
XS	3 XSLK	98.3	Fertilizer	T(M)
XS	4 XSLK	98.4	Cement	$(B)
XS	5 XSLK	98.5	Motor vehicles	$(B)
XS	6 XSLK	98.6	Aircraft	$(B)
XS	7 XSLK	98.7	Machinery	$(B)
XS	8 XSLK	98.8	Electric machinery	$(B)
Output variables				
XX	1 AGR	17.1	Residual agriculture	$(B)
XX	2 RSR	18.1	Residual resource activities	$(B)
XX	3 AGM	19.1	Agricultural margins (food)	$(B)
Resource margins (refining)				
XX	4 RSM	20.1	Petroleum refining	$(B)
XX	5 RSM	20.2	Primary metal processing	$(B)
Output of traded commodities				
XX	6 XT	21.1	Textiles, apparel	$(B)
XX	7 XT	21.2	Wood and cork	$(B)
XX	8 XT	21.3	Furniture, fixtures	$(B)
XX	9 XT	21.4	Paper	$(B)
XX	10 XT	21.5	Printing	$(B)
XX	11 XT	21.6	Rubber	$(B)
XX	12 XT	21.7	Industrial chemicals	$(B)
XX	13 XT	21.8	Fertilizer	T(M)
XX	14 XT	21.9	Miscellaneous chemical products	$(B)
XX	15 XT	21.10	Cement	$(B)
XX	16 XT	21.11	Glass	$(B)
XX	17 XT	21.12	Motor vehicles	$(B)
XX	18 XT	21.13	Shipbuilding	$(B)
XX	19 XT	21.14	Aircraft	$(B)
XX	20 XT	21.15	Metal products	$(B)
XX	21 XT	21.16	Machinery	$(B)
XX	22 XT	21.17	Electric machinery	$(B)
XX	23 XT	21.18	Professional instruments	$(B)
XX	24 XT	21.19	Watches, clocks	$(B)
Output of non-traded commodities				
XX	25 XNT	22.1	Electricity, water	$(B)
XX	26 XNT	22.2	Construction	$(B)
XX	27 XNT	22.3	Trade	$(B)
XX	28 XNT	22.4	Transport	$(B)
XX	29 XNT	22.5	Communication	$(B)
XX	30 XNT	22.6	Services	$(B)

Type of variable and variable symbol				Full name of variable	Unit of measurement

Cumulative resource output at end of period

CU	1	ECUMR	50.1	Copper	T (M)
CU	2	ECUMR	50.2	Bauxite	T (M)
CU	3	ECUMR	50.3	Nickel	T (000s)
CU	4	ECUMR	50.4	Zinc	T (M)
CU	5	ECUMR	50.5	Lead	T (M)
CU	6	ECUMR	50.6	Iron	T (M)
CU	7	ECUMR	50.7	Petroleum	T (M coal equivalent)
CU	8	ECUMR	50.8	Natural gas	T (M coal equivalent)
CU	9	ECUMR	50.9	Coal	T (M coal equivalent)

Dummy variables

DU	1	DUMMY	49.1	Dummy	
DU	2	DUMMY	49.2	Dummy	

Exports of selected agriculture

EE	1	EAGS	39.1	Meat and fish	T (M)
EE	2	EAGS	39.2	Oil-crops	T (M)
EE	3	EAGS	39.3	Grains	T (M)
EE	4	EAGS	39.4	Roots	T (M)
EE	5	EAGR	40.1	Exports of residual agriculture	$ (B)

Exports of selected resources

EE	6	ERSS	41.1	Copper	T (M)
EE	7	ERSS	41.2	Bauxite	T (M)
EE	8	ERSS	41.3	Nickel	T (000s)
EE	9	ERSS	41.4	Zinc	T (M)
EE	10	ERSS	41.5	Lead	T (M)
EE	11	ERSS	41.6	Iron	T (M)
EE	12	ERSS	41.7	Petroleum	T (M coal equivalent)
EE	13	ERSS	41.8	Natural gas	T (M coal equivalent)
EE	14	ERSS	41.9	Coal	T (M coal equivalent)
EE	15	ERSR	42.1	Exports of residual resources	$ (B)
EE	16	EAGM	43.1	Exports of agricultural margins	$ (B)

Exports of resource margins

EE	17	ERSM	44.1	Petroleum refining	$ (B)
EE	18	ERSM	44.2	Primary metal processing	$ (B)

Exports of traded goods

EE	19	EXT	45.1	Textiles, apparel	$ (B)
EE	20	EXT	45.2	Wood and cork	$ (B)
EE	21	EXT	45.3	Furniture, fixtures	$ (B)
EE	22	EXT	45.4	Paper	$ (B)
EE	23	EXT	45.5	Printing	$ (B)
EE	24	EXT	45.6	Rubber	$ (B)
EE	25	EXT	45.7	Industrial chemicals	$ (B)
EE	26	EXT	45.8	Fertilizer	T (M)
EE	27	EXT	45.9	Miscellaneous chemical products	$ (B)
EE	28	EXT	45.10	Cement	$ (B)
EE	29	EXT	45.11	Glass	$ (B)
EE	30	EXT	45.12	Motor vehicles	$ (B)
EE	31	EXT	45.13	Shipbuilding	$ (B)
EE	32	EXT	45.14	Aircraft	$ (B)
EE	33	EXT	45.15	Metal products	$ (B)
EE	34	EXT	45.16	Machinery	$ (B)
EE	35	EXT	45.17	Electric machinery	$ (B)
EE	36	EXT	45.18	Professional instruments	$ (B)
EE	37	EXT	45.19	Watches, clocks	$ (B)
EE	38	ESER	46.1	Exports of services	$ (B)
EE	39	ETR	52.1	Exports of transport	$ (B)
EE	40	EAID	48.1	Aid (inflow)	$ (B)
EE	41	ECAP	47.1	Foreign capital (inflow)	$ (B)

Emissions of abatable pollutants

EM	1	EMA	10.1	Pesticides	T (M)
EM	2	EMA	10.2	Particulates	T (M)
EM	3	EMA	10.3	Biological oxygen demand	T (M)
EM	4	EMA	10.4	Nitrogen water pollution	T (M)
EM	5	EMA	10.5	Phosphates	T (M)
EM	6	EMA	10.6	Suspended solids	T (M)
EM	7	EMA	10.7	Dissolved solids	T (M)
EM	8	EMA	10.8	Solid waste	T (M)

Type of variable and variable symbol			Full name of variable	Unit of measurement

Emissions of non-abatable pollutants

EM	9 EMNA	11.1	Pesticides	T (M)
EM	10 EMNA	11.2	Particulates	T (M)
EM	11 EMNA	11.3	Biological oxygen demand	T (M)
EM	12 EMNA	11.4	Nitrogen water pollution	T (M)
EM	13 EMNA	11.5	Phosphates	T (M)
EM	14 EMNA	11.6	Suspended solids	T (M)
EM	15 EMNA	11.7	Dissolved solids	T (M)
EM	16 EMNA	11.8	Solid waste	T (M)

Abatement determination

EM	17 ABDET	53.1	Air pollution control	T (M)
EM	18 ABDET	53.2	Primary water treatment	T (M)
EM	19 ABDET	53.3	Secondary water treatment	T (M)
EM	20 ABDET	53.4	Tertiary water treatment	T (M)
EM	21 ABDET	53.5	Solid waste disposal	T (M)

Investment and capital variables

IN	1 IEQP	21.1	Equipment investment	$ (B)
IN	2 IPLT	20.1	Plant investment	$ (B)
IN	3 INVCH	55.1	Inventory change investment equation	$ (B)
IN	4 SEQP	25.1	Equipment capital stock	$ (B)
IN	5 SPLT	24.1	Plant capital stock	$ (B)
IN	6 SINVY	54.1	Inventory stock equation	$ (B)
IN	7 SFAS	26.1	Stock of foreign assets	$ (B)
IN	8 SLAND	28.1	Cultivated land area	H (M)

Macro-economic variables

MA	1 GDP	1.1	Gross domestic product	$ (B)
MA	2 SAVE	2.1	Savings equation	$ (B)
MA	3 INV	3.1	Investment equation	$ (B)
MA	4 GOV	4.1	Government expenditures	$ (B)
MA	5 BAL	5.1	Balance of payments	$ (B)
MA	6 IMPRT	6.1	Total imports	$ (B)
MA	7 EXPRT	7.1	Total exports	$ (B)
MA	8 LABOR	8.1	Employment	MY (B)

Consumption of food nutrition

MA	9 NUTRN	9.1	Calories	(KCAL/DAY) (B)
MA	10 NUTRN	9.2	Proteins	(GRAMS/DAY)

Imports of selected agriculture

MM	1 MAGS	29.1	Meat and fish	T (M)
MM	2 MAGS	29.2	Oil-crops	T (M)
MM	3 MAGS	29.3	Grains	T (M)
MM	4 MAGS	29.4	Roots	T (M)
MM	5 MAGR	30.1	Imports of residual agriculture	$ (B)

Imports of selected resources

MM	6 MRSS	31.1	Copper	T (M)
MM	7 MRSS	31.2	Bauxite	T (M)
MM	8 MRSS	31.3	Nickel	T (000s)
MM	9 MRSS	31.4	Zinc	T (M)
MM	10 MRSS	31.5	Lead	T (M)
MM	11 MRSS	31.6	Iron	T (M)
MM	12 MRSS	31.7	Petroleum	T (M coal equivalent)
MM	13 MRSS	31.8	Natural gas	T (M coal equivalent)
MM	14 MRSS	31.9	Coal	T (M coal equivalent)
MM	15 MRSR	32.1	Imports of residual resources	$ (B)
MM	16 MAGM	33.1	Imports of agricultural margins	$ (B)

Imports of resource margins

MM	17 MRSM	34.1	Petroleum refining	$ (B)
MM	18 MRSM	34.2	Primary metal processing	$ (B)

Imports of traded goods

MM	19 MXT	35.1	Textiles, apparel	$ (B)
MM	20 MXT	35.2	Wood and cork	$ (B)
MM	21 MXT	35.3	Furniture, fixtures	$ (B)
MM	22 MXT	35.4	Paper	$ (B)
MM	23 MXT	35.5	Printing	$ (B)
MM	24 MXT	35.6	Rubber	$ (B)
MM	25 MXT	35.7	Industrial chemicals	$ (B)
MM	26 MXT	35.8	Fertilizer	T (M)
MM	27 MXT	35.9	Miscellaneous chemical products	$ (B)

Type of variable and variable symbol			Full name of variable	Unit of measurement
Imports of traded goods				
MM 28 MXT		35.10	Cement	$(B)
MM 29 MXT		35.11	Glass	$(B)
MM 30 MXT		35.12	Motor vehicles	$(B)
MM 31 MXT		35.13	Shipbuilding	$(B)
MM 32 MXT		35.14	Aircraft	$(B)
MM 33 MXT		35.15	Metal products	$(B)
MM 34 MXT		35.16	Machinery	$(B)
MM 35 MXT		35.17	Electric machinery	$(B)
MM 36 MXT		35.18	Professional instruments	$(B)
MM 37 MXT		35.19	Watches, clocks	$(B)
MM 38 MSER		36.1	Imports of services	$(B)
MM 39 MTR		51.1	Imports of transport	$(B)
MM 40 MAID		38.1	Aid (outflow)	$(B)
MM 41 MCAP		37.1	Foreign capital (outflow)	$(B)
Selected agricultural commodity				
SE 1 AGS		12.1	Meat and fish	T(M)
SE 2 AGS		12.2	Oil-crops	T(M)
SE 3 AGS		12.3	Grains	T(M)
SE 4 AGS		12.4	Roots	T(M)
Selected resources commodity balance				
SE 5 RSS		13.1	Copper	T(M)
SE 6 RSS		13.2	Bauxite	T(M)
SE 7 RSS		13.3	Nickel	T(000s)
SE 8 RSS		13.4	Zinc	T(M)
SE 9 RSS		13.5	Lead	T(M)
SE 10 RSS		13.6	Iron	T(M)
SE 11 RSS		13.7	Petroleum	T(M coal equivalent)
SE 12 RSS		13.8	Natural gas	T(M coal equivalent)
SE 13 RSS		13.9	Coal	T(M coal equivalent)
Output variables				
XX 1 AGR		14.1	Residual agriculture	$(B)
XX 2 RSR		15.1	Residual resource commodity balance	$(B)
XX 3 AGM		16.1	Agricultural margins (food)	$(B)
Resource margins (*refining*)				
XX 4 RSM		17.1	Petroleum refining	$(B)
XX 5 RSM		17.2	Primary metal processing	$(B)
Output of traded commodities				
XX 6 XT		18.1	Textiles, apparel	$(B)
XX 7 XT		18.2	Wood and cork	$(B)
XX 8 XT		18.3	Furniture, fixtures	$(B)
XX 9 XT		18.4	Paper	$(B)
XX 10 XT		18.5	Printing	$(B)
XX 11 XT		18.6	Rubber	$(B)
XX 12 XT		18.7	Industrial chemicals	$(B)
XX 13 XT		18.8	Fertilizer	T(M)
XX 14 XT		18.9	Miscellaneous chemical products	$(B)
XX 15 XT		18.10	Cement	$(B)
XX 16 XT		18.11	Glass	$(B)
XX 17 XT		18.12	Motor vehicles	$(B)
XX 18 XT		18.13	Shipbuilding	$(B)
XX 19 XT		18.14	Aircraft	$(B)
XX 20 XT		18.15	Metal products	$(B)
XX 21 XT		18.16	Machinery	$(B)
XX 22 XT		18.17	Electric machinery	$(B)
XX 23 XT		18.18	Professional instruments	$(B)
XX 24 XT		18.19	Watches, clocks	$(B)
Output of non-traded commodities				
XX 25 XNT		19.1	Electricity, water	$(B)
XX 26 XNT		19.2	Construction	$(B)
XX 27 XNT		19.3	Trade	$(B)
XX 28 XNT		19.4	Transport	$(B)
XX 29 XNT		19.5	Communication	$(B)
XX 30 XNT		19.6	Services	$(B)

THE MODEL IN CONVENTIONAL EQUATION FORM

Equations[a]

1: Gross domestic product
$$M * GNP = CONS + INV + GOV - IMPRT + EXPRT + P * URBAN + P * ABATE + INVCH.$$

2: Savings
$$DSAVE = \% * GNP - P * INV - P * INVCH - MAID + EAID + ECAP - MCAP.$$

3: Investment
$$INV = IEQP + IPLT + P * IIRR + P * ILAND.$$

4: Government expenditures
$$GOV = \% * GNP$$

5: Total imports
$$IMPRT = P * MFISH + P * MAGS + MAGR + P * MRSS + MRSR + MAGM + MRSM + P * MXT + MSER + MTR.$$

6: Total exports
$$EXPRT = P * EFISH + P * EAGS + EAGR + P * ERSS + ERSR + EAGM + ERSM + P * EXT + ESER + ETR.$$

7: Balance of payments
$$BAL = P * MFISH + P * EFISH + M * SFAS + INICF - P * MAGS - P * MAGR - P * MRSS - P * MRSR - P * MAGM - P * MXT - P * MSER - P * MTR - MAID + P * EAGS + P * EAGR + P * ERSS + P * ERSR + P * EAGM + P * ERSM + P * EXT + P * ESER + P * ETR + EAID + ECAP - MCAP.$$

8: Employment
$$LABOR = L * CONS + L * GOV + L * POP + L * URABN + L * XFISH + L * AGS + L * RSS + L * AGR + L * RSR + L * AGM + L * RSM + L * XT + L * XNT + L * ABATE + L * IIRR + L * ILAND.$$

9-10: Consumption of food nutrient units
$$NUTRN = M * CONS + M * POP.$$

11-15: Abatement determination
$$ABSLK = -M * ABATE.$$

16-23: Emissions of abatable pollutants
$$EMA = E * CONS + E * POP + E * URBAN + E * AGS + E * RSS + E * AGR + E * RSR + E * AGM + E * RSM + E * XT + E * XNT - M * ABATE.$$

24-31: Emissions of non-abatable pollutants
$$EMTOT = EMA + E * ABATE.$$

32-35: Selected agricultural commodity balance
$$AGS = -C * CONS - C * GOV - C * POP - U * URBAN + M * XFISH - M * NFISH + M * MFISH - M * EFISH + (I + @) * AGS + M * GMSUB + @ * RSS + @ * AGR + @ * RSR + @ * AGM + @ * RSM + @ * XT + @ * XNT$$

[a] See key to coefficient symbols, p. 84.

$$+ @ * ABATE - S * IEQP - S * IPLT - S * INVCH - S * IIRR - S * ILAND + MAGS - EAGS.$$

36: Residual agriculture
$$AGR = -C * CONS - C * GOV - C * POP - U * URBAN + @ * XFISH + @ * AGS + @ * RSS + (I + @) * AGR + @ * RSR + @ * AGM + @ * RSM + @ * XT + @ * XNT + @ * ABATE - S * IEQP - S * IPLT - S * INVCH - S * IIRR - S * ILAND + MAGR - EAGR.$$

37-45: Selected resource commodity balance
$$RSS = -C * CONS - C * GOV - C * POP - U * URBAN + @ * XFISH + @ * AGS + (I + @) * RSS + @ * AGR + @ * RSR + @ * AGM + @ * RSM + @ * XT + @ * XNT + @ * ABATE - S * IEQP - S * IPLT - S * INVCH - S * IIRR - S * ILAND + MRSS - ERSS.$$

46: Residual resource commodity balance
$$RSR = -C * CONS - C * GOV - C * POP - U * URBAN + @ * XFISH + @ * AGS + @ * RSS + @ * AGR + (I + @) * RSR + @ * AGM + @ * RSM + @ * XT + @ * XNT + @ * ABATE - S * IEQP - S * IPLT - S * INVCH - S * IIRR - S * ILAND + MRSR - ERSR.$$

47: Agricultural margins (food)
$$AGM = -C * CONS - C * GOV - C * POP - U * URBAN + @ * XFISH + @ * AGS + @ * RSS + @ * AGR + @ * RSR + (I + @) * AGM + @ * RSM + @ * XT + @ * XNT + @ * ABATE - S * IEQP - S * IPLT - S * INVCH - S * IIRR - S * ILAND + MAGM - EAGM.$$

48-49: Resource margins (refining)
$$RSM = -C * CONS - C * GOV - C * POP - U * URBAN + @ * XFISH + @ * AGS + @ * RSS + @ * AGR + @ * RSR + @ * AGM + (I + @) * RSM + @ * XT + @ * XNT + @ * ABATE - S * IEQP - S * EPLT - S * INVCH - S * IIRR - S * ILAND + MRSM - ERSM.$$

50-68: Output of traded commodities
$$XT = -C * CONS - C * GOV - C * POP - U * URBAN + @ * XFISH + @ * AGS + @ * RSS + @ * AGR + @ * RSR + @ * AGM + @ * RSM + (I + @) * XT + @ * XNT + @ * ABATE - S * IEQP - S * IPLT - S * INVCH - S * IIRR - S * ILAND + MXT - EXT.$$

69-74: Output of non-traded commodities
$$XNT = -C * CONS - C * GOV - C * POP - U * URBAN + @ * XFISH + @ * AGS + @ * RSS + @ * AGR + @ * RSR + @ * AGM + @ * RSM + @ * XT + (I + @) * XNT + @ * ABATE - S * IEQP - S * IPLT - S * IIRR - S * ILAND + M * MSER - M * MTR - M * ESER - M * ETR.$$

75: Equipment investment
$$IEQP = G * SEQP + G * HEQP.$$

76: Plant investment
IPLT = G * SPLT + G * HPLT.

77: Inventory change investment
INVCH = G * SINVY + G * HINVY.

78-86: Cumulative resource output at end of period
ECUMR = G * RSS + G * HRSS + SCUMR.

87: Equipment capital stock
SEQP = K * URBAN + K * XFISH + K * AGS + K
* RSS + K * AGR + K * RSR + K * AGM + K
* RSM + K * XT + K * XNT + K * ABATE + K
* IIRR + K * ILAND.

88: Plant capital stock
SPLT = K * CONS + K * POP + K * URBAN + K
* XFISH + K * AGS + K * RSS + K * AGR + K
* RSR + K * AGM + K * RSM + K * XT + K
* XNT + K * ABATE + K * IIRR + K * ILAND.

89: Inventory stock
SINVY = K * AGS + K * RSS + K * AGR + K * RSR
+ K * AGM + K * RSM + K * XT.

90: Stock of foreign assets
SFAS = G * BAL − SFAS + HFAS + G * HRFAS − G
* ECAP + G * MCAP.

91: Cultivated land area
SLAND = K * AGS + K * AGR.

92-95: Imports of selected agriculture
MAGS = A * AGS * T * MSLK.

96: Imports of residual agriculture
MAGR = A * AGR + T * MSLK.

97-105: Imports of selected resources
MRSS = A * RSS + MRSLK + T * MSLK.

106: Imports of residual resources
MRSR = A * RSR + T * MSLK.

107: Imports of agricultural margins
MAGM = D * MFISH + D * MAGS + D * MAGR + T
* MSLK.

108-109: Imports of resource margins
MRSM = D * MRSS + D * MRSR + T * MSLK + M
* CONST.

110-128: Imports of traded goods
MXT = A * XT + T * MSLK.

129: Imports of services
MSER = M * GDP + T * MSLK.

130: Imports of transport
MTR = M * GDP + M * IMPRT + M * EXPRT.

131: Foreign aid (outflow)
MAID = M * GDP.

132-135: Exports of selected agriculture
EAGS = T * ESLK + B * PAGS.

136: Exports of residual agriculture
EAGR = T * ESLK + B * PAGR.

137-145: Exports of selected resources
ERSS = T * ESLK + B * PRSS.

146: Exports of residual resources
ERSR = T * ESLK + B * PRSR.

147: Exports of agricultural margins
EAGM = D * EFISH + D * EAGS + D * EAGR − T
* ESLK + B * PAGM.

148-149: Exports of resource margins
ERSM = D * ERSS + D * ERSR − T * ESLK + M
* CONST + B * PRSM.

150-168: Exports of traded goods
EXT = T * ESLK + B * PXT.

169: Exports of services
ESER = T * ESLK + B * PSER.

170: Exports of transport
ETR = B * PTR.

171: Foreign aid (inflow)
EAID = B * PAID.

172: Foreign capital (inflow)
ECAP = M * GDP.

173: Foreign capital (outflow)
MCAP = B * PCAP.

174-175: Dummy equations
DUMMY = DUMA.

Key to coefficient symbols

A	Import to output ratios	P	Prices
B	World export pool shares	S	Structure of investment
C	Consumption coefficients		demand
D	Margin trade to physical	T	Marginal trade composition
	units	U	Urban amenities input
E	Emissions coefficients		structure
G	Growth rate type	X	Exogenous data for
	parameters		calibration 1970
K	Capital coefficients	%	Ratio applicable to context
L	Labour coefficients	@	I-A input-output
M	Miscellaneous parameters		coefficient

84

Annex V

TECHNICAL NOTES ON SCENARIO M

Section 1: Formulation

(a) Changes in import coefficients

In the general formulation of the model the relation between the volume of import, M, of a particular good and the level of domestic output, O, of that good, is controlled by the import coefficient m:

$$(1) \qquad m = \frac{M}{0}$$

In the formulation of scenario M the shift in m is actually described in terms of the corresponding ratio, $\overline{m}$, the volume of imports to the total domestic supply—that is, to domestic output plus imports:

$$(2) \qquad \overline{m} = \frac{M}{M+0}$$

Substituting from (1) into (2)

$$(3) \qquad \overline{m} = \frac{m0}{m0+0} = \frac{m}{m+1}$$

If $\overline{m}$ has to be multiplied by $\overline{\delta}$, what is the magnitude of the corresponding multiplier, say δ, for m? From (3)

$$(4) \qquad \overline{\delta}\,\frac{m}{m+1} = \frac{\delta m}{\delta m+1} \quad \text{solving for } \delta,$$

$$(5) \qquad \delta = \frac{\overline{\delta}}{1+m(1-\overline{\delta})}$$

(b) Change in export shares

Let the given proportional share of the export of a particular good from a particular region out of total world exports of that good be e and the new desired share be ē. If e is multiplied by say λ, then if the share of all the other countries, that is, $1-e$, is left unchanged, the sum total of all shares would become $1-e+e\lambda = 1-e(1-\lambda)$. Thus, the true new proportional share, ē, of the commodity in question would be not $e\lambda$ but rather

$$(1) \qquad \frac{e\lambda}{1-e(1-\lambda)} = e\overline{\lambda}$$

To determine the magnitude of the multiplier λ that would change the actual export share from e to $e\overline{\lambda}$ the above equation has to be solved for λ, in terms of $\overline{\lambda}$:

$$(2) \qquad \lambda = \frac{1-e}{1/\overline{\lambda}-e}$$

Section 2: Changes in import ratios and the export shares of Latin America (medium-income), Asia (low-income) and arid Africa

The import ratios $\left(\dfrac{\text{import}}{\text{domestic output}+\text{import}}\right)$ of the commodity groups listed below—as used in scenario X—were multiplied by the same factor $\overline{\delta}$, the magnitude of which declined with time in accordance with the following formula:

$$\overline{\delta} = (0.99)^{t-70}$$

$$\overline{\delta}^{80} = 0.90, \qquad \overline{\delta}^{90} = 0.82, \qquad \overline{\delta}^{2000} = 0.74$$

Import ratios reduced for   Grouping

| 2 MM 19 | Textiles, apparel (3) | LI (Light Industry) |
| 3 MM 20 | Wood and cork (4) | Mater + Chem (Materials + Chemicals) |

4 MM 21	Furniture, fixtures (5)	
5 MM 22	Paper (6)	
6 MM 23	Printing (7)	LI
7 MM 24	Rubber (8)	

8 MM 25	Industrial chemicals (9)	
9 MM 26	Fertilizers (10)	
10 MM 27	Miscellaneous chemical products (11)	Mater + Chem
11 MM 28	Cement (13)	
12 MM 29	Glass (14)	

13 MM 30	Motor vehicles (16)	
14 MM 31	Shipbuilding (17)	
15 MM 32	Aircraft (18)	M/E (Machinery + equipment)
16 MM 33	Metal products (19)	
17 MM 34	Machinery (20)	
18 MM 35	Electrical machinery (21)	
19 MM 36	Scientific instruments (22)	

| 20 MM 37 | Watches, clocks (23) | LI |

The actual export shares of *agricultural products* were stepped up only for medium-income Latin America by 3 per cent per year. The export shares used in projection X were multiplied by a factor $\overline{\lambda}$ computed for the three successive time periods according to the following general formula:

$$\overline{\lambda}_{ag} = (1.03)^{t-70}$$

$$\overline{\lambda}_{ag}^{80} = 1.34, \qquad \overline{\lambda}_{ag}^{90} = 1.91, \qquad \overline{\lambda}_{ag}^{2000} = 2.43$$

The export share of other goods listed below were multiplied for all three regions by the following factor

$$\overline{\lambda}_{man} = (1.01)^{t-70}$$

$$\overline{\lambda}_{man}^{80} = 1.10, \qquad \overline{\lambda}_{man}^{90} = 1.22, \qquad \overline{\lambda}_{man}^{2000} = 1.35$$

Export shares increased

MM 1	Exports of livestock	
MM 2	Exports of oilcrops	
MM 3	Exports of grains	LAM *only* $= (1.03)^{t-70}$
MM 4	Exports of roots	
MM 5	Exports of residual agriculture	

MM 19	Export of textiles	
MM 21	Export of furniture and fixtures	
MM 22	Exports of paper	$= (1.01)^{t-70}$
MM 23	Exports of printing	
MM 37	Export of watches, clocks	

Section 3: Sector aggregation used in scenario M

1. Agriculture	Livestock, oilcrops, grains, roots and residual agriculture
2. Resources	Copper, bauxite, nickel, zinc, coal, lead, iron, petroleum, natural gas
3. Materials	Wood and cork, rubber, industrial chemicals, fertilizer, miscellaneous chemical products, cement, glass
4. Light industry	Furniture, fixtures, paper, printing, textiles and apparel, watches and clocks
5. Machinery and equipment	Motor vehicles, shipbuilding, aircraft, metal products, machinery, electrical machinery, professional instruments
6. Invisibles	Transport and services

85

NUMERICAL RESULTS

Scenario X (fifteen regions)

	NORTH AMERICA				LATIN AMERICA MEDIUM				LATIN AMERICA LOW				WESTERN EUROPE HIGH			
	1970	1980	1990	2000	1970	1980	1990	2000	1970	1980	1990	2000	1970	1980	1990	2000
CONSUMPTION AND POPULATION																
GDP	1059.5	1537.6	2073.9	2720.2	113.7	191.4	392.3	891.0	39.9	68.4	141.1	326.0	728.9	1049.3	1626.9	2165.9
PERSONAL CONSUM.	681.5	966.3	1277.2	1660.8	78.5	130.9	253.0	547.0	27.7	44.8	93.7	211.8	478.7	685.1	989.4	1260.7
GOVERNMENT EXPENSE	192.1	278.6	375.9	492.7	20.7	34.9	71.0	161.9	7.3	12.5	25.7	59.3	132.4	190.4	294.9	392.5
POPULATION	229.1	251.9	278.6	299.9	191.4	250.0	325.0	414.6	90.0	120.7	160.2	206.7	282.0	297.5	311.6	324.1
URBAN POPULATION	169.5	198.1	230.6	258.9	115.4	168.8	231.0	325.2	42.6	67.9	99.8	139.8	203.9	227.8	250.7	272.6
EMPLOYMENT	91.4	113.6	135.3	153.3	44.6	67.2	152.6	194.3	29.4	39.0	60.8	113.5	121.5	133.6	137.9	153.8
GDP/HEAD	4624	6104	7440	9070	594	765	1200	2149	443	566	880	1577	2584	3527	5221	6682
CONSUMPTION/HEAD	2974	3836	4584	5537	409	523	780	1319	307	371	584	1024	1697	2302	3175	3889
CALORIES/DAY/HEAD	3.2	3.2	3.2	3.2	2.4	2.4	2.6	3.0	2.2	2.3	2.5	2.9	3.0	3.2	3.2	3.2
PROTEINS/DAY/HEAD	96	98	99	100	60	63	71	86	50	53	60	74	91	98	103	105
INVESTMENT AND CAPITAL																
INVESTMENT	174.3	278.4	373.3	500.4	13.2	29.4	78.7	220.7	4.1	8.8	29.0	90.0	108.6	165.6	297.7	345.4
EQUIPMENT	70.3	93.9	132.5	163.0	6.3	13.7	35.0	100.4	2.0	4.2	12.6	39.3	50.9	63.7	112.2	137.1
PLANT	103.5	184.3	240.5	337.2	6.4	15.3	43.1	119.8	2.1	4.5	16.2	50.6	57.6	101.8	185.4	208.0
IRRIGATION (AREA)	0.4	0.1	0.1	0.1	0.1	0.1	0.1	0.1	0.1	0.1	0.1	0.1	0.0	0.0	0.0	0.0
LAND (AREA)	0.7	0.8	0.8	0.8	2.0	1.8	2.0	2.4	0.3	0.3	0.4	0.4	0.0	0.0	0.0	0.0
INVENTORY CHANGE	8.7	8.9	10.5	12.4	1.5	2.9	7.1	15.5	0.6	0.8	2.2	6.0	7.0	4.5	11.4	11.7
CAPITAL STOCK	2251.7	3565.1	5277.7	7543.2	155.3	294.9	669.6	1649.1	48.5	92.4	227.8	628.5	1345.7	2098.3	3499.3	5021.8
EQUIPMENT	659.0	949.7	1356.2	1802.4	67.0	123.1	269.7	653.7	21.1	40.5	92.8	242.2	472.5	662.0	1037.9	1443.3
PLANT	1592.6	2615.3	3921.5	5740.8	88.2	171.7	399.9	995.5	27.4	51.9	134.9	386.4	873.2	1436.3	2461.4	3578.5
INVENTORY STOCK	193.2	268.1	358.4	466.1	29.1	50.8	100.7	207.5	10.9	17.9	33.7	73.9	151.3	191.7	284.5	385.2
LAND/YIELD INDEX	100	122	165	213	100	155	298	516	100	147	255	460	100	100	130	162
SURPLUS SAVINGS	-24.1	-46.6	-56.8	-80.8	2.0	-1.6	-19.5	-73.0	1.7	2.6	-4.0	-27.8	29.4	42.3	8.4	62.7
INTERNATIONAL TRANSACTIONS																
IMPORTS	64.0	100.6	152.8	222.0	9.9	21.3	46.9	107.9	8.1	13.0	30.5	76.0	148.8	233.7	439.5	668.7
EXPORTS	65.0	102.7	186.1	272.5	9.4	14.3	25.9	52.5	8.3	14.5	20.9	34.6	148.7	234.7	470.2	821.6
PAYMENTS SURPLUS	-2.3	-9.9	22.4	97.3	-0.0	-10.1	-68.5	-242.8	0.5	3.6	16.2	10.6	-1.9	-1.0	-66.8	-18.0
FOR. INVESTMENTS	.3	-6	187	1066	-1	-54	-491	-2142	0	-9	72	91	0	7	-252	-424
FOR. INCOME	4.9	4.4	19.9	90.2	-1.3	-6.5	-40.7	-172.7	0	-0.6	4.5	6.1	4.2	4.8	-16.0	-29.7

LEVEL OF ABATEMENT ACTIVITIES

	NORTH AMERICA 1970	1980	1990	2000	LATIN AMERICA MEDIUM 1970	1980	1990	2000	LATIN AMERICA LOW 1970	1980	1990	2000	WESTERN EUROPE HIGH 1970	1980	1990	2000
AIR	35.6	57.3	70.2	98.2	0.8	1.0	2.4	7.9	0.0	0.00	0.00	1.15	11.2	17.8	23.8	26.0
PRIMARY WATER	5.61	8.30	11.71	12.39	0.04	0.35	0.75	3.87	0.00	0.00	0.00	0.54	3.18	6.45	11.90	14.84
SECONDARY WATER	0.32	0.47	0.67	0.71	0.00	0.02	0.04	0.22	0.00	0.00	0.00	0.03	0.18	0.37	0.68	2.35
TERTIARY WATER	0.07	0.21	0.15	0.15	0.00	0.01	0.01	0.05	0.00	0.00	0.00	0.01	0.04	0.16	0.15	0.51
SOLID WASTE	197.1	257.4	324.0	393.5	0.0	48.1	78.6	279.1	0.0	0.0	0.0	53.0	188.0	237.9	306.0	367.1

NET TOTAL EMISSIONS

	NORTH AMERICA 1970	1980	1990	2000	LATIN AMERICA MEDIUM 1970	1980	1990	2000	LATIN AMERICA LOW 1970	1980	1990	2000	WESTERN EUROPE HIGH 1970	1980	1990	2000
PESTICIDES	0.99	2.03	2.41	2.56	0.04	0.23	0.54	0.95	0.11	0.22	0.47	1.20	0.38	0.52	0.68	0.84
PARTICULATES	4.21	4.21	4.21	4.21	1.09	1.23	2.51	0.78	0.34	0.66	1.76	1.74	1.22	1.87	1.22	1.22
BIOLOGICAL OXYGEN	9.35	10.04	10.66	11.74	1.41	2.57	4.85	7.54	0.60	0.60	1.30	2.28	6.54	6.87	7.50	7.92
NITROGEN (WATER)	0.19	0.21	0.24	0.27	0.01	0.03	0.07	0.11	0.00	0.01	0.01	0.02	0.23	0.29	0.46	0.58
PHOSPHATES	0.12	0.15	0.15	0.22	0.01	0.03	0.05	0.08	0.00	0.03	0.01	0.02	0.13	0.17	0.24	0.30
SUSPENDED SOLIDS	6.82	6.82	6.82	6.82	0.76	1.25	2.68	4.86	0.19	0.43	0.87	1.90	3.84	3.84	3.84	3.84
DISSOLVED SOLIDS	41.79	50.98	59.31	64.71	3.69	11.75	23.08	36.98	0.71	1.38	2.97	6.48	33.22	41.65	63.06	76.82
SOLID WASTE	0.00	0.00	0.00	0.00	59.46	48.07	78.65	36.00	19.51	34.35	60.08	53.05	0.00	0.00	0.00	0.00

RESOURCE OUTPUTS

	NORTH AMERICA 1970	1980	1990	2000	LATIN AMERICA MEDIUM 1970	1980	1990	2000	LATIN AMERICA LOW 1970	1980	1990	2000	WESTERN EUROPE HIGH 1970	1980	1990	2000
COPPER	2.2	3.0	4.3	6.0	0.8	1.5	3.2	10.0	0.2	0.5	1.4	3.6	0.2	0.1	0.2	0.2
BAUXITE	0.4	0.5	0.5	0.6	0.17	0.69	1.9	3.5	4.6	8.7	14.1	1.5	0.7	0.7	0.8	1.0
NICKEL	291	402	566	364	37	535	194	727	1	7	16	76	0.5	0.6	0.0	4.5
ZINC	1.7	2.7	6.6	2.4	0.3	0.6	0.9	1.2	0.2	0.7	0.4	0.3	0.5	0.4	1.0	3.9
LEAD	0.9	1.5	10.6	2.00	0.28	44	136	268	20	19	57	192	49	130	56	140
IRON	73	115	178	236	28				283	433	706	1026	211	211	21	612
PETROLEUM	737	1264	1838	2541	70	366	1272	3300	16	17	99	307	103	104	295	385
NATURAL GAS	912	1253	1676	2086	37	354	354	354	3	5	8	14	329	475	699	1033
COAL	554	888	1391	3195	37	370	748	1109								

CUMULATIVE RESOURCE OUTPUT AT END OF PERIOD

	NORTH AMERICA 1980	1990	2000	LATIN AMERICA MEDIUM 1980	1990	2000	LATIN AMERICA LOW 1980	1990	2000	WESTERN EUROPE HIGH 1980	1990	2000
COPPER	25	62	113	11	38	107	3	13	38	1	2	4
BAUXITE	2	6	12	3	12	35	63	174	252	6	14	23
NICKEL	3409	8286	12913	535	1852	6458	45	164	627	60	95	95
ZINC	22	68	113	5	9	17	5	10	14	5	13	40
LEAD	11	72	135	3	9	14	3	16	18	3	4	24
IRON	969	2397	4428	366	1272	3300	200	586	1388	897	1829	2810
PETROLEUM	10008	25520	47416	354	354	354	3586	9285	17948	212	422	3587
NATURAL GAS	10832	25482	44294	370	740	1109	169	752	2789	1038	3038	6444
COAL	7214	18614	41549	78	206	414	42	111	224	4023	9893	18557

	NORTH AMERICA				LATIN AMERICA MEDIUM				LATIN AMERICA LOW				WESTERN EUROPE HIGH			
OUTPUT LEVELS	1970	1980	1990	2000	1970	1980	1990	2000	1970	1980	1990	2000	1970	1980	1990	2000
ANIMAL PRODUCTS	46.3	53.8	62.6	69.5	14.6	21.4	34.9	55.5	4.6	7.0	12.5	21.4	37.7	45.3	55.1	61.8
HIGH PROTEIN CROPS	29.7	39.0	52.3	65.5	16.3	10.4	16.6	27.7	2.4	3.7	6.1	10.8	1.0	1.1	1.4	1.6
GRAINS	215.0	256.0	350.3	456.3	61.3	93.6	187.0	331.0	10.0	13.3	19.5	40.6	101.6	110.1	152.7	186.6
ROOTS	18.5	20.3	19.6	20.7	32.2	42.6	65.0	82.9	9.6	13.3	15.8	23.6	48.7	50.3	55.6	59.2
OTHER AGRICULTURE	28.7	37.9	49.7	65.1	12.5	21.2	40.2	69.2	5.3	9.4	15.8	33.6	47.3	37.2	40.7	52.8
OTHER RESOURCES	6.3	9.9	14.3	19.9	4.9	7.7	17.6	58.9	0.7	0.4	1.7	2.3	2.5	4.0	7.2	9.6
FOOD PROCESSING	71.3	92.3	115.3	141.9	49.3	71.7	179.7	33.6	1.7	2.0	4.7	16.0	48.0	91.1	104.8	127.0
PETROLEUM REFINING	19.1	27.5	36.4	45.4	8.7	4.4	10.3	33.6	0.5	1.8	3.2	10.7	25.7	37.7	68.8	99.2
PRIMARY METALS	42.4	66.6	104.7	124.6	6.6	13.4	25.4	49.4	2.8	4.0	8.3	17.6	45.1	50.7	66.8	92.5
TEXTILES,APPAREL	37.1	56.2	78.4	103.7	8.2	13.4	25.4	11.4	0.4	0.6	1.5	13.8	10.0	13.2	19.1	23.2
WOOD AND CORK	14.2	21.2	27.4	35.1	4.3	2.2	4.6	33.6	1.2	2.2	5.2	12.9	27.9	24.3	14.6	19.2
FURNITURE,FIXTURES	8.9	13.1	17.7	17.6	1.8	2.0	4.5	12.6	0.2	0.4	1.2	3.9	13.1	21.6	36.8	54.5
PAPER	24.2	35.9	52.1	74.3	1.8	2.7	4.3	13.1	0.2	0.4	1.8	1.5	13.4	23.2	42.3	59.3
PRINTING	26.5	39.3	55.9	74.5	2.1	2.7	8.0	8.1	0.5	0.2	0.5	5.3	8.0	14.0	28.5	41.6
RUBBER	16.6	24.2	33.7	44.2	2.1	4.9	8.8	20.0	0.5	0.8	1.7	5.3	19.9	28.1	47.3	70.8
INDUSTRIAL CHEM.	26.1	38.0	52.5	71.6	1.9	13.9	29.8	44.2	0.2	0.7	2.7	5.3	14.8	17.8	26.4	30.8
FERTILIZERS	17.1	21.8	24.7	28.1	1.0	3.2	6.0	16.1	0.4	0.4	1.3	4.5	15.4	25.7	45.5	67.4
OTHER CHEMICALS	23.6	33.7	45.1	60.5	1.0	2.5	6.2	17.9	0.3	0.6	1.9	1.0	13.0	21.9	40.0	57.0
CEMENT	2.3	3.7	5.1	7.7	3.0	5.7	6.3	11.5	0.2	0.1	0.4	0.9	25.6	42.6	82.9	121.9
GLASS	28.8	33.5	46.1	65.1	1.9	2.3	2.3	6.7	0.1	0.3	0.9	1.7	5.6	6.1	9.9	13.0
MOTOR VEHICLES	44.5	61.9	82.1	108.2	1.9	5.1	12.6	39.3	0.7	1.7	3.7	2.7	3.8	6.1	10.5	14.0
AIRCRAFT	14.4	20.7	29.7	41.1	0.5	6.0	15.7	49.8	0.1	0.1	2.3	12.2	33.3	54.0	102.5	135.0
OTHER TRANSP. EQ.	6.6	10.0	14.6	19.7	0.5	2.8	6.9	21.7	0.4	0.2	0.6	9.6	40.8	55.1	102.8	147.0
METAL PRODUCTS	63.1	94.9	128.7	171.6	2.8	6.0	16.0	25.8	0.5	0.7	2.1	2.1	24.6	40.8	75.9	113.1
MACHINERY	53.2	75.4	105.3	139.1	1.1	6.8	15.8	21.7	0.4	0.2	0.6	9.1	10.6	17.4	25.2	25.2
ELECTRICAL MACH.	45.3	63.0	87.7	117.3	1.4	6.6	11.4	5.8	0.5	0.7	1.6	4.1	18.5	21.6	30.5	30.5
INSTRUMENTS	10.4	15.2	20.6	28.1	0.5	2.8	5.9	26.2	0.4	0.1	1.6	4.1	21.8	39.2	68.2	85.0
OTHER MANUFACTURES	9.0	15.2	20.6	27.5	1.1	2.6	5.4	11.4	0.5	0.7	3.5	10.2	86.5	145.2	256.2	307.0
UTILITIES	35.7	56.5	84.4	106.6	5.7	3.6	9.8	26.2	0.7	1.5	3.5	67.1	118.5	217.6	332.8	418.8
CONSTRUCTION	139.6	235.6	314.9	436.0	11.5	23.7	65.3	163.0	3.7	7.5	22.7	59.5	136.2	145.2	256.2	307.0
TRADE	222.6	313.2	419.0	530.4	15.1	29.3	65.8	163.0	4.8	7.8	22.0	59.5	86.5	217.6	332.8	418.8
TRANSPORTATION	57.3	85.0	118.5	160.0	6.6	11.7	25.8	53.7	1.5	3.5	8.0	19.1	48.4	67.4	97.3	138.5
COMMUNICATIONS	25.6	35.7	47.5	61.5	1.5	2.7	5.8	15.0	0.5	2.0	2.0	5.2	11.4	21.5	38.8	49.7
SERVICES	336.1	499.3	704.1	955.0	24.4	46.4	107.7	245.9	8.0	15.0	38.9	101.6	180.8	302.3	523.2	702.9

FISH

FISH	1970	1980	1990	2000	1970	1980	1990	2000	1970	1980	1990	2000	1970	1980	1990	2000
FISH CATCH	3.8	3.8	3.8	3.8	2.2	2.2	2.2	2.2	12.2	12.2	12.2	12.2	7.2	7.9	7.2	7.2
NON-HUMAN USE	1.2	1.2	1.2	1.2	1.1	1.1	1.1	1.1	11.5	11.5	11.5	11.5	1.9	1.9	1.9	1.9
FISH IMPORTS	1.3	1.3	1.3	1.3	0.1	0.1	0.1	0.1	0.0	0.0	0.0	0.0	1.4	1.4	1.4	1.4
FISH EXPORTS	0.4	0.4	0.4	0.4	0.1	0.1	0.1	0.1	0.1	0.1	0.1	0.1	1.7	1.7	1.7	1.7

EXPORTS	NORTH AMERICA				LATIN AMERICA MEDIUM				LATIN AMERICA LOW				WESTERN EUROPE HIGH			
	1970	1980	1990	2000	1970	1980	1990	2000	1970	1980	1990	2000	1970	1980	1990	2000
LIVESTOCK	0.7	1.1	1.4	1.9	0.8	1.3	1.8	2.3	0.2	0.2	0.2	0.3	4.7	5.6	7.5	9.7
HIGH PROTEIN CROPS	14.3	22.4	32.0	42.1	0.4	1.3	1.1	2.4	0.2	0.4	0.6	0.9	1.5	1.8	2.6	3.4
GRAINS	47.8	68.5	103.6	145.1	7.3	10.7	16.5	22.6	0.4	0.4	0.9	0.3	19.5	18.8	28.5	39.9
ROOTS	2.4	2.8	3.7	4.5	2.3	0.4	0.3	0.6	0.2	0.2	0.2	0.3	5.0	5.8	7.6	9.3
OTHER AGRICULTURE	3.0	3.4	4.8	6.5	1.0	2.6	3.2	4.2	0.2	0.4	0.9	1.4	5.7	6.5	8.3	12.3
FOOD PROCESSING	2.1	2.7	3.6	5.6	0.2	1.5	1.4	3.2	0.5	0.6	0.5	1.5	4.8	5.7	8.3	12.2
TEXTILES,APPAREL	1.3	2.2	4.4	6.4	0.0	0.2	1.1	2.0	0.1	0.3	0.2	0.4	12.2	26.5	55.2	106.5
WOOD AND CORK	1.2	2.2	3.6	5.2	0.2	0.2	0.2	0.0	0.1	0.1	0.2	0.5	1.0	3.1	6.4	9.5
FURNITURE,FIXTURES	0.1	0.1	0.1	0.2	0.0	0.0	0.0	0.1	0.0	0.0	0.1	0.1	4.2	9.1	22.2	42.0
PAPER	3.4	7.2	13.5	24.2	0.0	0.0	0.0	0.5	0.0	0.0	0.0	0.5	1.3	2.6	6.3	12.3
PRINTING	0.4	0.4	1.8	2.3	0.0	0.0	0.0	0.0	0.0	0.0	0.1	0.1	1.3	2.4	5.4	11.5
RUBBER	0.3	0.5	0.8	1.3	0.0	0.0	0.0	1.0	0.1	0.0	0.2	0.2	9.6	15.1	29.6	49.5
INDUSTRIAL CHEM,	3.4	5.5	8.3	13.6	0.1	0.0	0.1	0.5	0.1	0.1	0.3	0.7	6.6	4.8	12.2	16.3
FERTILIZERS	1.9	3.5	7.4	9.4	0.1	0.1	0.2	1.8	0.1	0.1	0.1	0.5	2.6	9.3	20.2	40.6
OTHER CHEMICALS	1.3	2.5	4.6	8.3	0.1	0.2	0.3	0.5	0.1	0.1	0.3	0.7	0.6	0.2	0.7	1.7
CEMENT	0.1	0.1	2.1	0.3	0.1	0.1	0.1	0.4	0.0	0.0	0.1	0.2	0.1	5.6	0.7	27.6
GLASS	0.5	1.0	2.1	3.3	0.0	0.0	0.0	1.1	0.0	0.0	0.0	0.2	23.1	20.1	44.9	85.6
MOTOR VEHICLES	8.2	12.3	18.7	33.3	0.0	0.1	0.1	1.0	0.1	0.0	0.0	0.1	1.3	2.3	4.4	5.6
OTHER TRANSP. EQ.	0.2	0.3	0.3	0.5	0.0	0.0	0.0	0.1	0.0	0.0	0.0	0.0	1.3	2.2	4.0	8.6
AIRCRAFT	3.1	5.1	9.3	15.8	0.0	0.0	0.1	0.3	0.1	0.1	0.1	0.2	4.9	6.3	11.1	16.1
METAL PRODUCTS	1.6	2.8	3.3	4.5	0.0	0.0	0.1	2.7	0.1	0.1	0.1	0.2	18.9	31.2	66.4	113.1
MACHINERY	8.0	12.8	19.3	30.6	0.0	0.0	0.0	1.0	0.1	0.0	0.1	0.3	8.6	17.0	39.2	80.6
ELECTRICAL MACH,	3.1	5.9	11.3	22.1	0.0	0.0	0.0	0.2	0.1	0.1	0.1	0.1	3.2	5.7	13.2	22.9
INSTRUMENTS	1.8	3.2	5.3	8.7	0.0	0.0	0.0	0.2	0.0	0.0	0.0	0.2	4.4	7.4	13.2	20.3
OTHER MANUFACTURES	0.9	1.5	2.4	3.1	0.5	0.3	0.7	5.5	0.5	0.7	1.1	1.7	8.9	13.4	21.3	32.2
SERVICES	3.5	5.3	8.4	12.8	1.5	2.3	3.7	5.5	0.4	0.7	1.1	2.0	8.9	13.4	21.3	32.2
TRANSPORT	4.4	7.1	12.9	21.5	0.4	0.7	1.3	2.2	0.4	0.7	1.2	2.0	10.1	25.9	46.9	78.3
AID INFLOW	5.1	4.2	7.0	10.9	1.7	2.7	4.5	6.9	1.3	2.1	3.5	5.4	6.1	12.3	20.4	31.6
CAPITAL INFLOW	6.5	10.3	13.9	18.6	1.8	3.9	10.6	29.6	1.1	2.3	7.7	23.9	9.3	14.8	26.4	29.7

IMPORTS

	NORTH AMERICA				LATIN AMERICA MEDIUM				LATIN AMERICA LOW				WESTERN EUROPE HIGH			
	1970	1980	1990	2000	1970	1980	1990	2000	1970	1980	1990	2000	1970	1980	1990	2000
LIVESTOCK	1.8	2.0	2.4	2.6	0.2	0.2	0.8	0.7	0.2	0.3	0.6	1.0	5.1	6.2	7.5	8.4
HIGH PROTEIN CROPS	1.4	1.8	2.5	3.1	0.3	0.5	0.8	1.3	0.3	0.5	0.8	1.4	5.4	14.4	18.5	20.9
GRAINS	1.3	1.6	2.5	3.8	3.7	5.6	11.3	20.6	3.5	4.9	9.9	15.1	32.9	35.7	48.9	60.5
ROOTS	0.5	0.5	0.9	0.5	0.6	0.7	1.3	2.1	0.2	0.3	0.9	1.1	6.8	7.0	7.7	8.2
OTHER AGRICULTURE	4.6	6.0	7.0	10.3	0.4	0.4	0.9	2.2	0.4	0.6	0.8	1.6	11.5	9.1	9.9	12.9
FOOD PROCESSING	2.2	2.8	3.5	4.5	0.2	0.5	0.9	1.2	0.2	0.5	1.8	1.0	15.4	4.9	5.7	9.1
TEXTILES, APPAREL	4.6	11.1	17.0	29.1	0.1	0.5	0.8	2.2	0.1	0.8	1.0	4.6	10.4	21.3	52.1	100.8
WOOD AND CORK	0.2	0.5	0.6	0.8	0.3	0.1	0.3	0.8	0.1	0.1	0.5	0.5	1.2	4.2	8.3	11.3
FURNITURE, FIXTURES	1.2	2.0	3.6	3.3	0.1	0.1	0.6	1.9	0.1	0.5	0.2	0.2	0.7	0.8	8.7	11.0
PAPER	1.8	3.8	6.6	6.5	0.3	0.2	0.6	0.9	0.1	0.1	0.4	3.0	4.8	9.0	20.9	34.0
PRINTING	0.4	0.6	1.0	1.5	0.1	0.1	0.2	0.7	0.1	0.1	0.2	1.2	8.0	1.8	4.5	7.1
RUBBER	1.8	2.6	4.4	11.4	0.5	0.7	2.1	5.4	0.4	0.4	0.6	1.2	7.2	2.0	4.1	6.6
INDUSTRIAL CHEM.	1.8	3.0	4.1	7.3	0.5	1.3	2.1	7.3	0.1	0.2	1.6	3.8	40.8	11.8	21.6	34.9
FERTILIZERS	1.0	1.3	1.1	2.3	0.3	0.4	0.6	2.3	0.4	0.1	2.0	3.5	7.6	12.8	3.6	4.6
OTHER CHEMICALS	0.6	0.9	1.1	2.2	0.3	1.0	0.6	2.3	0.3	0.6	2.3	3.5	3.0	5.8	11.2	18.2
CEMENT	0.8	0.5	1.5	0.7	0.2	0.2	0.4	0.2	0.3	0.2	0.0	0.2	1.0	0.1	0.3	0.5
GLASS	10.8	18.2	30.4	47.8	0.7	1.4	4.4	15.7	0.8	0.2	0.7	1.7	8.4	4.4	10.9	17.5
MOTOR VEHICLES	0.1	0.2	0.4	0.7	0.2	0.5	4.7	1.4	0.1	0.5	0.2	6.5	1.7	16.0	34.1	57.9
OTHER TRANSP. EQ.	1.6	1.8	3.2	5.3	0.2	0.3	1.0	1.3	0.1	0.2	0.4	1.5	2.7	1.8	9.1	5.3
AIRCRAFT	1.6	2.2	2.9	3.5	0.2	0.4	0.6	4.3	0.1	0.5	1.1	2.3	3.2	4.8	7.8	13.9
METAL PRODUCTS	5.8	8.3	14.5	22.3	0.5	1.5	3.3	15.6	1.3	2.2	3.1	17.0	13.7	21.5	42.3	68.5
MACHINERY	3.8	6.6	11.5	18.3	1.0	2.4	7.5	9.3	1.1	1.0	6.1	9.3	7.0	14.7	31.2	54.6
ELECTRICAL MACH.	1.2	2.0	3.7	15.1	0.1	0.6	3.3	3.0	0.5	0.3	3.7	1.1	2.8	5.5	10.5	16.7
INSTRUMENTS	2.2	4.0	6.7	10.3	0.8	0.2	1.0	3.8	0.1	0.8	1.7	3.9	3.6	5.5	9.5	15.2
OTHER MANUFACTURES	6.4	9.2	12.4	16.3	1.8	1.6	3.1	7.7	0.5	0.8	1.7	3.7	10.1	14.6	22.6	30.1
SERVICES	4.2	6.2	9.3	12.8	0.9	1.5	3.1	6.9	0.9	1.6	3.0	6.7	13.0	19.4	33.5	49.7
TRANSPORT																

| AID OUTFLOW | 9.0 | 13.1 | 17.6 | 23.1 | 0.8 | 1.3 | 2.7 | 6.1 | 0.5 | 0.9 | 1.8 | 4.1 | 11.1 | 15.9 | 24.7 | 32.9 |
| CAPITAL OUTFLOW | 10.0 | 17.6 | 32.8 | 55.8 | 0.9 | 1.9 | 5.4 | 16.0 | 0.4 | 0.8 | 2.2 | 6.5 | 10.4 | 18.1 | 38.9 | 67.6 |

NET EXPORTS OF RESOURCES

	NORTH AMERICA				LATIN AMERICA MEDIUM				LATIN AMERICA LOW				WESTERN EUROPE HIGH			
	1970	1980	1990	2000	1970	1980	1990	2000	1970	1980	1990	2000	1970	1980	1990	2000
COPPER	0.4	0.5	1.0	-1.8	0.4	0.9	2.4	5.7	0.2	0.4	1.2	2.7	-1.7	-2.5	-4.6	-6.3
BAUXITE	-3.5	-5.4	-6.7	-8.5	-1.6	0.15	0.8	0.8	4.8	8.5	13.8	0.8	-2.4	-3.4	-7.2	-9.7
NICKEL	109.2	161.2	257.9	0.0	-1.2	3.5	48.8	307.1	0.0	3.5	17.0	51.2	-108.0	-153.4	-269.2	-336.8
ZINC	0.5	1.1	4.7	0.0	-0.2	0.7	0.0	0.0	0.0	0.7	0.3	0.0	-10.8	-1.2	-2.4	0.0
LEAD	-0.0	0.3	9.4	42.0	0.0	0.4	0.0	0.0	0.0	0.4	0.0	50.0	-0.8	-1.2	-2.8	0.0
IRON	3.7	6.2	23.4	42.9	20.1	27.8	90.2	164.6	12.4	15.4	46.8	71.6	-47.1	-158.5	153.3	
PETROLEUM	-274	-242	-184	0.0	44	-212	-462	-995	240	348	503	549	-767	-1312	-2300	-2358
NATURAL GAS	-20.1	0.0	299.0	481.4	4.7	-38.2	-145.0	-479.6	-0.5	-19.4	-9.3	0.0	-21.0	-81.0	-84.3	0.0
COAL	53.0	139.6			3.7	-9.7	-28.1	-84.4	0.5	-2.1	-0.4	-33.8	-40.8	-58.2	-2.8	-3.6
OTHER RESOURCES	0.6	1.1	2.3	3.6	0.1	0.1	0.2		0.1	0.2		0.5	-1.1	-1.6		
PETROLEUM REFINING	0.5	0.8	1.0	-0.0	-0.3	-1.9	-4.2	-9.3	0.3	1.3	2.8	5.2	-0.5	-5.7	-14.9	-22.1
PRIMARY METALS	-0.7	0.8	14.7	2.5	-0.2	0.5	1.0	5.1	0.0	0.9	0.7	2.3	1.8	-0.4	-6.1	-3.2

90

CONSUMPTION AND POPULATION

	WESTERN EUROPE MEDIUM				SOVIET UNION				EASTERN EUROPE				ASIA, CENTRALLY PLANNED			
	1970	1980	1990	2000	1970	1980	1990	2000	1970	1980	1990	2000	1970	1980	1990	2000
GDP	75.5	135.4	281.7	575.3	434.9	761.4	1372.0	1994.0	164.4	278.7	481.5	682.0	134.8	231.3	423.5	834.8
PERSONAL CONSUM.	52.2	94.1	169.2	374.9	266.8	471.6	793.3	1183.5	105.3	175.0	278.4	381.0	97.1	155.2	273.7	503.5
GOVERNMENT EXPENSE	13.8	24.6	51.2	104.4	79.1	138.3	248.8	361.3	29.9	50.6	87.4	123.8	24.6	42.2	77.2	152.1
POPULATION	108.1	124.9	145.1	165.5	242.8	268.5	297.0	321.2	105.1	112.6	119.5	126.0	808.4	954.0	1093.0	1205.9
URBAN POPULATION	50.2	67.4	87.4	109.8	137.3	172.0	210.0	245.0	55.5	67.0	78.5	90.1	175.1	267.5	380.0	508.9
EMPLOYMENT	28.9	40.7	69.8	81.8	112.9	137.0	142.5	158.0	54.7	58.1	63.9	67.2	58.3	107.3	198.9	335.7
GDP/HEAD	693	1084	1941	3476	1791	2835	4619	6207	1564	2475	4232	5419	166	242	387	680
CONSUMPTION/HEAD	487	753	1304	2265	1098	1756	2670	3684	1001	1554	2331	3025	120	162	250	410
CALORIES/DAY/HEAD	2.7	2.7	2.9	3.2	3.2	3.2	3.2	3.2	3.1	3.1	3.1	3.2	2.1	2.1	2.2	2.5
PROTEINS/DAY/HEAD	78	82	94	129	92	97	104	108	93	98	105	108	59	62	68	79

INVESTMENT AND CAPITAL

	WESTERN EUROPE MEDIUM				SOVIET UNION				EASTERN EUROPE				ASIA, CENTRALLY PLANNED			
	1970	1980	1990	2000	1970	1980	1990	2000	1970	1980	1990	2000	1970	1980	1990	2000
INVESTMENT	11.3	23.1	63.3	138.0	79.7	138.9	303.9	408.5	27.1	47.1	88.4	112.8	11.3	29.8	68.5	164.6
EQUIPMENT	5.2	9.9	27.6	50.6	38.7	58.0	115.3	143.4	13.7	20.9	36.8	47.8	6.2	16.1	34.5	85.3
PLANT	5.8	13.1	35.6	87.3	40.7	80.4	187.3	264.4	13.3	26.1	51.5	64.9	4.7	13.1	33.5	78.7
IRRIGATION (AREA)	0.3	0.1	0.2	0.2	0.2	0.4	0.6	0.6	0.1	0.1	0.1	0.1	0.2	0.5	0.6	0.6
LAND (AREA)	0.1	0.1	0.3	0.2	1.7	0.9	0.1	0.1	0.0	0.0	0.0	0.0	1.0	0.8	0.9	0.9
INVENTORY CHANGE	1.5	1.5	4.3	6.2	7.7	7.0	14.0	13.1	2.4	2.5	5.5	4.2	1.8	4.7	6.6	17.3
CAPITAL STOCK	115.7	226.5	518.6	1165.8	737.9	1383.5	2817.1	4752.5	288.4	505.7	920.6	1429.6	147.1	290.9	623.3	1420.7
EQUIPMENT	48.4	88.9	193.4	383.6	293.7	499.2	925.7	1390.4	115.2	187.5	319.0	471.1	73.4	145.2	299.2	679.1
PLANT	66.6	137.6	325.2	782.2	444.2	884.3	1891.7	3362.1	173.2	318.2	601.6	958.5	73.8	145.7	324.1	741.6
INVENTORY STOCK	22.0	34.2	65.0	111.4	110.2	173.2	270.5	380.3	42.0	63.0	100.7	136.0	42.0	75.9	126.6	249.9
LAND/YIELD INDEX	100	128	199	296	100	125	176	215	100	116	154	186	100	145	212	332
SURPLUS SAVINGS	1.2	1.4	-12.5	-27.1	2.7	17.4	-35.9	-31.6	-2.1	2.6	5.8	24.4	-1.7	-8.8	-20.2	-59.0

INTERNATIONAL TRANSACTIONS

	WESTERN EUROPE MEDIUM				SOVIET UNION				EASTERN EUROPE				ASIA, CENTRALLY PLANNED			
	1970	1980	1990	2000	1970	1980	1990	2000	1970	1980	1990	2000	1970	1980	1990	2000
IMPORTS	13.1	24.3	60.4	128.4	11.7	20.0	38.8	60.4	18.4	28.6	51.4	77.2	1.9	3.5	8.4	16.0
EXPORTS	10.2	16.2	34.0	80.0	12.5	22.5	47.8	84.5	17.5	31.3	72.3	137.0	1.8	2.9	5.7	13.1
PAYMENTS SURPLUS	0.7	-4.6	-44.9	-169.0	-0.4	2.5	31.8	106.2	-0.9	4.2	17.9	78.5	-0.2	-1.9	-7.8	-24.0
FOR. INVESTMENTS	3.3	-32	-310	-1438	0.0	13	181	866	17	128	610	-55	-214			
FOR. INCOME	0.6	-2.0	-24.3	-114.5	0.0	1.1	14.5	69.4	0.0	1.4	10.3	48.9	0.0	-0.7	-4.4	-17.1

WESTERN EUROPE MEDIUM   SOVIET UNION   EASTERN EUROPE   ASIA, CENTRALLY PLANNED

LEVEL OF ABATEMENT ACTIVITIES

	WEM 1970	WEM 1980	WEM 1990	WEM 2000	SU 1970	SU 1980	SU 1990	SU 2000	EE 1970	EE 1980	EE 1990	EE 2000	ASIA 1970	ASIA 1980	ASIA 1990	ASIA 2000
AIR	0.4	0.7	1.6	5.6	3.0	12.0	21.1	24.7	1.1	4.2	6.6	7.6	0.0	0.0	0.0	0.0
PRIMARY WATER	0.09	0.19	0.51	2.26	0.86	3.41	9.34	14.39	0.31	1.21	3.13	4.73	0.00	0.00	0.00	0.00
SECONDARY WATER	0.01	0.01	0.03	0.12	0.06	0.19	0.53	0.82	0.02	0.07	0.18	0.27	0.00	0.00	0.00	0.00
TERTIARY WATER	0.05	0.00	0.01	0.03	0.01	0.09	0.12	0.18	0.00	0.03	0.04	0.06	0.00	0.00	0.00	0.00
SOLID WASTE	13.8	21.9	36.0	114.0	54.2	165.2	244.6	320.6	21.0	60.8	86.5	111.6	0.0	0.0	0.0	0.0

NET TOTAL EMISSIONS

	WEM 1970	WEM 1980	WEM 1990	WEM 2000	SU 1970	SU 1980	SU 1990	SU 2000	EE 1970	EE 1980	EE 1990	EE 2000	ASIA 1970	ASIA 1980	ASIA 1990	ASIA 2000
PESTICIDES	0.21	0.40	0.78	1.05	0.16	0.38	0.70	0.84	0.25	0.44	0.51	0.53	0.00	0.02	0.21	0.70
PARTICULATES	0.45	0.82	1.54	2.55	3.72	4.70	6.37	7.59	1.41	2.12	2.41	2.49	0.96	2.13	3.74	6.02
BIOLOGICAL OXYGEN	0.82	1.53	2.54	3.86	4.78	6.20	6.87	7.59	2.12	2.10	2.43	2.49	1.73	4.28	6.81	11.79
NITROGEN (WATER)	0.02	0.03	0.07	0.12	0.13	0.23	0.19	0.49	0.07	0.08	0.11	0.13	0.01	0.04	0.04	0.12
PHOSPHATES	0.01	0.02	0.04	0.07	0.07	0.12	0.19	0.25	0.04	0.04	0.06	0.07	0.01	0.02	0.04	0.07
SUSPENDED SOLIDS	0.34	0.66	1.51	2.60	2.98	3.67	3.99	3.99	1.09	1.27	1.52	1.52	0.60	1.38	2.43	4.96
DISSOLVED SOLIDS	3.09	4.70	8.94	15.67	19.30	32.60	51.27	65.96	9.35	10.67	15.23	18.61	5.41	16.73	27.09	52.24
SOLID WASTE	13.79	21.92	36.00	0.00	54.22	0.00	0.00	0.00	20.97	0.00	0.00	0.00	54.51	96.62	165.29	276.71

RESOURCE OUTPUTS

	WEM 1970	WEM 1980	WEM 1990	WEM 2000	SU 1970	SU 1980	SU 1990	SU 2000	EE 1970	EE 1980	EE 1990	EE 2000	ASIA 1970	ASIA 1980	ASIA 1990	ASIA 2000
COPPER	0.2	0.2	0.3	0.4	0.9	1.4	1.7	2.3	0.1	0.2	0.3	0.4	0.0	0.2	0.2	0.3
BAUXITE	0.9	1.1	2.1	4.5	0.9	1.0	1.3	2.1	0.5	0.8	1.2	1.8	0.1	0.2	0.1	0.1
NICKEL	0.0	0.0	0.0	0.0	110	196	414	539	4	6	8					
ZINC	0.2	0.4	0.4	2.0	0.5	0.6	1.0	2.4	0.3	0.4	0.6	1.7	0.2	0.3	0.3	1.7
LEAD	0.2	0.13	0.0	2.2	0.5	0.3	1.0	2.6	0.4	0.3	0.6	1.3	0.2	0.3	0.3	1.4
IRON	6	13	36	78	117	203	425	633	7	12	24	24	26	54	68	123
PETROLEUM	8	0	0	0	458	781	1688	2284	26	24	24	24	26	53	107	240
NATURAL GAS	1	1	1	1	263	642	1440	2328	45	45	45	0	0	0	0	0
COAL	25	38	57	93	350	655	1083	1565	264	451	797	1012	393	608	1155	2128

CUMULATIVE RESOURCE OUTPUT AT END OF PERIOD

	WEM 1970	WEM 1980	WEM 1990	WEM 2000	SU 1970	SU 1980	SU 1990	SU 2000	EE 1970	EE 1980	EE 1990	EE 2000	ASIA 1970	ASIA 1980	ASIA 1990	ASIA 2000
COPPER	0	1	4	7	0	11	26	46	0	1	4	7	0	3	3	5
BAUXITE	0	10	26	59	0	9	20	37	0	6	17	32	0	1	3	5
NICKEL	0	88	133	133	0	1547	4618	9390	0	53	83	83	0	0	5	15
ZINC	0	6	6	18	0	5	14	31	0	3	8	20	0	3	5	14
LEAD	0	2	4	15	0	5	8	21	0	2	4	10	0	2	5	14
IRON	0	100	352	928	0	1603	4748	10044	0	59	158	320	0	400	1016	1978
PETROLEUM	0	42	42	42	0	6197	18547	38412	0	240	481	722	0	399	1205	2943
NATURAL GAS	0	11	21	31	0	4528	14940	33785	0	450	900	1125	0	0	0	0
COAL	0	322	802	1553	0	5032	13730	26975	0	3581	9828	18880	0	5009	13827	30248

OUTPUT LEVELS

	WESTERN EUROPE MEDIUM				SOVIET UNION				EASTERN EUROPE				ASIA, CENTRALLY PLANNED			
	1970	1980	1990	2000	1970	1980	1990	2000	1970	1980	1990	2000	1970	1980	1990	2000
ANIMAL PRODUCTS	13.1	17.6	25.6	37.1	27.2	36.3	48.5	58.2	13.2	16.3	20.8	23.6	18.7	29.4	47.2	80.2
HIGH PROTEIN CROPS	8.1	10.5	16.2	23.4	25.5	35.1	49.0	62.2	13.1	13.7	5.3	6.5	16.2	23.4	32.8	50.7
GRAINS	42.9	52.4	82.2	124.5	179.3	219.4	320.9	386.2	55.6	64.4	90.8	112.7	219.6	315.2	460.1	702.5
ROOTS	14.4	15.9	34.0	45.7	90.7	103.2	127.8	145.8	43.1	48.2	58.7	65.0	84.2	93.1	125.1	168.4
OTHER AGRICULTURE	9.3	14.7	23.4	24.0	38.6	48.5	34.6	50.2	14.6	17.0	15.4	16.5	8.6	21.2	34.5	79.2
OTHER RESOURCES	2.8	0.6	3.4	2.0	2.6	4.1	4.6	13.8	7.8	10.7	1.4	2.0	0.6	1.4	2.6	5.6
FOOD PROCESSING	2.7	5.0	9.3	50.0	20.2	47.1	86.0	115.1	2.4	13.2	36.7	40.1	2.3	4.4	8.7	22.7
PETROLEUM REFINING	0.7	1.0	2.0	16.2	2.6	12.0	25.4	36.6	2.4	9.2	20.7	7.8	1.2	2.3	4.0	11.0
PRIMARY METALS	5.7	10.0	18.5	29.8	15.7	28.5	63.2	98.4	11.4	18.1	23.7	34.4	11.8	5.3	10.9	27.0
TEXTILES, APPAREL	1.6	1.8	11.4	14.6	24.7	12.7	38.7	62.6	2.4	11.0	6.7	32.3	1.8	12.0	33.0	58.9
WOOD AND CORK	2.8	5.5	11.1	19.6	15.7	13.9	21.0	29.4	6.7	11.0	10.7	8.2	1.8	4.6	4.1	8.7
FURNITURE, FIXTURES	0.8	1.5	4.2	13.3	6.7	13.6	28.2	16.7	2.4	4.5	19.2	6.9	2.8	5.6	12.5	28.2
PAPER	0.8	1.7	4.5	18.2	6.8	13.9	33.2	42.2	2.1	4.5	9.8	12.8	1.1	2.3	4.8	11.1
PRINTING	0.4	1.5	5.9	11.5	6.0	7.6	22.4	52.5	1.5	3.3	8.0	15.8	0.6	1.1	2.3	5.6
RUBBER	1.3	2.2	6.7	18.5	10.2	18.7	32.4	34.0	3.9	6.3	10.8	12.8	3.2	4.1	11.5	24.2
INDUSTRIAL CHEM.	2.3	3.5	6.5	11.3	17.0	19.2	28.5	49.6	6.8	5.9	16.3	15.6	4.7	8.1	31.3	62.6
FERTILIZERS	1.0	2.0	4.5	8.4	7.5	13.9	31.8	34.7	3.3	5.2	10.1	6.6	1.1	3.0	6.8	15.2
OTHER CHEMICALS	0.3	0.2	5.0	12.4	7.5	14.7	34.9	43.7	2.7	5.4	11.5	15.7	4.1	0.3	6.8	5.5
CEMENT	0.3	0.7	2.9	10.4	11.5	25.6	67.8	51.4	4.3	10.5	25.5	16.6	0.5	2.8	5.5	12.4
GLASS	0.1	0.3	2.3	1.4	15.4	9.6	21.8	103.8	1.7	2.7	5.4	44.4	1.0	2.0	3.4	9.5
MOTOR VEHICLES	0.3	0.7	5.4	32.3	20.5	40.7	94.3	131.5	7.3	12.5	30.8	7.1	1.0	1.8	3.5	7.5
AIRCRAFT	2.3	3.7	6.2	26.0	25.4	42.9	82.9	137.0	11.6	20.3	43.5	44.3	4.4	7.3	13.0	35.1
OTHER TRANSP. EQ.	1.2	4.1	17.7	18.8	14.4	27.6	64.0	119.0	5.4	11.5	26.4	70.2	2.3	11.0	23.6	56.5
METAL PRODUCTS	1.2	2.6	13.7	13.5	9.7	6.4	13.9	90.2	1.3	3.8	5.2	44.7	0.6	1.5	10.2	25.5
MACHINERY	0.6	1.8	8.0	23.6	9.1	22.5	59.1	19.2	3.1	8.0	19.2	7.3	1.4	3.2	8.2	12.4
ELECTRICAL MACH.	1.1	2.0	46.2	109.6	54.8	107.2	242.4	353.6	19.1	36.0	70.8	92.6	7.7	18.0	43.1	119.5
INSTRUMENTS	11.5	18.6	54.4	123.4	74.2	139.8	280.4	402.6	28.5	51.0	93.8	132.6	11.3	22.0	50.2	99.5
OTHER MANUFACTURES	5.2	9.4	18.5	31.4	28.2	46.2	73.0	109.0	11.2	17.5	26.4	34.6	7.3	14.3	28.7	116.3
UTILITIES	1.1	2.0	5.1	12.8	12.3	33.4	47.9	703.7	2.4	4.4	15.8	212.0	19.4	39.7	95.7	217.4
CONSTRUCTION	19.3	37.4	83.9	184.8	103.2	193.4	443.8		39.6	70.0	136.2					

FISH

	WESTERN EUROPE MEDIUM				SOVIET UNION				EASTERN EUROPE				ASIA, CENTRALLY PLANNED			
	1970	1980	1990	2000	1970	1980	1990	2000	1970	1980	1990	2000	1970	1980	1990	2000
FISH CATCH	2.3	2.3	2.3	-0.2	6.7	6.7	6.7	6.7	0.8	0.8	0.8	0.8	7.9	7.9	7.9	7.9
NON-HUMAN USE	-0.2	-0.2	0.2	-0.2	0.6	0.6	0.6	0.6	0.2	0.2	0.2	0.2	0.1	0.1	0.1	0.1
FISH IMPORTS	-0.2	-0.1	-0.1	-0.1	0.4	0.4	0.4	0.4	0.0	0.0	0.0	0.0	0.0	0.0	0.0	0.0
FISH EXPORTS	0.3	0.3	0.3	0.3	0.4	0.4	0.4	0.4	0.0	0.0	0.0	0.0	0.1	0.1	0.1	0.1

WESTERN EUROPE MEDIUM   SOVIET UNION   EASTERN EUROPE   ASIA, CENTRALLY PLANNED

EXPORTS	1970	1980	1990	2000	1970	1980	1990	2000	1970	1980	1990	2000	1970	1980	1990	2000
LIVESTOCK																
HIGH PROTEIN CROPS																
GRAINS																
ROOTS																
OTHER AGRICULTURE																
FOOD PROCESSING																
TEXTILES, APPAREL																
WOOD AND CORK																
FURNITURE, FIXTURES																
PAPER																
PRINTING																
RUBBER																
INDUSTRIAL CHEM.																
FERTILIZERS																
OTHER CHEMICALS																
CEMENT																
GLASS																
MOTOR VEHICLES																
OTHER TRANSP. EQ.																
AIRCRAFT																
METAL PRODUCTS																
MACHINERY																
ELECTRICAL MACH.																
INSTRUMENTS																
OTHER MANUFACTURES																
SERVICES																
TRANSPORT																
AID INFLOW																
CAPITAL INFLOW																

WESTERN EUROPE MEDIUM · SOVIET UNION · EASTERN EUROPE · ASIA, CENTRALLY PLANNED

Columns (each region): 1970 1980 1990 2000

IMPORTS																
LIVESTOCK																
HIGH PROTEIN CROPS																
GRAINS																
ROOTS																
OTHER AGRICULTURE																
FOOD PROCESSING																
TEXTILES,APPAREL																
WOOD AND CORK																
FURNITURE,FIXTURES																
PAPER																
PRINTING																
RUBBER																
INDUSTRIAL CHEM.																
FERTILIZERS																
OTHER CHEMICALS																
CEMENT																
GLASS																
MOTOR VEHICLES																
OTHER TRANSP. EQ.																
AIRCRAFT																
METAL PRODUCTS																
MACHINERY																
ELECTRICAL MACH.																
INSTRUMENTS																
OTHER MANUFACTURES																
SERVICES																
TRANSPORT																
AID OUTFLOW																
CAPITAL OUTFLOW																

NET EXPORTS OF RESOURCES

COPPER																
BAUXITE																
NICKEL																
ZINC																
LEAD																
IRON																
PETROLEUM																
NATURAL GAS																
COAL																
OTHER RESOURCES																
PETROLEUM REFINING																
PRIMARY METALS																

CONSUMPTION AND POPULATION

	JAPAN 1970	1980	1990	2000	ASIA LOW 1970	1980	1990	2000	MIDDLE EAST 1970	1980	1990	2000	ARID AFRICA 1970	1980	1990	2000
GDP	199.8	373.8	594.2	840.9	122.6	201.6	396.7	761.1	36.2	137.6	407.6	989.4	26.9	36.2	54.6	90.1
PERSONAL CONSUM.	111.5	222.9	353.3	480.8	91.6	154.1	290.7	547.7	20.9	60.3	212.2	552.6	19.8	27.9	41.2	67.7
GOVERNMENT EXPENSE	36.3	67.9	107.8	152.4	22.4	36.8	72.4	138.8	6.6	25.1	74.1	179.6	4.9	6.6	10.8	16.4
POPULATION	104.3	117.5	126.2	132.9	1023.2	1327.0	1714.9	2156.0	126.5	171.0	234.6	318.0	131.2	173.0	231.8	307.6
URBAN POPULATION	55.5	72.0	86.2	98.5	207.1	309.7	472.3	704.4	34.9	59.0	95.5	148.2	34.5	77.2	115.3	168.4
EMPLOYMENT	50.6	59.1	58.4	62.8	52.7	84.0	191.2	364.0	12.6	36.1	90.7	188.2	9.8	13.1	24.8	46.3
GDP/HEAD	1915	3181	4708	6327	119	151	231	353	286	804	1737	3111	205	209	235	292
CONSUMPTION/HEAD	1068	1897	2799	3617	89	116	169	254	158	352	904	1737	151	161	177	220
CALORIES/DAY/HEAD	2.4	2.7	3.2	3.2	2.0	2.1	2.2	2.4	2.0	2.1	2.5	3.2	2.5	2.4	2.4	2.3
PROTEINS/DAY/HEAD	71	87	112	117	52	54	58	64	53	60	79	106	72	71	69	70

INVESTMENT AND CAPITAL

	JAPAN 1970	1980	1990	2000	ASIA LOW 1970	1980	1990	2000	MIDDLE EAST 1970	1980	1990	2000	ARID AFRICA 1970	1980	1990	2000
INVESTMENT	44.7	74.6	110.9	137.6	10.8	18.5	60.9	123.0	3.3	36.0	120.2	342.4	2.4	2.7	6.8	13.6
EQUIPMENT	20.9	28.4	39.6	53.5	5.1	9.0	31.2	61.5	1.6	17.7	52.8	132.5	1.0	1.3	3.4	6.5
PLANT	23.7	46.2	71.3	84.2	4.1	8.4	28.8	60.6	1.8	18.1	67.0	209.8	1.0	1.2	3.2	6.8
IRRIGATION (AREA)	0.0	0.0	0.0	0.0	1.7	0.4	1.0	1.0	0.1	0.5	0.1	0.1	0.1	0.1	0.1	0.1
LAND (AREA)	0.0	0.0	0.0	0.0	2.9	1.1	1.3	1.3	0.0	0.5	0.5	0.5	1.0	0.8	0.9	0.9
INVENTORY CHANGE	4.2	4.4	4.0	5.8	2.0	2.4	8.1	11.4	1.0	4.2	11.2	21.2	0.4	0.2	1.2	1.2
CAPITAL STOCK	313.2	661.1	1187.7	1817.5	110.4	198.3	485.4	1082.1	26.7	160.1	642.5	2116.8	26.6	38.1	70.9	137.1
EQUIPMENT	124.7	228.2	363.7	532.0	53.8	92.9	229.9	504.4	11.8	74.6	265.2	764.2	12.6	17.4	32.4	61.3
PLANT	188.4	432.9	824.7	1285.6	56.3	105.4	255.6	577.7	14.9	85.4	377.4	1352.6	14.1	20.7	38.5	75.8
INVENTORY STOCK	39.5	71.5	104.5	152.7	38.1	57.4	118.4	204.0	12.0	36.6	101.7	239.5	7.3	9.3	18.4	28.1
LAND/YIELD INDEX	100	148	207	268	100	140	234	354	100	207	400	803	100	120	213	314
SURPLUS SAVINGS	3.0	9.2	13.9	17.6	2.8	4.4	-18.4	-39.7	1.3	-11.1	-40.6	-131.9	0.7	2.0	0.2	-0.6

INTERNATIONAL TRANSACTIONS

	JAPAN 1970	1980	1990	2000	ASIA LOW 1970	1980	1990	2000	MIDDLE EAST 1970	1980	1990	2000	ARID AFRICA 1970	1980	1990	2000
IMPORTS	18.4	39.5	72.2	108.6	19.8	33.0	78.1	142.3	8.3	28.1	87.7	240.6	3.4	4.2	9.0	15.7
EXPORTS	21.0	42.7	89.5	171.9	15.6	22.7	42.6	82.4	13.6	40.1	77.6	133.3	2.4	3.0	4.4	6.8
PAYMENTS SURPLUS	0.7	1.8	-28.6	-41.8	0.5	-4.4	-55.2	-187.4	1.8	15.6	187.2	418.4	0.1	-0.0	-3.3	-12.2
FOR. INVESTMENTS	0.0	.31	-44	-259	0.0	.26	-344	-1599	0.0	65	996	3781	0.0	0.0	-17	-96
FOR. INCOME	-0.4	2.1	3.9	-21.1	-0.8	-2.9	-28.4	-128.8	-3.9	1.4	75.8	298.6	-0.2	-0.2	-1.6	-7.9

96

LEVEL OF ABATEMENT ACTIVITIES

	JAPAN 1970	JAPAN 1980	JAPAN 1990	JAPAN 2000	ASIA LOW 1970	ASIA LOW 1980	ASIA LOW 1990	ASIA LOW 2000	MIDDLE EAST 1970	MIDDLE EAST 1980	MIDDLE EAST 1990	MIDDLE EAST 2000	ARID AFRICA 1970	ARID AFRICA 1980	ARID AFRICA 1990	ARID AFRICA 2000
AIR	2.4	5.0	7.5	6.7	0.00	0.00	0.00	0.00	0.0	0.8	3.4	12.5	0.0	0.0	0.0	0.0
PRIMARY WATER	0.80	2.50	3.61	3.33	0.00	0.00	0.00	0.00	0.00	0.11	0.82	3.69	0.00	0.00	0.00	0.00
SECONDARY WATER	0.05	0.14	0.84	2.14	0.00	0.00	0.00	0.00	0.00	0.01	0.09	0.21	0.00	0.00	0.00	0.00
TERTIARY WATER	0.01	0.06	0.18	0.47	0.00	0.00	0.00	0.00	0.00	0.00	0.03	0.05	0.00	0.00	0.00	0.00
SOLID WASTE	45.5	72.2	100.9	129.8	0.0	0.0	0.0	0.0	0.0	17.1	75.3	147.3	0.0	0.0	0.0	0.0

NET TOTAL EMISSIONS

	JAPAN 1970	JAPAN 1980	JAPAN 1990	JAPAN 2000	ASIA LOW 1970	ASIA LOW 1980	ASIA LOW 1990	ASIA LOW 2000	MIDDLE EAST 1970	MIDDLE EAST 1980	MIDDLE EAST 1990	MIDDLE EAST 2000	ARID AFRICA 1970	ARID AFRICA 1980	ARID AFRICA 1990	ARID AFRICA 2000
PESTICIDES	0.12	0.28	0.72	1.25	0.16	0.39	1.95	3.77	0.05	0.36	1.57	3.35	0.05	0.17	0.59	1.00
PARTICULATES	0.23	0.23	0.23	0.23	0.64	1.04	2.47	3.44	0.15	1.02	6.63	1.71	0.19	0.26	0.56	0.67
BIOLOGICAL OXYGEN	1.18	1.42	1.65	1.71	1.38	2.89	5.62	8.79	0.21	0.82	3.82	5.56	0.31	0.53	1.46	1.98
NITROGEN (WATER)	0.02	0.03	0.03	0.05	0.01	0.01	0.03	0.08	0.00	0.01	3.04	5.09	0.00	0.00	0.02	0.02
PHOSPHATES	0.01	0.02	0.03	0.05	0.01	0.01	0.03	0.04	0.05	0.03	0.03	0.06	0.05	0.12	0.18	0.02
SUSPENDED SOLIDS	0.95	0.95	0.95	0.95	0.35	0.63	1.64	3.08	0.41	0.39	2.44	4.63	0.18	0.27	0.48	0.65
DISSOLVED SOLIDS	5.69	9.63	15.87	21.82	3.69	5.51	10.92	34.08	2.67	2.67	13.03	27.30	0.94	1.53	6.87	8.99
SOLID WASTE	0.00	0.00	0.00	0.00	56.72	92.86	167.19	295.07	13.44	17.13	75.32	0.00	11.66	26.26	41.18	65.52

RESOURCE OUTPUTS

	JAPAN 1970	JAPAN 1980	JAPAN 1990	JAPAN 2000	ASIA LOW 1970	ASIA LOW 1980	ASIA LOW 1990	ASIA LOW 2000	MIDDLE EAST 1970	MIDDLE EAST 1980	MIDDLE EAST 1990	MIDDLE EAST 2000	ARID AFRICA 1970	ARID AFRICA 1980	ARID AFRICA 1990	ARID AFRICA 2000
COPPER	0.1	0.2	0.2	0.3	0.2	0.2	0.4	0.3	0.0	0.0	0.0	0.3	0.0	0.0	0.0	0.0
BAUXITE	0.0	0.0	0.0	0.0	0.7	1.1	1.8	3.0	0.0	0.0	0.0	0.3	0.0	0.0	0.0	0.0
NICKEL	0.3	0.4	0.4	3.5	156	256	557	1025	0.1	0.1	0.0	1.2	0.1	0.1	0.1	0.1
ZINC	0.1	0.1	0.1	1.1	0.2	0.0	0.1	1.4	0.1	0.1	0.0	1.5	0.1	0.2	0.7	1.2
LEAD	0.1	0.1	0.1	1.2	0.2	0.0	0.5	0.5	0.1	0.6	0.9	1.24	0.1	0.4	0.7	0.4
IRON	1	1	2	1	22	34	104	185	16	24	9	287	38	41	92	154
PETROLEUM	1	1	2	1	75	75	75	75	1241	2545	5567	9526	0	0	0	0
NATURAL GAS	0	0	0	0	13	13	13	13	30	317	913	1557	0	0	0	0
COAL	39	59	87	142	87	164	414	911	0	0	1	1	0	0	0	1

CUMULATIVE RESOURCE OUTPUT AT END OF PERIOD

	JAPAN 1970	JAPAN 1980	JAPAN 1990	JAPAN 2000	ASIA LOW 1970	ASIA LOW 1980	ASIA LOW 1990	ASIA LOW 2000	MIDDLE EAST 1970	MIDDLE EAST 1980	MIDDLE EAST 1990	MIDDLE EAST 2000	ARID AFRICA 1970	ARID AFRICA 1980	ARID AFRICA 1990	ARID AFRICA 2000
COPPER	0	1	3	6	2	2	4	8	0	0	0	0	0	0	0	0
BAUXITE	0	0	0	0	7	9	24	48	0	0	0	1	0	0	0	0
NICKEL	0	0	0	0	156	2063	6132	14046	0	0	0	0	0	1	1	3
ZINC	0	3	4	22	0	0	0	0	0	1	1	7	0	0	1	3
LEAD	0	0	1	8	0	0	0	3	0	0	1	9	0	0	1	2
IRON	0	9	21	38	22	286	983	2437	39	18931	59496	134866	56	114	171	287
PETROLEUM	0	10	19	29	75	751	1501	2251	0	18931	59496	134866	398	1065	2296	
NATURAL GAS	0	0	0	0	13	131	261	391	0	1741	7896	20251	5	1	1	
COAL	0	494	1229	2381	87	1259	4154	10785	0	5	13	28	5	14	28	

OUTPUT LEVELS

	JAPAN				ASIA LOW				MIDDLE EAST				ARID AFRICA			
	1970	1980	1990	2000	1970	1980	1990	2000	1970	1980	1990	2000	1970	1980	1990	2000
ANIMAL PRODUCTS		8	14	18	13	22	42	69	2	7	15	32	3	5	7	10
HIGH PROTEIN CROPS																
GRAINS																
ROOTS																
OTHER AGRICULTURE																
OTHER RESOURCES																
FOOD PROCESSING																
PETROLEUM REFINING																
PRIMARY METALS																
TEXTILES,APPAREL																
WOOD AND CORK																
FURNITURE,FIXTURES																
PAPER																
PRINTING																
RUBBER																
INDUSTRIAL CHEM.																
FERTILIZERS																
OTHER CHEMICALS																
CEMENT																
GLASS																
MOTOR VEHICLES																
AIRCRAFT																
OTHER TRANSP. EQ.																
METAL PRODUCTS																
MACHINERY																
ELECTRICAL MACH.																
INSTRUMENTS																
OTHER MANUFACTURES																
UTILITIES																
CONSTRUCTION																
TRADE																
TRANSPORTATION																
COMMUNICATIONS																
SERVICES																

FISH

	JAPAN				ASIA LOW				MIDDLE EAST				ARID AFRICA			
	1970	1980	1990	2000	1970	1980	1990	2000	1970	1980	1990	2000	1970	1980	1990	2000
FISH CATCH																
NON-HUMAN USE																
FISH IMPORTS																
FISH EXPORTS																

EXPORTS

	JAPAN				ASIA LOW				MIDDLE EAST				ARID AFRICA			
	1970	1980	1990	2000	1970	1980	1990	2000	1970	1980	1990	2000	1970	1980	1990	2000
LIVESTOCK																
HIGH PROTEIN CROPS																
GRAINS																
ROOTS																
OTHER AGRICULTURE																
FOOD PROCESSING																
TEXTILES, APPAREL																
WOOD AND CORK																
FURNITURE, FIXTURES																
PAPER																
PRINTING																
RUBBER																
INDUSTRIAL CHEM.																
FERTILIZERS																
OTHER CHEMICALS																
CEMENT																
GLASS																
MOTOR VEHICLES																
OTHER TRANSP. EQ.																
AIRCRAFT																
METAL PRODUCTS																
MACHINERY																
ELECTRICAL MACH.																
INSTRUMENTS																
OTHER MANUFACTURES																
SERVICES																
TRANSPORT																
AID INFLOW																
CAPITAL INFLOW																

Table with column groups: JAPAN, ASIA LOW, MIDDLE EAST, ARID AFRICA — each with years 1970, 1980, 1990, 2000.

IMPORTS	JAPAN 1970	JAPAN 1980	JAPAN 1990	JAPAN 2000	ASIA LOW 1970	ASIA LOW 1980	ASIA LOW 1990	ASIA LOW 2000	MIDDLE EAST 1970	MIDDLE EAST 1980	MIDDLE EAST 1990	MIDDLE EAST 2000	ARID AFRICA 1970	ARID AFRICA 1980	ARID AFRICA 1990	ARID AFRICA 2000
LIVESTOCK																
HIGH PROTEIN CROPS																
GRAINS																
ROOTS																
OTHER AGRICULTURE																
FOOD PROCESSING																
TEXTILES, APPAREL																
WOOD AND CORK																
FURNITURE, FIXTURES																
PAPER																
PRINTING																
RUBBER																
INDUSTRIAL CHEM.																
FERTILIZERS																
OTHER CHEMICALS																
CEMENT																
GLASS																
MOTOR VEHICLES																
OTHER TRANSP. EQ.																
AIRCRAFT																
METAL PRODUCTS																
MACHINERY																
ELECTRICAL MACH.																
INSTRUMENTS																
OTHER MANUFACTURES																
SERVICES																
TRANSPORT																
AID OUTFLOW																
CAPITAL OUTFLOW																

NET EXPORTS OF RESOURCES

	JAPAN 1970	JAPAN 1980	JAPAN 1990	JAPAN 2000	ASIA LOW 1970	ASIA LOW 1980	ASIA LOW 1990	ASIA LOW 2000	MIDDLE EAST 1970	MIDDLE EAST 1980	MIDDLE EAST 1990	MIDDLE EAST 2000	ARID AFRICA 1970	ARID AFRICA 1980	ARID AFRICA 1990	ARID AFRICA 2000
COPPER																
BAUXITE																
NICKEL																
ZINC																
LEAD																
IRON																
PETROLEUM																
NATURAL GAS																
COAL																
OTHER RESOURCES																
PETROLEUM REFINING																
PRIMARY METALS																

CONSUMPTION AND POPULATION

	TROPICAL AFRICA 1970	1980	1990	2000	SOUTHERN AFRICA 1970	1980	1990	2000	OCEANIA 1970	1980	1990	2000
GDP	23.7	31.9	48.6	81.5	16.9	29.6	62.7	148.2	43.1	64.0	110.7	161.5
PERSONAL CONSUM.	16.6	21.0	24.9	49.8	11.8	20.7	43.0	100.1	27.7	41.2	68.7	105.9
GOVERNMENT EXPENSE	4.3	5.8	8.9	14.9	3.1	5.6	11.9	26.9	7.8	11.6	20.1	29.3
POPULATION	141.4	184.6	247.1	332.1	21.5	28.6	37.9	50.0	15.4	18.4	21.5	24.5
URBAN POPULATION	17.8	38.8	67.2	109.4	10.3	15.0	21.9	32.0	12.9	16.0	19.2	22.4
EMPLOYMENT	15.6	13.0	21.1	38.0	8.8	11.1	19.7	25.6	5.7	7.6	9.0	12.7
GDP/HEAD	167	172	196	245	786	1034	1654	2964	2798	3478	5148	6591
CONSUMPTION/HEAD	117	113	100	149	546	722	1134	2002	1801	2237	3196	4322
CALORIES/DAY/HEAD	2.2	2.2	2.2	2.3	2.8	2.8	2.9	3.2	3.2	3.2	3.2	3.2
PROTEINS/DAY/HEAD	62	61	59	64	79	81	90	127	91	94	97	100

INVESTMENT AND CAPITAL

	TROPICAL AFRICA 1970	1980	1990	2000	SOUTHERN AFRICA 1970	1980	1990	2000	OCEANIA 1970	1980	1990	2000
INVESTMENT	1.9	2.0	5.1	10.8	2.5	4.5	14.2	39.1	6.8	10.7	25.0	35.3
EQUIPMENT	1.0	1.1	3.0	6.0	1.2	2.0	6.2	15.0	3.2	4.4	9.0	10.9
PLANT	0.8	1.8	1.9	4.5	1.0	2.5	8.0	24.0	3.5	6.1	15.8	24.0
IRRIGATION (AREA)	0.0	0.0	0.0	0.7	0.0	0.1	0.0	0.0	0.5	0.4	0.6	0.6
LAND (AREA)	1.0	1.0	1.7	1.3	0.3	0.3	1.0	2.4	0.5	0.3	1.1	1.0
INVENTORY CHANGE	0.4	0.2	0.5	1.3								
CAPITAL STOCK	21.2	29.5	53.5	105.1	27.0	48.8	114.2	294.3	79.3	127.9	248.4	416.3
EQUIPMENT	10.3	14.3	27.6	54.4	11.4	19.3	42.8	100.7	28.9	43.3	77.6	111.3
PLANT	10.5	15.2	25.9	50.7	15.6	29.6	71.4	193.7	50.5	84.7	170.8	305.0
INVENTORY STOCK	8.5	10.1	14.6	24.5	14.3	26.8	13.6	29.8	10.9	13.6	21.0	29.1
LAND/YIELD INDEX	100	119	183	321	100	133	224	421	100	128	205	292
SURPLUS SAVINGS	0.3	1.6	0.7	-1.0	0.8	2.1	0.5	-1.0	2.8	4.5	2.3	4.7

INTERNATIONAL TRANSACTIONS

	TROPICAL AFRICA 1970	1980	1990	2000	SOUTHERN AFRICA 1970	1980	1990	2000	OCEANIA 1970	1980	1990	2000
IMPORTS	5.8	6.9	12.2	22.8	4.2	6.2	15.3	37.9	6.5	10.4	21.0	32.7
EXPORTS	6.2	9.8	21.5	27.6	3.5	4.8	8.4	17.5	6.5	10.4	17.0	22.5
PAYMENTS SURPLUS	0.4	5.3	24.5	73.4	-0.5	-2.2	-14.0	-49.7	0.3	-0.3	-10.1	-39.0
FOR. INVESTMENTS	0.0	27	176	663	-20	-120	-492		-17	-104	-409	
FOR. INCOME	-0.4	1.8	13.6	52.6	-0.5	-2.1	-10.1	-39.9	-0.9	-2.3	-9.3	-33.7

LEVEL OF ABATEMENT ACTIVITIES

	TROPICAL AFRICA				SOUTHERN AFRICA				OCEANIA			
	1970	1980	1990	2000	1970	1980	1990	2000	1970	1980	1990	2000
AIR	0.0	0.0	0.0	0.0	0.1	0.2	0.4	1.5	0.5	0.8	1.3	1.1
PRIMARY WATER	0.00	0.00	0.00	0.00	0.02	0.05	0.11	0.56	0.15	0.42	0.68	0.66
SECONDARY WATER	0.00	0.00	0.00	0.00	0.00	0.00	0.01	0.01	0.01	0.02	0.17	0.26
TERTIARY WATER	0.00	0.00	0.00	0.00	0.00	0.00	0.00	0.01	0.00	0.01	0.04	0.06
SOLID WASTE	0.0	0.0	0.0	0.0	3.0	4.8	8.5	31.2	12.3	16.6	23.3	30.1

NET TOTAL EMISSIONS

	TROPICAL AFRICA				SOUTHERN AFRICA				OCEANIA			
	1970	1980	1990	2000	1970	1980	1990	2000	1970	1980	1990	2000
PESTICIDES	0.02	0.04	0.08	0.42	0.01	0.01	5.62	0.05	0.02	0.02	0.03	0.04
PARTICULATES	0.12	0.22	0.47	0.45	0.11	0.17	0.32	0.15	0.05	0.05	0.05	0.05
BIOLOGICAL OXYGEN	0.14	0.18	0.30	0.53	0.18	0.27	0.60	1.11	0.30	0.26	0.25	0.30
NITROGEN (WATER)	0.01	0.00	0.00	0.00	0.01	0.11	0.02	0.02	0.00	0.00	0.01	0.01
PHOSPHATES	0.08	0.20	0.60	0.68	0.09	0.13	0.01	0.02	0.00	0.00	0.00	0.01
SUSPENDED SOLIDS	0.08	0.20	0.69	0.68	0.09	0.13	0.32	0.71	0.18	0.18	0.18	0.18
DISSOLVED SOLIDS	0.40	0.29	0.59	1.10	0.68	1.04	2.50	5.16	1.17	1.24	1.80	2.49
SOLID WASTE	5.19	11.41	20.81	37.16	2.96	4.82	8.49	5.00	1.00	1.00	1.00	2.00

RESOURCE OUTPUTS

	TROPICAL AFRICA				SOUTHERN AFRICA				OCEANIA			
	1970	1980	1990	2000	1970	1980	1990	2000	1970	1980	1990	2000
COPPER	1.1	2.1	5.4	6.9	0.1	0.1	0.1	0.2	0.2	0.2	0.5	0.7
BAUXITE	0.7	0.8	2.0	8.7	0.1	0.1	0.1	0.0	1.8	3.2	6.4	21.6
NICKEL	0.2	0.3	1.3	0.0	1.0	15	2.0	0.4	29	45	86	102
ZINC	0.2	0.1	0.0	0.02	0.1	0.1	0.1	0.2	0.5	0.9	2.0	10.3
LEAD	0.1	0.1	0.6	102	0.0	7	14	42	0.4	0.9	0.7	0.3
IRON	23	23	0	0	5	5	0	0	32	36	57	56
PETROLEUM	6	33	33	33	0	0	0	0	11	11	11	11
NATURAL GAS	4	7	17	28	0	4	0	0	2	2	2	2
COAL	4	7	17	28	54	64	93	234	50	94	170	245

CUMULATIVE RESOURCE OUTPUT AT END OF PERIOD

	TROPICAL AFRICA				SOUTHERN AFRICA				OCEANIA			
	1970	1980	1990	2000	1970	1980	1990	2000	1970	1980	1990	2000
COPPER	0	16	53	114	0	10	2	3	0	1	5	11
BAUXITE	0	7	21	74	0	0	0	0	0	25	73	213
NICKEL	0	99	144	144	0	137	216	216	0	375	1036	1985
ZINC	0	2	1	17	0	4	5	1	0	6	22	34
LEAD	0	1	1	1	0	0	0	0	0	6	11	12
IRON	0	234	684	1526	0	64	175	460	0	345	814	1383
PETROLEUM	0	33	33	33	0	0	0	0	0	110	220	330
NATURAL GAS	0	0	0	0	0	0	0	0	0	20	40	60
COAL	0	59	185	414	0	594	1380	3017	0	724	2047	4124

OUTPUT LEVELS

	TROPICAL AFRICA				SOUTHERN AFRICA				OCEANIA			
	1970	1980	1990	2000	1970	1980	1990	2000	1970	1980	1990	2000
ANIMAL PRODUCTS	3.5	4.7	6.4	11.7	0.9	1.5	2.9	8.6	5.1	6.8	9.2	11.1
HIGH PROTEIN CROPS	6.9	8.6	12.2	26.5	0.8	1.5	2.9	2.8	13.5	17.6	20.3	10.3
GRAINS	19.6	23.9	41.2	72.4	0.8	1.3	1.7	33.3	13.1	17.6	28.3	40.3
ROOTS	43.1	53.5	73.4	99.3								
OTHER AGRICULTURE		4.4	5.4	9.3				1.5	4.2	3.7	1.3	1.4
OTHER RESOURCES		0.2	0.6	0.6				0.8	0.3		4.6	6.7
FOOD PROCESSING		0.5	0.7	1.0				12.8	3.7	6.0	8.6	11.3
PETROLEUM REFINING												
PRIMARY METALS	1.4	1.5	1.6	6.7				4.0		2.4	5.6	5.9
TEXTILES, APPAREL	2.2	2.3	1.6	6.1				5.2	0.6	2.8	3.5	5.0
WOOD AND CORK	2.4	2.5						1.6				1.5
FURNITURE, FIXTURES										0.5	1.4	1.8
PAPER								2.4				3.9
PRINTING										1.0	2.1	2.3
RUBBER											1.1	2.8
INDUSTRIAL CHEM.		0.3						5.0		0.7	5.5	2.4
FERTILIZERS								2.0			2.3	3.3
OTHER CHEMICALS										1.0	3.4	3.6
CEMENT								3.5		1.1	2.4	3.4
GLASS								10.3				
MOTOR VEHICLES								17.8		1.3	3.5	4.3
AIRCRAFT												
OTHER TRANSP. EQ.								7.8		2.9	6.5	0.8
METAL PRODUCTS		0.3		1.0				4.7		1.1	5.5	0.9
MACHINERY								2.0			3.7	4.8
ELECTRICAL MACH.		0.1		1.0				3.5		0.7	3.5	4.0
INSTRUMENTS												
OTHER MANUFACTURES		0.4	0.8	1.4				3.5		0.6	1.0	1.6
UTILITIES											4.8	6.8
CONSTRUCTION	1.7	2.4		8.7				30.5		2.4	20.5	31.1
TRADE	1.9	2.3	3.1	7.6				30.5	5.2	8.7	23.3	34.3
TRANSPORTATION	0.2	1.3	2.3	4.5				2.6	8.3	13.3	5.2	8.1
COMMUNICATIONS		0.3		0.9					2.3	1.3	2.6	3.0
SERVICES	3.6	5.0	9.1	18.5	5.1	9.1	20.0	46.3	10.6	18.2	36.8	58.0

FISH

	1970	1980	1990	2000	1970	1980	1990	2000	1970	1980	1990	2000
FISH CATCH	1.9	1.9	1.9	1.9	2.2	2.2	2.2	2.2	0.2	0.0	0.2	0.2
NON-HUMAN USE	0.6	0.6	0.6	0.6	0.2	0.2	0.2	0.0	0.0	0.0	0.0	0.0
FISH IMPORTS	0.1	0.1	0.1	0.1	0.0	0.0	0.0	0.0	0.0	0.0	0.0	0.0
FISH EXPORTS	0.1	0.1	0.1	0.1	0.0	0.0	0.0	0.0	0.0			

EXPORTS

	TROPICAL AFRICA					SOUTHERN AFRICA					OCEANIA			
	1970	1980	1990	2000		1970	1980	1990	2000		1970	1980	1990	2000
LIVESTOCK														
HIGH PROTEIN CROPS														
GRAINS														
ROOTS														
OTHER AGRICULTURE														
FOOD PROCESSING														
TEXTILES, APPAREL														
WOOD AND CORK														
FURNITURE, FIXTURES														
PAPER														
PRINTING														
RUBBER														
INDUSTRIAL CHEM.														
FERTILIZERS														
OTHER CHEMICALS														
CEMENT														
GLASS														
MOTOR VEHICLES														
OTHER TRANSP. EQ.														
AIRCRAFT														
METAL PRODUCTS														
MACHINERY														
ELECTRICAL MACH.														
INSTRUMENTS														
OTHER MANUFACTURES														
SERVICES														
TRANSPORT														
AID INFLOW														
CAPITAL INFLOW														

	TROPICAL AFRICA				SOUTHERN AFRICA				OCEANIA			
	1970	1980	1990	2000	1970	1980	1990	2000	1970	1980	1990	2000
IMPORTS												
LIVESTOCK	0.1	0.2	0.3	0.5	0.0	0.1	0.1	0.1	0.1	0.2	0.3	0.4
HIGH PROTEIN CROPS	2.2	0.2	0.3	0.7	0.0	0.0	0.1	0.2	0.1	0.2	0.3	0.4
GRAINS	2.5	3.0	5.4	9.4	0.5	0.7	0.3	2.0	0.1	0.1	0.1	0.1
ROOTS	0.2	0.3	0.2	0.4	0.0	0.1	0.1	0.5	0.2	0.1	0.2	0.3
OTHER AGRICULTURE	0.3	0.3	0.5	0.4	0.1	0.2	0.3	0.3	0.2	0.2	0.2	0.3
FOOD PROCESSING	0.6	1.3	0.5	4.2	0.4	0.5	0.7	2.6	1.6	0.7	1.6	3.3
TEXTILES, APPAREL	0.2	0.1	2.1	4.0	0.5	0.2	0.2	1.9	0.3	0.0	0.3	0.4
WOOD AND CORK	0.2	0.2	0.1	0.0	0.1	0.1	0.1	0.6	0.1	0.3	0.7	0.0
FURNITURE, FIXTURES	0.1	0.1	0.2	0.5	0.0	0.2	0.2	0.1	0.0	0.1	0.4	0.7
PAPER	0.1	0.2	0.3	0.3	0.2	0.1	0.2	0.6	0.4	0.3	0.2	0.6
PRINTING	0.1	0.1	0.2	0.7	0.1	0.1	0.1	0.1	0.2	0.1	0.1	0.2
RUBBER	0.2	0.1	0.4	1.0	0.2	0.2	0.2	0.6	0.5	0.5	0.7	0.6
INDUSTRIAL CHEM.	0.2	0.3	0.4	0.0	0.1	0.1	0.1	1.4	0.2	0.5	1.0	1.2
FERTILIZERS	0.2	0.2	0.5	1.0	0.1	0.2	0.2	0.0	0.4	0.1	0.1	0.0
OTHER CHEMICALS	0.2	0.3	0.3	1.0	0.4	0.2	0.3	0.4	0.3	0.3	0.7	1.0
CEMENT	0.1	0.1	0.1	0.0	0.1	0.1	0.1	0.0	0.1	0.2	0.1	0.0
GLASS	0.6	0.6	0.2	0.6	0.8	0.1	0.1	0.8	0.6	0.2	0.5	0.7
MOTOR VEHICLES	0.6	0.6	0.4	0.3	0.1	0.2	0.2	1.4	2.1	1.2	2.7	4.2
OTHER TRANSP. EQ.	0.1	0.1	0.6	0.5	0.2	0.1	0.1	0.1	0.1	0.1	0.2	0.3
AIRCRAFT	0.3	0.3	0.2	0.0	0.1	0.1	0.1	0.6	0.1	0.1	0.1	0.3
METAL PRODUCTS	0.7	0.3	0.6	0.0	0.6	0.1	0.1	0.6	0.2	0.2	0.2	0.5
MACHINERY	0.3	0.8	2.6	4.2	0.2	0.1	0.2	0.3	1.6	2.0	2.3	3.7
ELECTRICAL MACH.	0.1	0.3	0.2	1.4	0.1	0.1	0.2	0.3	0.3	0.3	0.3	0.9
INSTRUMENTS	0.1	0.1	0.2	0.3	0.1	0.1	0.1	0.3	0.2	0.2	0.2	0.6
OTHER MANUFACTURES	0.1	0.2	0.2	0.1	0.4	0.1	0.2	0.6	0.9	0.6	0.6	0.4
SERVICES	0.1	0.8	0.4	0.1	0.1	0.3	0.7	1.3	0.6	0.6	1.0	1.7
TRANSPORT	0.6	0.8	1.4	2.2	0.4	0.6	1.3	3.1	0.9	1.4	2.6	3.7
AID OUTFLOW	0.5	0.7	1.0	1.8	0.2	0.3	0.7	1.7	0.5	0.8	1.4	2.1
CAPITAL OUTFLOW	0.2	0.3	0.6	1.3	0.1	0.1	0.2	0.8	0.1	0.3	0.6	1.2
NET EXPORTS OF RESOURCES												
COPPER	1.1	2.1	5.3	6.9	0.1	0.1	0.2	0.7	0.1	0.1	0.3	0.5
BAUXITE	5.9	0.8	2.0	8.1	1.6	0.5	0.2	8.6	0.5	2.8	5.5	20.0
NICKEL	10.9	9.3	0.0	0.0	6.0	3.0	6.0	0.0	1.0	3.7	7.0	0.0
ZINC	0.2	0.3	0.3	0.0	2.2	0.2	0.2	0.0	0.4	0.8	0.2	0.3
LEAD	0.4	0.1	0.5	0.2	2.5	1.1	0.2	0.0	0.4	0.8	0.2	0.8
IRON	18.8	23.1	65.5	100.1	2.4	1.6	0.0	0.0	20.4	20.0	28.1	14.3
PETROLEUM	4.9	-18	-32	-64	-15	-26	-55	-130	-27	-54	-119	-17.4
NATURAL GAS	0.3	0.0	0.0	0.3	0.9	2.3	0.5	0.5	0.5	1.5	4.5	-7.1
COAL	0.3	0.0	0.0	0.3	9.1	2.0	8.0	0.0	8.1	44.2	85.2	130.1
OTHER RESOURCES	0.1	0.1	0.2	0.3	0.1	0.2	0.3	0.1	0.1	0.1	0.2	0.3
PETROLEUM REFINING	-0.1	-0.2	-0.3	-0.6	0.1	0.1	0.4	1.2	0.0	0.2	-0.8	-1.6
PRIMARY METALS	0.1	1.3	5.6	5.9	0.1	0.0	0.1	0.1	0.0	0.9	1.4	-0.2

105

Scenario A (three aggregated regions and world total)

	WORLD				DEVELOPED COUNTRIES				DEVELOPING				DEVELOPING - CLASS I				DEVELOPING - CLASS II			
	1970	1980	1990	2000	1970	1980	1990	2000	1970	1980	1990	2000	1970	1980	1990	2000	1970	1980	1990	2000
CONSUMPTION AND POPULATION																				
GDP	3220	4881	7697	11072	2630	3939	6122	8173	589	941	1574	2898	99	268	636	1322	490	673	938	1576
PERSONAL CONSUM.	2286	3164	4774	6913	1671	2516	3727	5038	414	647	1046	1873	64	155	385	833	350	492	661	1040
GOVERNMENT EXPENSE	585	886	1396	2027	477	714	1109	1480	107	170	286	526	18	48	115	240	89	122	171	286
POPULATION	3625	4420	5344	6495	978	1066	1154	1228	2640	3333	4189	5175	357	476	642	856	2283	2857	3547	4319
URBAN POPULATION	1322	1824	2445	3233	634	753	875	987	687	1070	1569	2245	95	165	262	397	592	905	1307	1848
EMPLOYMENT	692	861	1121	1425	436	498	541	585	255	362	579	839	52	101	188	320	203	261	391	519
GDP/HEAD	889	1149	1440	1728	2687	3694	5304	6652	278	563	990	1543	278	563	990	1543	214	235	264	364
CONSUMPTION/HEAD	576	719	893	1079	1707	2360	3229	4101	179	325	599	972	179	325	599	972	153	172	186	240
CALORIES/DAY/HEAD	2.4	2.4	2.4	2.5	3.1	3.1	3.2	3.2	2.2	2.3	2.5	2.8	2.2	2.3	2.5	2.8	2.1	2.2	2.2	2.3
PROTEINS/DAY/HEAD	66	68	70	74	90	96	103	106	56	63	73	85	56	63	73	85	58	58	59	63
INVESTMENT AND CAPITAL																				
INVESTMENT	501	783	1449	2047	440	663	1193	1438	60	119	255	608	9	56	154	383	51	63	101	225
EQUIPMENT	227	312	559	786	197	254	439	513	29	57	119	273	4	26	66	151	25	31	53	122
PLANT	269	467	885	1256	241	408	752	924	27	58	132	332	4	29	87	232	23	29	45	100
IRRIGATION (AREA)	11	7	9	9	3	2	1	1	2	2	1	1	0	2	2	0	2	1	1	1
LAND (AREA)	42	37	66	90	30	25	42	39	9	5	5	5	2	2	2	2	2	4	5	5
INVENTORY CHANGE													2	5	13	24	7	7	10	26
CAPITAL STOCK	5693	9230	15897	25205	5016	8045	13568	20080	677	1184	2328	5124	96	325	978	2677	581	859	1350	2447
EQUIPMENT	2003	3027	4990	7578	1694	2496	3982	5465	309	530	1008	2112	43	145	400	979	266	385	608	1133
PLANT	3689	6203	10907	17626	3522	5549	9586	14614	367	655	1320	3011	53	182	578	1698	314	473	742	1313
INVENTORY STOCK	721	1030	1549	2257	547	758	1104	1450	173	270	444	807	31	67	152	316	142	203	292	491
LAND/YIELD INDEX	100	131	189	276	100	120	165	205	100	150	246	420	100	168	307	567	100	132	185	272
SURPLUS SAVINGS	20	78	-63	-33	11	64	-54	77	8	14	-9	-110	3	-11	-39	-117	5	25	30	7
INTERNATIONAL TRANSACTIONS																				
IMPORTS	342.7	543.0	995.5	1589.2	268.6	413.5	741.7	1058.6					22.2	55.3	137.9	313.1	51.8	74.1	115.9	217.5
EXPORTS	342.7	542.0	993.5	1587.6	271.2	422.6	779.4	1222.3					28.1	58.1	104.5	153.1	42.6	61.4	109.7	212.2
PAYMENTS SURPLUS	-0.7	-1.6	0.2	0.6	-3.8	-4.0	-128.5	-200.0					2.7	3.1	129.9	201.6	0.5	-0.7	-1.4	-1.0
FOR. INVESTMENTS	0.0	-0.8	0.0	0.3	3.0	0.29	-490	-1832					-5.6	-15	516	1843	-2.2	-.21	-.25	-.8
FOR. INCOME	0.0	-0.6	0.0	0.3	7.8	10.2	-31.4	-138.8					-5.6	-6.9	35.6	141.8	-2.2	-3.9	-4.2	-2.8

LEVEL OF ABATEMENT ACTIVITIES

	WORLD 1970	WORLD 1980	WORLD 1990	WORLD 2000	DEVELOPED 1970	DEVELOPED 1980	DEVELOPED 1990	DEVELOPED 2000	DEVELOPING I 1970	DEVELOPING I 1980	DEVELOPING I 1990	DEVELOPING I 2000	DEVELOPING II 1970	DEVELOPING II 1980	DEVELOPING II 1990	DEVELOPING II 2000
AIR	54.3	93.0	123.4	165.0	53.8	91.0	121.8	146.7	0.0	0.8	0.0	12.7	0.4	1.3	1.7	5.7
PRIMARY WATER	11.0	21.0	39.1	55.2	10.9	20.9	38.5	47.9	0.0	0.1	0.0	4.1	0.1	0.0	0.6	3.2
SECONDARY WATER	2.6	1.2	2.4	4.5	0.6	1.2	3.7	4.0	0.0	0.0	0.0	0.2	0.0	0.0	0.0	-0.4
TERTIARY WATER	0.1	0.5	3.7	1.0	0.1	0.5	0.7	1.0	0.0	0.0	0.0	0.1	0.0	0.0	0.0	-0.1
SOLID WASTE	534.9	902.1	1208.5	1977.2	518.2	810.1	1085.4	1352.6	0.0	17.1	0.0	200.3	16.8	74.8	123.1	424.3

NET TOTAL EMISSIONS

	WORLD 1970	WORLD 1980	WORLD 1990	WORLD 2000	DEVELOPED 1970	DEVELOPED 1980	DEVELOPED 1990	DEVELOPED 2000	DEVELOPING I 1970	DEVELOPING I 1980	DEVELOPING I 1990	DEVELOPING I 2000	DEVELOPING II 1970	DEVELOPING II 1980	DEVELOPING II 1990	DEVELOPING II 2000
PESTICIDES	2.6	5.4	13.4	16.0	1.9	3.6	4.9	5.9	0.2	0.7	2.2	5.0	0.5	1.1	6.3	5.1
PARTICULATES	14.9	13.3	22.7	16.2	10.9	7.3	7.4	7.4	0.6	2.1	8.7	2.6	3.4	4.5	6.6	6.3
BIOLOGICAL OXYGEN	29.6	36.6	44.6	55.3	24.1	27.3	29.6	31.1	0.7	1.8	5.4	7.7	5.8	9.6	15.5	21.3
NITROGEN (WATER)	0.7	1.0	1.8	1.9	0.4	0.8	1.2	1.0	0.0	0.2	0.0	0.1	0.1	0.1	0.1	0.2
PHOSPHATES	0.4	0.8	0.8	1.1	0.7	0.5	0.7	0.8	0.3	1.1	0.0	0.1	0.2	0.3	0.5	0.5
SUSPENDED SOLIDS	18.5	21.7	26.3	31.3	15.5	17.2	17.3	17.3	1.5	4.5	4.6	6.4	1.5	0.0	4.4	7.6
DISSOLVED SOLIDS	129.4	181.3	268.7	358.9	110.5	142.4	195.4	234.3	1.4	4.1	15.4	29.0	17.5	34.8	57.9	95.6
SOLID WASTE	312.4	353.4	653.0	727.5	75.2	0.0	0.0	0.0	38.1	62.9	156.2	90.2	199.1	290.5	496.8	637.3

RESOURCE OUTPUTS

	WORLD 1970	WORLD 1980	WORLD 1990	WORLD 2000	DEVELOPED 1970	DEVELOPED 1980	DEVELOPED 1990	DEVELOPED 2000	DEVELOPING I 1970	DEVELOPING I 1980	DEVELOPING I 1990	DEVELOPING I 2000	DEVELOPING II 1970	DEVELOPING II 1980	DEVELOPING II 1990	DEVELOPING II 2000
COPPER	6.4	9.3	16.5	23.6	3.6	4.9	6.6	8.8	1.4	2.5	6.2	8.2	1.4	1.9	3.6	6.7
BAUXITE	11.4	16.7	27.9	38.5	4.3	5.8	9.7	23.5	5.3	6.3	15.1	8.8	1.8	2.6	3.1	6.3
NICKEL	668	954	1602	2135	441	638	1039	954	12	16	15	57	214	299	548	1127
ZINC	5.4	7.5	12.4	17.8	3.4	5.3	10.2	13.5	0.4	1.1	1.0	1.4	0.8	1.1	0.8	3.0
LEAD	3.5	5.4	9.7	14.7	2.4	3.6	9.3	10.3	0.4	0.7	0.2	1.7	0.7	1.0	0.4	2.7
IRON	424	660	1111	1612	282	481	712	994	45	50	121	170	97	128	277	447
PETROLEUM	3703	4998	9340	14136	1253	2104	3515	5292	1531	2736	5616	6552	218	157	208	293
NATURAL GAS	1426	2336	4262	5910	1327	1980	3293	4402	47	304	917	1457	51	51	51	51
COAL	2165	3307	5232	8313	1589	2561	4065	6568	7	17	34	54	568	728	1132	1690

CUMULATIVE RESOURCE OUTPUT AT END OF PERIOD

	WORLD 1970	WORLD 1980	WORLD 1990	WORLD 2000	DEVELOPED 1970	DEVELOPED 1980	DEVELOPED 1990	DEVELOPED 2000	DEVELOPING I 1970	DEVELOPING I 1980	DEVELOPING I 1990	DEVELOPING I 2000	DEVELOPING II 1970	DEVELOPING II 1980	DEVELOPING II 1990	DEVELOPING II 2000
COPPER	0.0	78.2	207.1	407.9	0.0	42.3	99.9	177.0	0.0	19.3	62.9	135.0	0.0	16.7	44.3	95.8
BAUXITE	0.0	140.5	363.6	695.6	0.0	50.3	127.7	293.6	0.0	68.1	185.4	304.5	0.0	22.1	50.5	97.5
NICKEL	0	8113	20921	39592	0	5403	13792	23742	0	145	304	670	0	2567	6804	15180
ZINC	0.0	64.5	164.3	315.7	0.0	45.9	123.3	241.9	0.0	8.9	21.9	36.2	0.0	9.7	19.0	37.6
LEAD	0.0	44.7	119.6	241.8	0.0	30.2	94.1	192.6	0.0	5.5	9.5	18.0	0.0	8.9	16.0	31.1
IRON	0	5425	14287	22908	0	3820	9791	18324	0	477	1336	2798	0	1128	3160	6785
PETROLEUM	0	40048	111700	229293	0	16786	44863	88919	0	21338	63104	133950	0	1883	3712	6222
NATURAL GAS	0	18818	51813	102676	0	16540	42011	81392	0	1763	7877	19749	0	514	1024	1534
COAL	0	27362	70060	137794	0	20754	53688	107062	0	125	387	834	0	6481	15784	29897

OUTPUT LEVELS

	WORLD				DEVELOPED COUNTRIES				DEVELOPING - CLASS I				DEVELOPING - CLASS II			
	1970	1980	1990	2000	1970	1980	1990	2000	1970	1980	1990	2000	1970	1980	1990	2000
ANIMAL PRODUCTS	209.5	277.1	373.2	499.0	132.8	165.2	209.7	240.9	11.1	22.4	39.6	67.6	64.6	89.5	123.9	190.5
HIGH PROTEIN CROPS	136.9	184.1	261.9	369.0	60.7	84.4	110.9	138.7	12.3	19.6	34.1	52.9	64.0	84.2	116.9	167.6
GRAINS	1217.6	1537.2	2191.5	3029.0	503.6	686.1	968.1	1203.8	51.1	78.2	138.7	244.6	582.8	772.7	1084.8	1581.5
ROOTS	458.6	543.3	716.5	926.5	215.5	243.6	296.4	283.0	64.3	89.2	130.3	206.0	178.8	210.7	290.1	387.4
OTHER AGRICULTURE	206.0	256.4	296.6	457.8	147.5	162.6	254.8	203.0	12.1	21.8	51.6	96.4	46.4	69.8	91.1	158.4
OTHER RESOURCES	15.9	25.4	45.6	67.5	12.6	17.0	34.5	46.2	1.2	2.6	4.5	10.0	2.3	6.3	6.6	11.2
FOOD PROCESSING	172.9	321.5	428.4	590.2	159.3	278.3	304.5	478.2	1.9	5.2	17.4	66.6	11.7	18.0	24.5	45.4
PETROLEUM REFINING	146.2	72.9	312.9	178.0	40.6	55.5	81.4	104.1	11.7	10.6	33.9	66.7	5.4	4.8	6.8	11.4
PRIMARY METALS	103.1	169.2	311.9	466.5	97.1	153.6	276.3	370.3	5.4	15.3	17.9	52.0	10.3	10.3	17.7	44.2
TEXTILES, APPAREL	180.3	256.9	350.9	539.2	133.3	187.5	237.1	337.8	6.7	12.9	30.0	60.8	41.1	56.6	82.6	140.6
WOOD AND CORK	42.2	63.5	97.5	131.6	36.8	54.9	82.2	100.4	2.3	1.7	4.0	11.1	4.7	6.7	10.4	19.5
FURNITURE, FIXTURES	82.8	116.2	106.7	168.1	67.0	90.1	59.2	72.4	2.4	7.6	21.6	49.3	12.7	18.2	25.9	46.5
PAPER	54.2	87.5	148.2	217.0	50.0	81.2	136.4	191.0	3.0	7.8	5.4	5.0	3.8	5.6	8.0	20.3
PRINTING	35.5	59.3	109.8	255.9	51.1	55.7	154.3	218.6	2.1	1.3	2.1	5.3	1.9	3.0	5.3	12.6
RUBBER	77.6	117.1	186.5	246.0	33.3	55.7	122.3	143.6	1.6	2.8	6.9	20.7	2.1	3.1	8.0	42.7
INDUSTRIAL CHEM.	66.7	106.8	173.7	228.0	67.9	100.3	155.7	219.1	1.5	3.5	17.3	24.7	9.9	14.1	22.3	110.5
FERTILIZERS	60.5	93.8	159.3	228.8	54.2	84.2	143.7	195.7	1.1	3.1	13.0	32.3	13.0	37.0	69.0	25.5
OTHER CHEMICALS	60.7	93.8	159.3	228.8	54.2	84.2	143.7	195.7	1.5	1.2	3.0	7.6	5.0	8.4	13.1	25.5
CEMENT	5.7	9.6	18.6	23.7	5.2	8.7	16.7	23.7	0.8	2.4	0.7	2.7	0.5	1.1	2.7	2.7
GLASS	53.7	89.6	165.5	247.8	49.7	80.9	147.4	201.4	2.0	2.7	7.7	23.9	4.5	6.3	10.4	22.2
MOTOR VEHICLES	94.7	152.8	294.6	433.1	93.6	150.5	235.9	400.4	0.6	0.9	4.3	20.7	1.8	1.7	4.3	12.0
AIRCRAFT	27.4	41.5	72.8	104.1	25.4	38.6	64.9	84.5	0.9	0.3	3.9	12.5	1.1	2.6	3.9	7.1
OTHER TRANSP. EQ.	21.4	31.0	50.1	77.7	19.4	25.6	45.4	56.6	0.3	0.9	4.8	10.9	1.8	2.7	4.4	9.8
METAL PRODUCTS	149.4	239.6	440.8	644.2	135.3	215.7	391.4	515.0	1.4	5.9	20.2	68.0	12.7	18.6	28.6	60.6
MACHINERY	159.5	226.4	394.4	588.0	146.8	205.4	349.2	465.8	1.2	4.5	17.2	53.9	12.2	16.5	28.6	68.6
ELECTRICAL MACH.	105.6	165.9	301.4	439.0	99.6	156.4	282.4	388.1	2.1	1.4	15.2	21.0	1.5	18.1	13.9	30.9
INSTRUMENTS	26.1	38.8	69.2	99.3	24.3	35.6	62.4	84.4	0.1	0.6	7.2	6.0	1.6	2.3	3.7	8.9
OTHER MANUFACTURES	39.7	58.8	89.2	139.0	32.2	46.2	68.0	98.3	1.1	0.9	7.2	16.2	6.5	9.8	18.0	25.3
UTILITIES	78.3	150.4	289.0	415.0	71.8	136.7	256.7	333.5	1.0	3.9	15.1	48.7	5.5	9.8	18.8	33.6
CONSTRUCTION	384.8	646.3	1188.8	1733.1	337.2	556.3	1000.3	1276.3	7.9	37.3	108.7	295.1	39.7	52.7	79.8	161.7
TRADE	562.7	890.6	1454.2	2090.5	521.8	784.3	1250.0	1647.0	9.1	31.4	95.4	244.9	51.7	74.5	108.8	198.5
TRANSPORTATION	189.2	284.2	433.3	632.3	159.2	232.1	335.9	456.9	3.0	13.4	37.2	80.3	26.5	38.7	57.3	95.0
COMMUNICATION	56.8	92.2	165.2	239.5	50.2	79.1	144.1	193.1	3.0	5.0	8.5	22.8	8.1	8.1	12.4	23.0
SERVICES	819.3	1329.6	2383.6	3679.5	713.9	1142.4	1990.2	2822.8	16.1	52.8	154.9	440.8	89.3	136.3	229.5	415.9

FISH

	WORLD				DEVELOPED COUNTRIES				DEVELOPING - CLASS I				DEVELOPING - CLASS II			
	1970	1980	1990	2000	1970	1980	1990	2000	1970	1980	1990	2000	1970	1980	1990	2000
FISH CATCH	66.0	66.0	66.0	66.0	26.9	26.9	26.8	26.9	14.5	14.5	14.5	14.5	24.5	24.5	24.5	24.5
NON-HUMAN USE	22.0	22.0	22.0	22.0	5.8	5.8	5.8	5.8	11.9	11.9	11.9	11.9	4.3	4.3	4.3	4.3
FISH IMPORTS	4.0	4.0	4.1	4.1	3.2	3.2	3.2	3.2	0.2	0.2	0.2	0.2	0.6	0.6	0.6	0.6
FISH EXPORTS	4.1	4.1	4.1	4.1	3.0	3.0	3.0	3.0	0.2	0.2	0.2	0.2	0.8	0.8	0.8	0.8

EXPORTS

	WORLD				DEVELOPED COUNTRIES				DEVELOPING - CLASS I				DEVELOPING - CLASS II			
	1970	1980	1990	2000	1970	1980	1990	2000	1970	1982	1990	2000	1970	1982	1990	2000
LIVESTOCK	9.7	12.5	16.4	20.7	8.4	10.6	14.0	17.6		0.2	0.3	0.4	1.2	1.6	2.2	2.7
HIGH PROTEIN CROPS	25.0	33.3	47.9	61.4	17.3	25.0	35.5	46.1	2.9	2.9	4.1	5.3	4.9	5.4	7.7	9.1
GRAINS	103.3	126.1	184.9	251.4	86.7	107.0	156.8	213.2	1.7	1.0	1.5	2.1	15.5	18.1	26.6	36.1
ROOTS	13.2	15.0	18.9	22.8	9.8	11.0	13.9	16.8	5.1	5.7	11.6	19.5	2.0	3.1	3.9	4.7
OTHER AGRICULTURE	27.4	32.4	35.3	50.8	12.2	13.0	15.8	22.7	5.1	5.1	6.6	9.1	10.0	11.7	12.9	18.6
FOOD PROCESSING	13.1	15.7	20.4	29.2	9.8	10.6	14.2	20.4	1.0	1.2	1.5	2.2	3.0	3.7	4.7	7.0
TEXTILES,APPAREL	23.2	50.7	106.2	212.4	18.0	40.0	82.0	154.4	4.3	2.0	2.5	6.7	4.8	9.4	21.7	51.3
WOOD AND CORK	4.7	8.8	16.2	26.7	3.4	7.1	13.3	19.7	0.8	0.3	0.6	1.0	0.8	1.4	3.0	5.8
FURNITURE,FIXTURES	1.5	2.0	2.9	4.3	1.8	2.4	3.6	3.8	0.0	0.2	0.2	0.2	0.0	0.7	2.1	6.5
PAPER	9.3	17.5	37.9	68.5	8.7	16.0	35.6	61.4	0.0	0.1	0.1	0.6	0.0	0.4	1.0	2.5
PRINTING	1.8	4.1	9.6	17.2	1.9	3.7	8.5	15.1	0.0	0.0	0.2	0.4	0.0	0.3	0.8	2.2
RUBBER	2.1	3.9	8.6	17.2	1.4	3.0	7.7	14.0	0.1	0.1	0.3	0.7	0.6	1.1	2.6	7.1
INDUSTRIAL CHEM.	15.1	24.9	43.2	71.6	14.4	23.7	40.8	63.3	0.2	0.3	1.5	1.1	0.4	1.0	2.3	3.6
FERTILIZERS	6.6	11.5	23.2	51.0	5.8	10.1	20.4	25.9	0.0	0.2	0.5	0.9	0.4	1.0	2.3	4.6
OTHER CHEMICALS	6.8	13.6	27.5	51.0	6.3	12.6	25.9	45.2	0.2	0.2	0.3	1.2	0.3	0.6	2.3	4.6
CEMENT	5.3	10.6	15.2	2.1	3.2	4.6	3.2	2.1	0.0	0.1	0.2	0.4	0.3	0.6	2.3	0.8
GLASS	3.9	8.5	20.9	37.6	3.6	7.9	18.5	33.4	0.0	0.1	0.2	0.7	0.3	0.6	1.5	3.7
MOTOR VEHICLES	26.5	40.7	81.1	144.2	26.1	40.0	78.9	136.9	0.2	0.1	0.2	0.7	0.4	0.5	1.9	6.5
OTHER TRANSP. EQ.	4.8	7.3	12.4	20.3	4.5	6.8	11.7	16.7	0.2	0.1	0.2	0.2	0.3	0.5	1.1	3.5
AIRCRAFT	5.6	9.1	17.4	26.9	5.1	8.8	16.1	25.2	0.2	0.1	0.1	0.3	0.4	0.3	0.2	0.4
METAL PRODUCTS	7.6	11.8	19.4	26.6	7.1	11.0	17.3	23.5	0.2	0.1	0.2	0.3	0.6	0.7	1.5	3.1
MACHINERY	35.6	59.2	110.7	182.6	34.9	56.0	107.3	171.3	0.2	0.1	0.2	0.5	0.8	1.2	3.2	10.7
ELECTRICAL MACH.	16.8	32.3	66.7	127.3	16.6	30.8	63.3	118.9	0.2	0.1	0.2	0.8	0.8	1.4	3.3	8.0
INSTRUMENTS	8.1	10.7	21.2	35.0	6.5	10.5	20.3	33.2	0.3	0.4	0.5	0.8	0.2	0.2	0.5	1.7
OTHER MANUFACTURES	8.5	13.5	22.5	34.3	6.6	10.1	17.3	27.5	0.6	1.2	1.8	2.5	1.7	2.5	4.3	7.9
SERVICES	19.8	28.1	42.5	58.5	12.8	18.1	27.4	37.7	1.2	1.2	1.8	2.5	6.2	8.8	13.3	18.3
TRANSPORT	26.8	41.1	70.1	126.3	22.9	35.1	59.9	90.8	1.1	1.7	2.8	4.3	2.8	4.3	7.4	11.2
AID INFLOW	27.0	40.5	64.8	97.6	11.8	16.8	27.0	36.8	3.2	5.0	7.9	11.4	12.0	18.7	29.9	47.3
CAPITAL INFLOW	26.5	43.7	83.7	136.6	19.2	27.8	49.4	54.2	1.9	9.8	25.3	59.5	5.4	6.1	9.0	22.8

	WORLD				DEVELOPED COUNTRIES				DEVELOPING				DEVELOPING – CLASS I				DEVELOPING – CLASS II			
	1970	1980	1990	2000	1970	1980	1990	2000	1970	1980	1990	2000	1970	1980	1990	2000	1970	1980	1990	2000
IMPORTS																				
LIVESTOCK	9.7	12.5	16.5	20.7	8.2	9.9	12.5	14.1	0.5	1.1	2.0	3.6	1.0	1.1	2.0	3.6	3.1	2.0	2.4	3.1
HIGH PROTEIN CROPS	25.8	33.3	47.4	61.4	20.1	26.7	37.6	45.7	1.7	1.9	3.2	6.2	3.7	1.9	3.2	6.2	9.4	4.7	6.4	9.4
GRAINS	103.3	126.1	184.9	251.8	68.6	78.9	112.7	139.8	8.9	13.2	23.2	38.4	26.0	13.2	23.2	38.4	73.4	34.0	48.8	73.4
ROOTS	13.2	15.0	18.9	22.8	10.1	10.7	12.7	13.0	0.4	1.5	5.2	13.0	3.2	1.5	5.2	13.0	5.6	4.6	4.0	5.6
OTHER AGRICULTURE	27.1	30.4	35.3	50.8	23.4	23.6	24.1	30.8	0.7	2.3	4.9	10.1	2.0	2.3	4.9	10.1	9.5	2.0	6.5	9.5
FOOD PROCESSING	13.1	15.7	20.6	29.3	11.2	10.7	12.7	14.5	1.7	2.3	4.9	9.0	2.9	2.3	3.5	9.0	5.5	2.1	3.5	5.5
TEXTILES,APPAREL	23.2	52.7	106.2	212.4	18.2	39.7	63.7	165.5	1.1	4.5	11.6	25.0	3.6	4.5	11.6	25.0	22.0	6.7	11.0	22.0
WOOD AND CORK	4.7	8.0	16.0	26.4	4.1	7.2	13.2	17.0	1.1	0.8	2.6	7.6	0.4	0.8	1.1	7.6	2.1	0.1	1.1	2.1
FURNITURE,FIXTURES	1.5	2.6	3.7	68.5	1.6	2.3	2.0	4.5	0.2	0.8	0.6	7.5	0.2	0.8	0.6	7.5	2.2	2.0	1.1	2.2
PAPER	8.3	17.5	37.0	68.5	6.4	13.7	28.0	44.8	0.8	1.5	5.6	16.4	0.3	1.5	5.6	16.4	7.3	3.3	3.0	7.3
PRINTING	1.8	4.1	8.6	17.7	1.1	3.2	7.6	11.4	0.7	0.8	1.5	7.2	0.3	0.8	1.5	7.2	1.5	3.7	0.8	1.5
RUBBER	12.1	24.9	43.6	71.2	11.0	21.8	38.4	47.6	0.5	0.7	2.2	11.6	0.3	0.7	2.2	11.6	13.6	0.8	7.0	13.6
INDUSTRIAL CHEM.	15.1	24.9	43.2	71.4	13.8	17.6	30.5	41.0	0.9	2.6	4.8	7.4	2.5	2.6	4.8	7.4	16.1	5.3	12.6	16.1
FERTILIZERS	6.5	11.5	23.2	31.6	3.8	4.6	6.4	8.4	0.9	1.6	3.6	21.4	2.0	1.6	3.6	21.4	16.1	2.5	13.6	16.1
OTHER CHEMICALS	6.8	13.6	27.3	51.4	4.0	8.2	15.0	23.4	1.3	2.2	8.6	21.4	1.6	2.2	8.6	21.4	0.5	0.1	3.2	0.5
CEMENT	2.3	3.6	9.6	9.9	2.5	8.2	8.7	10.9	1.3	1.3	4.1	2.4	1.6	1.3	4.1	2.4	0.5	0.9	0.4	0.5
GLASS	3.9	8.5	20.2	37.0	3.6	6.3	14.9	21.5	2.2	1.3	4.1	13.0	3.1	1.3	4.1	13.0	16.1	3.3	6.1	16.1
MOTOR VEHICLES	26.5	40.7	81.0	144.2	20.5	35.3	66.8	103.3	2.2	2.1	8.1	24.8	3.7	2.1	8.1	24.8	15.5	1.7	6.1	15.5
OTHER TRANSP. EQ.	4.8	7.3	12.0	20.3	2.3	5.1	8.8	13.3	2.3	0.5	0.5	1.4	1.2	0.5	0.5	1.4	4.2	1.2	2.7	4.2
AIRCRAFT	5.6	9.0	17.0	25.7	5.3	7.3	13.7	19.1	0.5	0.5	1.0	2.4	1.8	0.5	1.0	2.4	2.8	1.9	1.9	2.8
METAL PRODUCTS	35.6	59.2	110.7	182.6	25.6	38.3	70.8	102.8	3.1	11.8	26.5	11.2	1.3	11.8	26.5	11.2	27.5	0.8	13.7	27.5
MACHINERY	35.6	59.2	110.7	182.6	12.4	22.8	45.8	72.6	1.5	5.1	13.7	52.2	3.6	5.1	13.7	52.2	15.2	0.4	13.7	15.2
ELECTRICAL MACH.	16.8	32.3	66.7	127.0	14.0	22.6	45.3	72.6	1.3	1.4	13.7	39.6	1.5	1.4	13.7	39.6	4.5	4.4	2.0	4.5
INSTRUMENTS	6.1	10.7	21.2	35.0	4.8	7.6	15.3	22.4	1.3	1.6	3.7	8.1	1.2	1.6	3.7	8.1	4.6	2.0	3.0	4.6
OTHER MANUFACTURES	8.5	13.5	22.2	34.3	6.5	10.6	17.4	26.5	1.7	1.6	3.8	3.1	1.7	1.6	3.8	3.1	5.2	2.1	2.8	5.2
SERVICES	19.0	28.1	42.5	58.5	17.5	24.4	36.2	46.6	0.7	2.0	3.5	6.7	1.7	2.0	3.5	6.7			2.8	
TRANSPORT	26.8	41.1	70.1	106.3	20.6	30.8	51.6	72.1	2.1	4.7	9.7	18.1	4.0	4.7	9.7	18.1	16.1	5.6	8.7	16.1
AID OUTFLOW	27.0	40.5	64.8	97.6	22.1	31.1	46.2	59.7	1.9	5.3	13.1	28.2	3.1	5.3	13.1	28.2	9.6	4.2	5.6	9.6
CAPITAL OUTFLOW	26.5	43.7	83.7	136.6	23.2	37.2	66.8	96.7	0.8	1.8	5.4	13.6	2.5	1.8	5.4	13.6	26.2	4.6	11.5	26.2
NET EXPORTS OF RESOURCES																				
COPPER	0.0	0.0	0.0	0.0	-1.9	-3.2	-7.8	-10.0	1.3	2.3	5.7	6.8	0.6	1.0	2.1	3.2	3.2	1.0	2.1	3.2
BAUXITE	0.0	0.0	0.0	0.0	-15.5	-8.8	-14.7	-7.6	5.0	8.1	14.4	6.9	0.5	0.7	0.3	0.7	0.7	0.7	0.3	0.7
NICKEL	0.0	0.0	0.0	0.0	-102.6	-169.5	-346.3	-724.0	10.9	10.9	3.1	32.3	92.1	158.6	343.3	692.5	692.5	158.6	343.3	692.5
ZINC	0.0	0.0	0.0	0.0	0.5	1.1	-1.4	-0.0	0.6	0.6	1.5	0.0	0.2	0.1	-0.7	0.0	0.0	0.1	-0.7	0.0
LEAD	0.0	0.0	0.0	0.0	-75.9	-89.7	-241.6	-276.0	32.3	37.0	84.6	70.1	0.2	52.7	157.0	205.9	205.9	52.7	157.0	205.9
IRON	0.0	0.0	0.0	0.0	-126.0	-187.0	-3586.0	-3945.0	141.7	2227	4129	4995	43.6	-348	-542	-1050	-1050	-348	-542	-1050
PETROLEUM	0.0	0.0	0.0	0.0	-8.4	-140.0	-41.4	-32.9	3.1	55.1	103.4	236.6	-156	-15.1	-62.0	-203.7	-203.7	-15.1	-62.0	-203.7
NATURAL GAS	0.0	0.0	0.0	0.0	-1.0	-1.6	-42.0	124.3	-1.6	-7.5	-27.7	-77.0	5.3	-12.8	-14.5	-47.3	-47.3	-12.8	-14.5	-47.3
COAL	0.0	0.0	0.0	0.0	-1.0	-1.6	-2.8	-3.3	0.6	-7.8	1.4	1.7	-8.3	-10.8	1.4	1.7	1.7	-10.8	1.4	1.7
OTHER RESOURCES	0.0	0.0	0.0	0.0									0.5							
PETROLEUM REFINING	0.0	0.0	0.0	0.0	-0.1	-6.0	-22.5	-37.0	0.4	8.1	26.4	46.9	-0.3	-2.0	-3.9	-9.9	-9.9	-2.0	-3.9	-9.9
PRIMARY METALS	0.0	0.0	0.0	0.0	3.4	0.8	-1.9	-6.0	-0.7	1.1	4.1	4.8	-2.7	-2.0	-2.2	1.1	1.1	-2.0	-2.2	1.1

TABLE 3. SINGLE REGION BLOCK OF THE WORLD MODEL (*inside*)

Key to rows in table 3

(Abbreviations for classes of equations)

GDP	1[a]	Gross domestic product	SEQP	1	Equipment capital stock
SAVE	1	Savings equation	SPLT	1	Plant capital stock
INV	1	Investment equation	SINVY	1	Inventory stock equation
GOV	1	Government expenditures	SFAS	1	Stock of foreign assets
IMPRT	1	Total imports	SLAND	1	Cultivated land area
EXPRT	1	Total exports	MAGS	4	Imports of selected agriculture
BAL	1	Balance of payments	MAGR	1	Imports of residual agriculture
LABOR	1	Employment	MRSS	9	Imports of selected resources
NUTRN	2	Consumption of food nutrition units	MRSR	1	Imports of residual resources
ABDET	5	Abatement determination	MAGM	1	Imports of agricultural margins
EMA	8	Emissions of abatable pollutants	MRSM	2	Imports of resource margins
EMNA	8	Emissions of non-abatable pollutants	MXT	19	Imports of traded goods
AGS	4	Selected agricultural commodity balance	MSER	1	Imports of services
AGR	1	Residual agriculture	MTR	1	Imports of transport
RSS	9	Selected resource commodity balance	MAID	1	Aid outflows
RSR	1	Residual resource commodity balance	EAGS	4	Exports of selected agriculture
AGM	1	Agricultural margins (food)	EAGR	1	Exports of residual agriculture
RSM	2	Resource margins (refining)	ERSS	9	Exports of selected resources
XT	19	Output of traded commodities	ERSR	1	Exports of residual resources
XNT	6	Output of non-traded commodities	EAGM	1	Exports of agricultural margins
IEQP	1	Equipment investment	ERSM	2	Exports of resource margins
IPLT	1	Plant investment	EXT	19	Exports of traded goods
INVCH	1	Inventory change investment equation	ESER	1	Exports of services
ECUMR	9	Cumulative resource output at end of period	ETR	1	Exports of transport
			EAID	1	Aid inflow
			ECAP	1	Capital inflow
			MCAP	1	Capital outflow
			DUMMY	2	Dummy equations

[a] The number following each symbol indicates how many equations of this type are contained in each regional set.

Key to columns in table 3

(Abbreviations for classes of variables)

GDP	1[a]	GDP $ (B)[b]	HRSS	9	Historical selected resource output ***
CONS	1	Consumption level $ (B)	ECUMR	9	Cumulative resource output at end of period ***
DSAVE	1	Excess savings potential $ (B)	SCUMR	9	Cumulative resource output at start of period ***
INV	1	Investment level $ (B)	HEQP	1	Historical equipment capital stock $ (B)
GOV	1	Government expenditures $ (B)	HPLT	1	Historical plant capital stock $ (B)
BAL	1	Balance of payments (capital inflow) $ (B)	HINVY	1	Historical inventory stock $ (B)
IMPRT	1	Total imports $ (B)	HFAS	1	Historical stock of foreign assets $ (B)
EXPRT	1	Total exports $ (B)	HRFAS	1	Historical net inward capflow $ (B)
POP	1	Population (M)	INICF	1	1970 net foreign investment income $ (B)
URBAN	1	Urban population (M)	MAGS	4	Imports of selected agriculture T (M)
LABOR	1	Employment MY (M)	MAGR	1	Imports of residual agriculture $ (B)
NUTRN	2	Consumption of food nutrition units ***	MRSS	9	Imports of selected resources ***
EMA	8	Net emissions of abatable pollutants ***	MRSR	1	Imports of residual resources $ (B)
EMTOT	8	Net total emissions ***	MAGM	1	Imports of agricultural margins $ (B)
XFISH	1	Fish catch T (M)	MRSM	2	Imports of resource margins $ (B)
NFISH	1	Non-human consumption of fish T (M)	MXT	19	Imports of traded goods $ (B)
MFISH	1	Fish imports T (M)	MSER	1	Imports of services $ (B)
EFISH	1	Fish exports T (M)	MTR	1	Imports of transport $ (B)
AGS	4	Selected agricultural activities T (M)	MAID	1	Aid outflow $ (B)
GMSUB	1	Grain substituted for meat T (M)	MSLK	1	Import slack $ (B)
RSS	9	Selected resource activities T (M)	EAGS	4	Exports of selected agriculture T (M)
MRSLK	9	Resource import slacks (= imports) $ (B)	EAGR	1	Exports of residual agriculture $ (B)
AGR	1	Residual agriculture $ (B)	ERSS	9	Exports of selected resources ***
RSR	1	Residual resource activities $ (B)	ERSR	1	Exports of residual resources $ (B)
AGM	1	Agricultural margins (food) $ (B)	EAGM	1	Exports of agricultural margins $ (B)
RSM	2	Resource margins (refining) $ (B)	ERSM	2	Exports of resource margins $ (B)
XT	19	Output of traded commodities $ (B)	EXT	19	Exports of traded goods $ (B)
XNT	6	Output of non-traded commodities $ (B)	ESER	1	Exports of services $ (B)
ABATE	5	Level of abatement activities T (M)	ETR	1	Exports of transport $ (B)
ABSLK	5	Abatement equipment slacks T (M)	EAID	1	Aid inflow $ (B)
IEQP	1	Equipment investment $ (B)	ESLK	1	Export slack $ (B)
IPLT	1	Plant investment $ (B)	ECAP	1	Capital inflow $ (B)
INVCH	1	Inventory change investment $ (B)	MCAP	1	Capital outflow $ (B)
IIRR	1	Irrigation investment H (M)	CONST	1	Constant vector ***
ILAND	1	Land development H (M)	DUMA	2	Dummy vectors ***
SEQP	1	Equipment capital stock $ (B)	PAGS	4	Export pool of selected agriculture T (M)
SPLT	1	Plant capital stock $ (B)	PAGR	1	Export pool of residual agriculture $ (B)
SINVY	1	Inventory stocks $ (B)	PRSS	9	Export pool of selected resources ***
SFAS	1	Stock of foreign assets $ (B)	PRSR	1	Export pool of residual resources $ (B)
SLAND	1	Cultivated land area H (M)	PAGM	1	Export pool of agricultural margins $ (B)
			PRSM	2	Export pool of resource margins $ (B)
			PXT	19	Export pool of traded goods $ (B)
			PSER	1	Export pool of services $ (B)
			PTR	1	Export pool of transport $ (B)
			PAID	1	Export pool of aid inflow $ (B)
			PCAP	1	Pool of capital inflow $ (B)
			DUMMY	2	Dummy vectors ***

[a] The number following each symbol indicates the number of variables of this type contained in each regional set of equations.

[b] See *Key to units of measurement used for classes of variables* (overleaf) for explanation of the units used for each of the variables.

(*Continued overleaf*)

INVY36   MAGR 44   MxT 58   EAGS 81   ERSM 97   ESLK 21   PAGS 27   PRSM 43   PCAP 67
 HFAS 37   MRSS 45   MSER 77   EAGR 85   EXT 99   ECAP 22   PAGR 31   PXT 45   DUMMY68
  HRFAS38   MRSR 54   MTR 78   ERSS 86   ESER 18   MCAP 23   PRSS 32   PSER 64   0
   INICF39   MAGM 55   MAID 79   ERSR 95   ETR 19   CONST24   PRSR 41   PTR 65   0
35   MAGS 40   MRSM 56   MSLK 80   EAGM 96   EAID 20   DUMA 25   PAGM 42   PAID 66   0

```
        :           :         -   :          :         + :   + -      :           :           :
        :           :             :          :           :           :           :           :
  + P :     P P P P : P P P -   : P P P P : P P P P + :   + -      :           :           :
    P :     + P + + + : P + +     :           :           :           :           :           :
        :           :             : P + P + + : + P + +   :           :           :           :
        :           :             :          :           :           :           :           :
        :           :             :          :           :           :           :           :
    + :           :             :  -       :           :           :           :           :
        :       + :             :   -      :           :           :           :           :
        :         +   :             :           :  -      :           :           :           :
        :          + :  +          :           :   -  +   :           :           :           :
        :             : M M       :           :       M M :           :           :           :
        :           :             :          :           :           :           :           :
        :           :             :          :           :           :           :           :
        :           :             :          :           :           :           :           :
  + G :           :             :          :           : G G       :           :           :
    - :           :        T :   :          :           :           :           :           :
        :      - :        T :   :          :           :           :           :           :
    D :     D D D - :        T :   :          :           :           :           :           :
        :             :        T :   :          :           :           :           :           :
        :           : + :        T :   :          :           :       M :           :           :
        :           :  -   -  T :   :          :           :           :           :           :
        :           :      -   :   :          :  -       :       B :           :           :
        :           :             :   -      :  T        :           :           :           :
        :           :    -  :   : T       :   B       :           :       B :           :
        :           :             : T       :       B   :           :         B :           :
        :           : D D - :   : T     M :           :         B :           :
        :           :   D D :  -   : T       :           :           :       B       :
        :           :             :    -  : T       :           :         B :           :
        :           :             :      -  : T       :           :           B :           :
        :           :             :        - :   :          :           :             B :   :
        :           :             :          :  -       :           :           :       B
        :           :             :       -  :   :          :           :           :
```

TABLE 3. SINGLE REGION B

```
       GNP   1      BAL    6     LABOR11      NFISH31      RSS  39      RSM  60     IEQP 97      SEQP  2      HRSS  7
           CONS  2     IMPRT 7     NUTRN12      MFISH32     MRSLK48      XT   62     IPLT 98      SPLT  3     ECUMR16
          DSAVE 3     EXPRT 8      EMA  14     EFISH33      AGR  57     XNT  81     INVCH99     SINVY 4     SCUMR25
           INV   4     POP   9    EMTOT22      AGS  34     RSR  58     ABATE87     IIRR  0     SFAS  5     HEQP 34
           GOV   5    URBAN10     XFISH30     GMSUB38      AGM  59     ABSLK92     ILAND 1     SLAND 6     HPLT

 1 GNP    M  +   + +  :   - +    P  :         :         :         :         P   :      +    :         :
 2 SAVE   %      P  :         :         :         :         :         :      P     :         :
 3 INV           -  :         :         :         :         :  + +   P P :         :
 4 GOV    %        -  :         :         :         :         :         :         :
 5 BAL             :  -       :         : P P     :         :         :         M   :

 6 IMPRT          :    -     :         : P       :         :         :         :
 7 EXPRT          :      -   :         :   P     :         :         :         :
 8 LABOR  L    L  :    L L  : -        L  :    L  : L  L L L : L L L L :      L L :
 9 NUTRN  M       :    M    :    -     :         :         :         :         :
 1 EMA    E       :    E E  :      -   :    E  : E  E E E : E E E M :         :

 9 EMNA           :         :  + -     :         :         :    E    :         :
 7 ABDET          :         :         :         :         :    M -  :         :
42 AGS    C    C  :    C U  :    M  : M M M @ M : @  @ @ @ : @ @ @ @ : S S S S S :
36 RSS    C    C  :    C U  :    @  :       @  : @  @ @ @ : @ @ @ @ : S S S S S :
45 AGR    C    C  :    C U  :    @  :       @  : @  @ @ @ : @ @ @   : S S S S S :

46 RSR    C    C  :    C U  :    @  :       @  : @  @ @ @ : @ @ @ @ : S S S S S :
47 AGM    C    C  :    C U  :    @  :       @  : @  @ @ @ : @ @ @ @ : S S S S S :
48 RSM    C    C  :    C U  :    @  :       @  : @  @ @ @ : @ @ @ @ : S S S S S :
50 XT     C    C  :    C U  :    @  :       @  : @  @ @ @ : @ @ @ @ : S S S S S :
59 XNT    C    C  :    C U  :    @  :       @  : @  @ @ @ : @ @ @ @ : S S   S S :

75 IEQP           :         :         :         :         :    -    :     G   :        G :
76 IPLT           :         :         :         :         :      -  :   G     :      G :
77 INVCH          :         :         :         :         :     -   :    G    :
78 ECUMR          :         :         : G       :         :         :  G - +  :
87 SEQP           :    K    : K       :    K  : K  K K K : K K K K :      K K : -

88 SPLT   K       :    K K  : K       :    K  : K  K K K : K K K K :      K K :  -
89 SINVY          :         :         :    K  : K  K K K : K K     :         :
90 SFAS           : G       :         :         :         :         :      -  :
91 SLAND          :         :         :    K  :    K     :         :         :   -
92 MAGS           :         :         :    A  :         :         :         :

96 MAGR           :         :         :       A  :       :         :         :
97 MRSS           :         :         : A +     :         :         :         :
 6 MRSR           :         :         :       A :        :         :         :
 7 MAGM           :         :    D    :         :         :         :         :
 8 MRSM           :         :         :         :         :         :         :

10 MXT            :         :         :         : A       :         :         :
29 MSER   M       :         :         :         :         :         :         :
30 MTR    M       :  M M    :         :         :         :         :         :
31 MAID   M       :         :         :         :         :         :         :
32 EAGS           :         :         :         :         :         :         :

36 EAGR           :         :         :         :         :         :         :
37 ERSS           :         :         :         :         :         :         :
46 ERSR           :         :         :         :         :         :         :
47 EAGM           :         :    D    :         :         :         :         :
48 ERSM           :         :         :         :         :         :         :

50 EXT            :         :         :         :         :         :         :
69 ESER           :         :         :         :         :         :         :
70 ETR            :         :         :         :         :         :         :
71 EAID           :         :         :         :         :         :         :
72 ECAP   M       :         :         :         :         :         :         :

73 MCAP           :         :         :         :         :         :         :
74 DUMMY          :         :         :         :         :         :         :
```

Key to Coefficient Symbols in Table 3

A	Import to output ratios		M	Miscellaneous parameters
B	World export pool shares		P	Prices
C	Consumption coefficients		S	Structure of investment demand
D	Margin trade to physical units		T	Marginal trade composition
E	Emissions coefficients		U	Urban amenities input structure
G	Growth rate type parameters		X	Exogenous data for calibration 1970
K	Capital coefficients		%	Ratio applicable to context
L	Labour coefficients		@	I-A input-output coefficient

Key to units of measurement used for classes of variables

$	1970 dollars for real magnitudes; current dollars for financial magnitudes
MY	man-years
T	metric tons
H	hectares
(B)	billions, i.e. 10^9
(M)	millions, i.e. 10^6
***	diverse physical units applying to individual variables within the general class